Healing Eating Disorders
with Psychodrama and
Other Action Methods

Healing Eating Disorders with Psychodrama and Other Action Methods

Beyond the Silence and the Fury

Karen Carnabucci and Linda Ciotola

Jessica Kingsley *Publishers*
London and Philadelphia

First published in 2013
by Jessica Kingsley Publishers
116 Pentonville Road
London N1 9JB, UK
and
400 Market Street, Suite 400
Philadelphia, PA 19106, USA

www.jkp.com

Library of Congress Cataloging in Publication Data
A CIP catalog record for this book is available from the Library of Congress

British Library Cataloguing in Publication Data
A CIP catalogue record for this book is available from the British Library

ISBN 978 1 84905 934 3
eISBN 978 0 85700 728 5

Printed and bound in Great Britain

Contents

Preface

Food, like air and water, gives us life. People who deny themselves food deny themselves the nourishment of life. People who take in too much food are striving to take in life—but in a distorted form that damages the body and spirit.

Eating disorders result from a complicated interaction of biological, psychological and social factors and a relationship with food that is out of balance. People with eating disorders are intensely preoccupied with food, weight and appearance, jeopardizing their health and adversely affecting their relationships. The use of psychodrama and other action methods is especially helpful with the treatment of the classic eating disorders—anorexia, bulimia and compulsive binge eating—as well as dieting struggles and a range of difficulties with body image. The psychodramatic group is another plus, since people with eating disorders are often isolated from others and tend to use or misuse food to avoid relationships with people.

The person with the eating disorder is able to experience his or her relationship with the disorder and learn more about its role in his or her life. Experientially, people are able to move out of their heads and into a fuller experience of self, at which time they can view their problems with clarity and compassion. As clients participate in role play, art, movement, choice making and imagery, they expand their sense of self and replace compulsive activities with internal safety and creativity.

Action approaches vary greatly according to the individual styles of the practitioner, as well as the setting. We use the terms *protagonist* for the person enacting a drama and *director* for the professional who is working closely with the protagonist. These words accurately represent the fact that psychodrama is not a therapy but rather a method with numerous applications. Although we are mindful that many of our readers will be psychotherapists, counselors, psychologists, physicians, nurses, dietitians, nutritionists, body workers, midwives and other treatment and healing professionals, we are choosing to stay true to the original terminology because we know that more professionals, including educators, community and group leaders, social activists, and other like-minded professionals, will find these concepts extremely valuable. As authors and psychodrama trainers, we are actual representatives of these variations—Karen is a licensed clinical social worker, psychotherapist and facilitator of family constellation work, and Linda is an educator, wellness counselor and fitness and yoga instructor.

This book is designed for professionals who have knowledge and training in psychodrama, the expressive arts therapies or other experiential modalities and techniques. We hope more will be intrigued by the immense possibilities of action methods to educate, treat and heal these struggling clients. Although some of the action structures appear simple, we do not recommend that readers pick up this book and begin to use action methods without adequate training and supervision. Training in the judicious use of psychodramatic techniques of role reversal, doubling, mirroring, concretization, scene setting and others as well as role theory and role development is essential to understanding how to use these methods ethically and effectively.

We hope that our readers will be inspired by this book and consider collaboration with professionals in other disciplines, evaluate and use the benefits of creativity within multiple educational and psychotherapeutic settings, and design multi-modal interventions that address mind, body and spirit.

Whatever your discipline or level of experience, an atmosphere of safety, mindfulness, attention to moment-to-moment experiencing, respectful pacing and noticing the subtle interacions of mind, body and spirit are fundamental to this work.

Acknowledgements

Our work with people with eating disorders, dieting struggles and body image distortions draws from many teachers, mentors, colleagues and professional writings and presentations that we have found invaluable.

We thank J.L. Moreno, who developed the marvelous action method of psychodrama, and his widow and collaborator Zerka Moreno, who refined the method through the decades and remains one of our most wise and respected teachers and role models. We have taken inspiration from Kate Hudgins and her Therapeutic Spiral Model, which is a safe and elegant way of working with containment to heal survivors of trauma.

Others who have helped to refine our thoughts, ideas and phrases of language are Kathy Amsden, who contributed the "self-soothing voice" and "truth-telling voice," and has generously shared her work with rhythm and music. We also are grateful to Kim (Kamala) Burden, who co-created the Therapeutic Spiral Model "body workshops" with Linda. Karen Drucker also kindly offered many helpful suggestions for this book.

We are grateful to Mary Bellofatto and Colleen Baratka, psychodramatists who specialize in eating disorder treatment, for sharing their food atom procedures, as well as Kathy Metcalf for developing with Linda the food atom we highlight in this book. We thank Connie Lawrence James of the Cleveland Psychodrama Institute for developing and sharing her Caring Observer, which we find useful in working with highly critical clients. We thank Rebecca M. Ridge for introducing us to the Polyvagal Theory.

Thanks to Angelica Gonzalez and Lissa Garcia who offered favorite interventions at the 2012 conference of the American Society of Group Psychotherapy and Psychodrama; Nancy Bailey who graciously shared the preliminary results of her dissertation research; and Karin Dremel who taught her 1 – 1 constellation process with the use of cups.

We have found the "stages of change" developed by James Prochaska, John Norcross and Carlo DiClemente in their book *Changing for Good: A Revolutionary Six-Stage Program for Overcoming Bad Habits and Moving Your Life Positively Forward* a great model to help our clients understand the process of change, and we recognize Natalie Miller who presented her version of the Wheel of Change at the 2006 conference of the American Society of Group Psychotherapy and Psychodrama, and Chevese Turner, founder of the Binge Eating Disorders Association, who teaches so much about the socio-political aspects of weight prejudice.

We appreciate the writings from Bonnie Badenoch, Donna Fahri, Thich Nhat Hanh, Gabor Maté, Deanna Minich, and Daniel Siegel, pioneers in health and healing. Great thanks too to Alma Nugent, an extraordinary artist and poet who has consistently provided inspirational photographs for our work, plus introducing the idea of celebrating the crone and for making Linda's crone staff, which has been added to through the years.

More thanks to Nancy Alexander, Adam Blatner, Heike Bloom, Terri Brewer, Mario Cossa, Patti Desert, Mercedes Dzindzeleta, Antoinette Fiumos, Linda Grande, Joan Lewin, Joe Kenna, Connie Miller, Marie de Marco, Cathy Nugent, Amy Pershing, Rita Preller, Edie Seashore, Gerda Swearengen, JoAnn Thacker, Gerald Tremblay, Carolyn Zahner, Victoria Wood and the members of the Mid-Atlantic Chapter of the American Society of Group Psychotherapy and Psychodrama.

Our gratitude goes to the skillful editors at Jessica Kingsley Publishers who have made the process of editing and publishing pleasant, smooth and seamless.

Linda thanks her husband Joe and family for their support in writing this book. Karen thanks her husband Richard Wilson and family for their support.

Finally, we give heartfelt appreciation to our clients, trainees and protagonists for the past two decades. As we teach them what we know, we recognize that in many ways they have been our most profound teachers.

Chapter 1

The Body as a Battleground

Our illness is often our healing.

Mooji

Eating disorders are a collection of curious and mysterious ailments that expands to a wide landscape where great numbers of people stand with fear, sadness, silence and shame. Disorders with eating behaviors affect children and adults, males and females. They cross racial, ethnic and socioeconomic lines, and the sufferers include—but are not limited to—athletes, models, dancers, truck drivers, chefs, bankers, exercise instructors, computer programmers, royalty, department store clerks, business persons and ministers. Although eating disorders have been typically linked to the struggles of adolescent girls, they afflict young adults and older adults, some with significant mental health problems, some who appear well functioning, some highly sociable with many friends, others who are desperately isolated. In brief:

- It is estimated that at least 8 million people in the United States have an eating disorder.

- One in 200 American women suffers from anorexia.

- Two to three in 100 American women suffer from bulimia.

- The number of males and children diagnosed with eating disorders is rising.

The past decade has seen rapid changes in this landscape, as battle lines appear to grow fierce on many fronts. The internet offers a multitude of sites that support teen eating disorders. Energy drinks—beverages with high levels of caffeine, sugar and various herbal supplements—are being embraced by people of many ages. People diagnosed with diabetes learn to manipulate their insulin dosage to purge calories from the body. The deluge of magazines and pornographic images raise the bar of unrealistic body types for men and women.

Hundreds more images of faces and bodies stream into our lives daily with the ubiquitous presence of mobile devices. Breast implants are increasingly common, as are the altering of body parts through surgery, cosmetic fillers, botox, tanning, inking and piercing.

The upcoming fifth edition of the *Diagnostic and Statistical Manual of Mental Disorders (DSM)*, the official manual published by the American Psychiatric Association that describes mental illnesses, will have revisions of eating disorders, beginning to remove the stereotype of eating disorders as an illness of women and confirming that binge eating is a pervasive health condition that has long been ignored. At the time of this writing, the changes in the *DSM-5* include:

- Anorexia nervosa is an eating disorder of self-starvation, often life-endangering, characterized by a distorted body image, excessively low weight and the relentless pursuit of thinness.

- Bulimia nervosa combines binge eating with purging behaviors such as self-induced vomiting, laxative abuse or excessive exercise in an attempt to avoid weight gain.

- Binge eating involves recurrent episodes of quickly eating large amounts of food in a short amount of time while feeling out of control.

- Eating Disorder Not Otherwise Specified (EDNOS) signals serious variations of disordered eating that do not meet diagnostic criteria for other eating disorders but require treatment.

We have learned to look at these diagnoses as guidelines, due to the diversity of our clients and the fact that many people have an intense preoccupation with food, weight and shape, even if they do not starve, purge or overeat. In our own practices, we have worked with people who have had different behaviors and symptoms at different times in their lives, and we have learned that different solutions and treatments promote healing and change.

Serious health concerns

Truly, the human body has become a battleground. Helping professionals who treat eating disorders know there are serious health concerns that devastate the mind, body and spirit. Physical complications affect the heart, blood pressure, the gastrointestinal system, teeth and gums, and liver and kidneys. Amenorrhea and malnutrition increase the risk of osteoporosis. Compulsive eaters and yo-yo dieters often suffer from heart disease, diabetes and other health consequences. Anorexia has the highest mortality rate of any mental illness; some studies show that as many as 20 percent of eating disorder clients die as a result of their eating disorder.

Although people with eating disorders may layer clothes to hide the shape of their bodies, many malnourished people feel intense sensitivity to cold and heat due to a lowered core body temperature. Headaches, fatigue, weakness, dizziness, fainting, low energy, loss of hair and decreased resistance to infection are common. Excessive weight contributes to joint problems—the ankles and knees can hold only so much weight—and athletes with eating disorders suffer frequent orthopedic injuries due to compromised bone health and the effects of malnutrition on muscles and connective tissues and the functioning of internal organs.

The intellect and the mind are affected. Biochemical imbalances due to malnutrition, anemia and fluctuating blood sugars impair concentration and learning and contribute to distorted thoughts. Irrational thinking presents a challenge since clients have an impaired ability to see themselves accurately and to reason clearly. Use of experiential methods can sometimes bypass these limitations; however, as malnutrition becomes more severe, medical intervention is mandatory.

Diet and mood

Eating disorders often result from an attempt to regulate mood, especially anxiety and depression. Ironically, acting on this attempt has the opposite effect: changes in brain biochemistry can intensify mood swings, disturb sleep patterns and deregulate the appetite. Obsessive thoughts about food, weight and appearance increase as the eating disorder intensifies. In addition, persons with a family history of mood disorders, physical abuse, sexual abuse, chemical dependency or eating disorders appear at higher risk for the development of eating disorders. New research suggests that there is not one type of brain pattern but rather multiple patterns for depression, attention deficit and bipolar disorder, which often are connected to overeating. In *The Amen Solution: The Brain Healthy Way to Lose Weight and Keep It Off* (2011) by physician David Amen, he describes at least five brain patterns related to overeating, including eating when sad, eating when anxious and eating when impulsive, and then recommends differing supplements, medications or combinations to calm and balance brain chemicals of dopamine, serotonin, GABA and the natural pleasure-enhancing endorphins.

Behaviors and characteristics

Not everyone who is thin is anorexic and not everyone who is fat is an overeater. People's shapes and sizes vary for a number of reasons beyond lifestyle, including genetics; malnourishment due to alcoholism, drug addiction and digestive disorders; hormonal imbalances; food allergies and sensitivities; and a history of yo-yo dieting and certain illnesses.

We have identified five common areas of behavior that are typically practiced by people with eating and body image disorders. From the psychodramatic perspective, these are roles that people take when the use of food becomes distorted and body diversity is devalued, limiting body images to a narrow set of rigid ideals. Looking at these behaviors as roles, rather than as cemented pathology, means that they can be altered and new roles can be rehearsed, learned and integrated.

Not everyone practices all of these behaviors, but these categories offer a quick overview:

- A distorted relationship with food and eating, including constant dieting, restriction of food, fasting, binge eating, purging, practice of food rituals and counting calories.

- Patterns of relationships with people that involve isolating, difficulty asking for help and high levels of seeking validation from others.

- Thinking is "all or nothing," along with a distorted body image, such as feeling fat when thin or perceiving a distorted body weight and size.

- Behaviors that involve perfectionism, poor impulse control, restlessness and self-harm actions or suicide attempts.

- Emotional struggles such as difficulty identifying and expressing feelings, irritability and low tolerance of frustration, anxiety, depression and low self-esteem.

The perspective of relationships and roles

Psychodrama, the action method developed by Dr. J.L. Moreno and his wife Zerka Moreno, teaches the importance of relationships and the social roles that we employ within these relationships. With this perspective, we see that relationships with food and the body can be explored and changed, becoming less damaging and increasing emotional, physical and spiritual health. As we name the roles, rather than pathological behaviors, we identify the sufferer as the one who binges, the one who restricts food, the one who purges, the one who isolates, the one who is anxious, the one who diets, the one who fears being fat, and so on.

At the same time, we recognize that the people with whom we work are resourceful, with strengths, supporters and spiritual connections. A great part of their resilience and strength comes from the fact that they carry additional roles within themselves—the observant one, the compassionate one, the tenacious one, the brave one—that can be recognized, fortified and expanded to address and solve personal problems.

Entering eating disorder treatment is often difficult for the person with the eating disorder because the maladaptive behaviors relating to the use of food are experienced as useful roles to deal with emotional distress. When we investigate the person's relationship with food, we learn that food also plays roles: the one that numbs the body and the spirit, the one that distracts from underlying painful feelings, the one that fills the body, substituting for emotional needs. This learning is not merely intellectual understanding but an understanding that comes from an experience of body, brain and spirit.

In addition, the individual's beliefs and behaviors that are entrenched in roles join the interplay with this battleground, along with the family role dynamics—the daughter, the son, the spouse. Studies (Brewerton, 2005) have established a correlation between eating disorders and emotional, physical and sexual abuse and other trauma, and others (Schwartz, Galperin and Gleiser, 2009) describe problems with secure attachment of child to nurturer. Together, they present a multitude of issues: fear of certain foods, body image distortions, relationship problems, patterns of control, mistrust, and painful memories stored deeply within the body.

Finally, socio-cultural influences contaminate an environment where a person with low esteem is encouraged to seek external validation by attempting to conform to unrealistic images of body in the media. Admiration and praise are directed to people who lose weight or follow excessive exercise regimens. Persons involved in a sport, art or profession with emphasis on weight or appearance—such as models, actors, gymnasts, divers, body builders, jockeys, wrestlers, distance runners and ballet dancers—are at a higher risk for eating disorders because they feel pressure to perform or compete at their "best" level.

Denial

Denial is a common reaction when health professionals, family members or others voice concern or recommend treatment. Anorexics usually deny having a problem, saying that everything is "under control," and claiming, "You're only trying to make me fat." Bulimics may talk about exercise as healthful and report they only use high-quality laxatives. Compulsive or binge eaters may say, "I really like food…" or, "I just don't have the discipline," or, "Life is too short to deny these pleasures of food." Underneath the denial, however, bulimics and compulsive eaters often know their behaviors are problematic but experience intense feelings of shame and guilt, denying the behaviors to maintain secrecy. Anorexics suffer such immense body image distortions and impaired cognitive processes due to malnutrition that their denial is reinforced.

With the psychodramatic perspective, people who deny their problems are less likely to be labeled as resistant but rather seen as holding a role—"the one who denies"—that must be transformed, perhaps initially into "the curious one" or the "open-minded one." Pathologies that are normally considered to be defeated are now considered roles that can be identified, sorted, rehearsed, changed and integrated—and can bring a new life to a client with eating disorders or body distress.

Medications and surgery are not enough

Traditional talk therapy may help the suffering person understand the components that contribute to the eating disorder or body dissatisfaction. This kind of therapy offers tools to remedy distorted thinking but often leaves the sufferer frustrated in the attempt to make lasting behavior changes.

The biochemical imbalances may be treated with a prescription for antidepressants or other medications. Although the medications are helpful at times, their efficacy is diminished due to malnutrition. They also have side effects, such as anxiety, insomnia, fatigue and sometimes weight gain, and not everyone can tolerate them. Surgery—whether the full bariatric procedure or the less drastic gastric band option—is sometimes successful and sometimes not. Some sufferers find surgery eliminates multiple medical conditions and mediates severe body image dissatisfaction; the gastric band is less effective in reducing medical concerns like diabetes. However, the surgical procedure does not eliminate obsessions about food and body appearance, and depression sometimes results when people realize their problems do not disappear. People who no longer use food to deal with feelings may become drawn to alcohol abuse, compulsive shopping, gambling and other compulsions. Furthermore, these kinds of surgeries can stress the body and cause various levels of pain; many post-bariatric patients report feeling chronic hunger that they cannot satisfy.

We believe that medications and surgery are not the cure for eating disorders because eating disorders result from a complicated interplay of bio-psycho-social factors that demand integrative treatment by multiple disciplines. With these challenges and changes, we believe that helping professionals need new tools to assess and treat eating disorders.

A holistic approach to treatment

The Western model of treatment has traditionally looked to defeat troubling symptoms, problems and illnesses with language that reinforces themes of war and battling, as we discuss earlier in the chapter. Our perspective is that, when we face an eating disorder, the purpose is not to fight, defeat, or kill but rather to discover, heal and transform.

Here is where the action method of psychodrama—as well as other action-oriented and experiential therapies—helps professional and client walk away from the battleground, finding peace and a new relationship with food, self and the body. To be sure, action therapies do not stand-alone: our clients need medical care; individual, group, expressive, cognitive behavioral and family therapy; body image treatment; stress management; nutrition and exercise education; and exercise trainers with knowledge of eating disorders.

Confidential support groups, such as Overeaters Anonymous and other 12-step programs, are helpful adjuncts to treatment. Yoga, tai chi, qigong and other appropriate and mindful movement offer valuable ways to experience the strength of the body. Complementary therapies like acupuncture, naturopathy and homeopathy help balance the brain's biochemistry, adjusting for circadian and seasonal rhythms, stimulating detoxification and reducing cravings. Medicinal herbs, often used by practitioners of Chinese medicine and naturopathic physicians, support detoxification from sugar and additives that often contribute to cravings.

We encourage our clients to stay with the healing process as long as necessary. Relapses are an expected part of recovery, and clients are encouraged to consider deeper explorations and alternative options if they re-engage in eating disordered behaviors. This approach allows the relapse to become a learning experience rather than a sign of failure.

Recovery from eating disorders is a process, sometimes long term. Many persons recover and live full and productive lives. Action and experiential methods, including psychodrama, contribute greatly to the recovery process because they not only address the cognitive distortions but also support the practice of new behaviors and assist in embracing lost parts of self.

Chapter 2

The New Neuroscience

*We are slowed down sound and light waves, a walking bundle
of frequencies, tuned to the music of the cosmos. We are souls
dressed up in sacred, biochemical garments, and our bodies are
the instruments through which our souls play their music.*

Albert Einstein

Awareness, which is the basis of change, does not create change. Knowing about the pattern of unhealthy behaviors does not stop automatic behaviors seemingly beyond our conscious control.

In the past two decades, researchers have learned a great deal of information about the human brain's development and functioning, how the brain is connected to the body's intelligence and why insight and awareness are not enough to heal the impact of traumatic experiences and our automatic responses to them.

We now know about the delicate nature of the brain as it develops from the very beginning of life. Certain experiences—a stressed mother, a community trauma, a family crisis—appear to inhibit the circuitry of the developing brain. Yet the brain is not "fixed" into any specific configuration for life. The brain has an amazing plasticity, continuing to constantly change, alter and adapt as it responds to new experiences later in life. These experiences change not only the brain's physical structure but also the functional organization.

The "smart" vagus nerve

New attention is directed to the so-called "smart vagus," the tenth cranial nerve, which gives us a fascinating perspective to understand the healthy development of our brain, our sensory systems and our ability to regulate our emotions (Banks, 2011; Porges, 2011a, b; Ridge, 2012).

The vagus nerve is actually not a single nerve but a group of some thousands of neural pathways that originate in several areas of the brain stem. It is a primary component of the autonomic nervous system, the part of the nervous system that is beyond our conscious control, and regulates the heart, the gastrointestinal tract and other organs and systems. It streams information about the body's viscera to the brain and is crucial to the infant's developing ability to self-soothe and engage in social interaction. A detailed discussion of Polyvagal Theory and its implications for attachment, self-regulation and eating disorders is beyond the scope of this book. However, it is important to know that the engagement of the primary caregiver with the infant, developing limbic resonance and empathic attunement, creates a healthy vagus.

We might imagine the vagus nerve as a giant cluster of electrical wires covered by a wrapping of insulation. The insulation protects the vagus so that it does not metaphorically spark when touched or stimulated, creating a cascade of uncontrolled stress responses. Social engagement and empathic attunement provide the insulation, which protects the infant from the impact of stressors. If a parent is stressed—even if the parent does not show it—the child senses danger rather than safety; this sensing can impair the child's development of a well-toned vagus and his or her ability to attach to the caregiver and ultimately self-regulate and socially engage. Messages to young children to "toughen up" and prematurely separate from the primary caregiver interfere with the development of healthy vagal tone.

Vagal tone refers to an impulse sent from the vagus to the heart, inhibiting the frequency of the heart's beats so that we feel more calm and balanced. When vagal tone is impaired, we struggle to find safety and stability and search outside of ourselves with alcohol and drug use and compulsive behaviors.

In his 2010 book, *In the Realm of the Hungry Ghosts*, physician Dr. Gabor Maté speaks of our tendency to feel empty and seek satisfaction from the outside, desperately wanting soothing in the short term yet feeling unable to meet our need for satiety. We see many clients who attempt to fill the emptiness and find self-regulation with binge eating. Maté is among many experts who recommend certain conditions that promote optimal reconfiguration of the brain so that anxieties can be properly soothed. He speaks of the necessity to provide children—and we presume adults if they were not able to receive these prerequisites as children—with a non-stressed environment, an empathic group of caregivers and consistent nurturing so that brain circuitry can properly develop.

Conditions and activities that promote healing of the brain

Adults with healthy vagal tone are able to experience anxiety, anger and other emotional upsets without withdrawing or becoming aggressive. Porges, the developer of Polyvagal Theory, suggests strategies to create a sense of safety, such as retreating to a quiet environment, listening to music or playing musical instruments, singing, talking softly and respecting the messages of the body instead of forcing it to perform (Dykema, 2006). Play dampens the automatic defensive responses because it includes face-to-face social engagement with an expressive face and wide-open eyes (Porges, 2011a). Since so much of psychodrama involves play and experimentation, it is ideal to gradually take people from a frozen state to a re-regulated nervous system.

Habits of isolating from others or engaging in high-intensity exercise—rather than moderate exercise—actually create a greater retraction of the social engagement system; it puts us in the state of analgesia, so we no longer feel the stress, as opposed to stimulating a sense of safety and security. This has obvious implications for our clients who exercise obsessively.

Brain development is linked to relationships with others. Dr. Daniel Siegel, the author of *Mindsight* (2010a) and *The Developing Mind* (2012), has coined the phrase "interpersonal neurobiology," which suggests that social relationships shape the brain's development. Certain kinds of relationships promote a special kind of attunement that creates resilience, compassion and well-being in us and relationships. This attuned relationship is beyond the task of caretaking—rather, it is what psychotherapist Bonnie Badenoch calls right-brain to right-brain bodily based regulatory experiences (2008), producing a mindful and calming presence that infuses internal stability in the midst of external stressors and modeling self-soothing that emerges from within. Knowing this, directors will want to stay in sustained and regulating contact with protagonists and create warm ups that support this good vagal tone, opening up spontaneous opportunities for social engagement and using techniques in dramatic scenes that gradually empower the protagonist to integrate the brain.

About attachment

This brain development research parallels research on attachment and how a child's insecure attachment to caregivers leads to eating disorders. In his presentation "Attachment as a Mediator of Eating Disorder: Implications for Treatment" at the 2009 Psychotherapy Networker Conference, psychologist Mark Schwartz identified two styles of insecure attachment: dismissing the need for attachment and preoccupation with wanting attachment. He theorizes that eating disorder symptoms are a mirror of the attachment difficulty—ritualized ways of negating needs while expressing extreme demands for attention through life-threatening symptoms.

Schwartz advocates for experiential psychotherapy because of its ability to activate the limbic system and access the unconscious internal models of relationships to provide developmental repair.

What creates change?

So it appears that action, not analysis, is the maker of change. Porges, Maté, Siegel, Badenoch, Schwartz and others maintain that reparative enactments of early attachment experiences, co-created by helping professional and client, are fundamental to healing. Here is where the importance of multi-modal emotional learning is so valuable—a longtime concept of psychodrama that is now appreciated and validated by a range of experts.

In his 2009 book, *The End of Overeating: Taking Control of the Insatiable American Appetite*, David A. Kessler notes that habit reversal happens through a combination of awareness, recognition of competing behavior and competing thoughts, support and emotional learning. Just as the eating disordered person has learned to attach emotions to experiences of eating—or not eating—he or she may begin to practice new emotional connections to new cues, overlaying unhealthy patterns with new ones.

With practice in redirecting the neuronal excitement away from the unhealthy habit, the new responses eventually become automatic as well. Here, the process of role training can facilitate this redirection. Through experience, people learn to derive emotional satisfaction in new ways.

Neurological basis for action methods

Trauma expert and physician Bessel van der Kolk, the eminent psychiatrist who has studied post-traumatic stress disorder for the past 20 years, was among the first to maintain that trauma experiences create neurological changes within the brain, particularly affecting a person's ability to soothe the self (2003). There is an inability to put the internal experience of disorganized sensations and action patterns into words because Broca's area, the speech center in the left brain, is deactivated by trauma. The stress hormone cortisol is depleted, exhausting the adrenal glands and often boosting reliance on caffeine, other stimulants and sugar to substitute for genuine energy. Hyperarousal of the brain's amygdala, which plays a primary role in the processing and storing of emotions, creates a cycle of intense feeling followed by numbness and dissociation.

As we learn that traumatic memories are stored in the non-verbal right side of the brain, we realize that talk therapy has limitations and that new ways are needed to stabilize the brain and the body. Experiential treatment, which uses non-verbal and verbal approaches, is prescribed to heal body–mind connections, rather than simply managing the symptoms of eating disorders. Kathryn Zerbe, in her comprehensive 2008 book *Integrated Treatment of Eating Disorders: Beyond the Body Betrayed*, notes that experiential treatments including psychodrama, when employed with expertise, can have a substantial impact on helping a client integrate body and mind.

Van der Kolk also has identified experiential therapy as the treatment of choice for trauma survivors and suggests improvisation and theater as superior to traditional talk therapy. Van der Kolk (van der Kolk, 2002; Wyley, 2004) calls for a system of experiential psychotherapy to treat post-traumatic stress disorder because it has been shown anecdotally to be a treatment of choice for the non-verbal and body-based symptoms that comprise the diagnosis of trauma.

Meditation

An increasing number of studies show that mindfulness meditation creates positive changes in the brain. In the Harvard Medical School study reported in *Psychiatry Research: Neuroimaging* (Hözel *et al.*, 2011), researchers report that those who meditated for about 30 minutes a day for eight weeks had measurable changes in gray-matter density in parts of the brain associated with memory, sense of self, empathy and stress. Brain scans taken before and after the participants' meditation regimen showed increased gray matter in the hippocampus, an area important for learning and memory. The images also showed a reduction of gray matter in the amygdala, the brain region connected to anxiety and stress. Overall, learning and memory processes, regulation of emotions, self-referential processing and perspective taking were affected; a control group that did not practice meditation showed no change.

Although meditation appears passive, we consider it action oriented in the broadest sense, because it activates the presence of the observing self—the Witness role—that notices when thoughts begin to intrude upon the process of rhythmic breathing and gently returns the self to the breath. Meditation, which emphasizes staying in the present moment, is akin to the psychodrama standard of attending to the here-and-now, so experiences can be metabolized and integrated.

Creating a new reality

A study by Tali Sharot and Elizabeth Phelps found that directing our thoughts towards a positive future is a result of the brain's frontal cortex's communicating with subcortical regions. Sharot's book, *The Optimism Bias: A Tour of the Irrationally Positive Brain* (2011a), demonstrates that the same neural system that recalls the past also imagines the future, suggesting that recollection is designed as a reconstructive process. Neural mechanisms seem to engender hope, but there is more: stress and anxiety are reduced, physical and mental health are improved, and motivation to take productive action is enhanced. Sharot maintains that, in order to progress, we need to be able to imagine alternative realities, realties that are better and within our reach.

Guided imagery supports this optimism, but psychodrama offers more: rather than simply imagining a future scene with an optimistic outcome, action methods like psychodrama present the opportunity to set the scene in great detail, then step into the scene and actually experience it. As part of the enactment, which psychodramatists call surplus reality, we are also able to prepare ourselves to function well in that alternative reality.

For example, we may identify a person who has specific goals—to have recovery from his or her eating disorder, to have a greater sense of spirituality and to make a career change. The person believes that his or her eating disorder prevents personal growth and professional change but has difficulty imagining a different kind of life. By enacting a scene where the eating disorder is concretized as the obstacle on the path, the person is able to gather allies and physically approach and pass the obstacle, then create the future scenes with his or her future self fully in his or her new career, having gained spiritual growth. Standing in the future, as the fully healed self, he or she speaks from that role to his or her present self about remembering what it was like to be there and how he or she got to this new place.

Education about the brain: Brain Chairs

Many people struggle with their inability to control irrational anger or chronic anxiety, and trauma survivors often blame themselves when they are not able to override automatic reactions or chase intrusive images from their waking and sleeping hours. They are often frustrated that they overreact to certain triggers even though they intellectually know that the trauma is in the past.

Karen uses an extremely simple activity, Brain Chairs, which explains the hemispheres of the brain and helps people become more compassionate and understanding of their triggered responses. Karen begins with two chairs placed side by side and explains that one chair is the left brain, the other is the right brain.

The left-brain chair is pasted with sticky notes that describe its functions: logical, analytical, proficient with words, meaning and sentences. The right-brain chair is pasted with sticky notes that describe its functions: emotional, creative, body oriented, feelings and the like.

Two people are invited to sit on the two chairs, each portraying a hemisphere of the brain, and Karen gives them a scarf to hold, with each person holding an end of the scarf. The scarf, Karen says, represents the corpus callosum, the thick band of nerve fibers that is the link between the two hemispheres. In a well-functioning brain, the right brain is able to quickly detect a new sensation—a brightly colored scarf that Karen waves in front of the right-brain player—and immediately sends a signal to the left brain to determine the level of threat or safety. The left-brain player says, "Everything is all right," and the right-brain player breathes easily.

In the trauma-altered brain, the link between the hemispheres is weaker and the message cannot easily get through. Karen instructs the two players to drop the scarf to their laps, brings in a third person (or pillow or chair) to stand as Trauma and waves the brightly colored scarf again. Now the emotional brain becomes chaotic, and the message gets scrambled so that it is unclear if the sensation is threatening or not. The right-brain player shakes or waves hands, looking overwhelmed. The left-brain player looks puzzled. Karen points out that the trauma experiences are activated in the brain but cannot be clearly processed.

Because psychodrama is geared to spontaneity and the needs of the group and the individual, we are providing additional variations throughout the book to demonstrate how these structures can be adapted and personalized.

■ VARIATION

If there are sufficient group members, use additional participants to portray the brain hemispheres and represent functions of each hemisphere, holding signs.

■ VARIATION

In an individual session, use empty chairs with sticky notes or signs and other props as needed.

■ VARIATION

If there is more time and interest and the director has an in-depth knowledge of the brain, the nervous system may be more fully sculpted with the thalamus, the amygdala, the hippocampus and the pre-frontal cortex along with the vagus nerve, with each part of the brain receiving a more complex function.

Chapter 3

How Action Methods Help Move Beyond the Silence and the Fury

*When you work in interior work, the work is
not done by method, but by intensity.*

Kabir

For those afflicted with eating disorders, actions speak louder than words. The disorder becomes friend and foe, enemy and lifeboat. Food becomes the primary relationship, serving many functions such as comforting, numbing, empowering, punishing or surviving.

Psychodrama and action methods (Blatner, 2000; Dayton, 1994, 1997, 2000) are powerful ways to concretize the relationship between people, their eating patterns and internal and external experiences. Psychodrama was developed by Dr. J.L. Moreno and Zerka Moreno and uses improvisation, role play and other techniques to facilitate the shift from narration of a story to physical representation—showing and experiencing the story with the body and the voice. Action methods refer to a form of personal and professional growth work derived from psychodrama.

The client, called the protagonist, puts his or her truth into action with the assistance of a trained professional, called the director, and other participants, called auxiliaries. The director may pick from a variety of options, which may include simple posed scenes called sculptures, brief enactments known as vignettes or full-length dramas with multiple scenes.

Psychodrama should not be viewed as a single therapy, but rather as a complex method of concepts and techniques that can be adapted for use with many types of problems and issues. It is most powerful when combined with sociometry, the science and art of evaluating roles as they are played out in social relationships, which Moreno also developed and refined through the years.

Although psychodrama has been closely linked to psychotherapy, it is employed successfully in education, law, business, theology, coaching and other fields. Psychodrama is one of the first modern body-based methods, stimulating multi-modal learning and deep change; like the experiential and expressive arts therapies—such as drama therapy, music therapy, art therapy, dance and movement therapy, and poetry therapy—it engages both hemispheres of the brain.

Helping heal eating disorders

The sociometric and experiential nature of these methods helps eating disorder clients in several ways. From the sociometric perspective, the understanding of roles the client plays—including the self-destructive roles—is a first step in identifying new roles that are healthy and self-caring. Action methods help people bring their inner worlds to the stage and find words that are hidden behind the binge eating, purging and restricting. They are able to rehearse making new choices for the developing self, access strengths, address obstacles to problem solving and gain opportunities to enliven creativity.

There is an increasing number of models of experiential treatment, with the Therapeutic Spiral Model the leading psychodramatic model of trauma treatment (Hudgins, 2002; Kellermann and Hudgins, 2000), and the one that we believe most closely applies to those with eating disorders. The Therapeutic Spiral Model draws on theoretical foundations from clinical psychology and research in experiential psychotherapy and modifies classical psychodrama interventions to prevent uncontrolled regression.

Limited research

Psychodramatists who specialize in eating disorders report many testimonials and anecdotal support about psychodrama's usefulness, some of it published in Colleen Baratka's chapter in *Healing World Trauma with the Therapeutic Spiral Model: Psychodramatic Stories from the Frontlines* (Hudgins and Toscani, 2013). However, there is very limited evidence-based research about psychodrama and eating disorders. One current study, developed by Nancy Bailey for her PhD dissertation at Capella University is "The healing experiences of women: Psychodrama and eating disorders" in 2012. Her study documented in-depth interviews of ten women, aged 18 to 65, who were diagnosed with an eating disorder and whose treatment included participation in at least one session of psychodrama during their treatment experience. Several prominent themes were revealed:

- The women expressed fear of being connected emotionally, physically, relationally or personally to themselves or others.

- They also mentioned an overwhelming need for safety in the therapeutic process—with groups and with the facilitators of the groups.

- All the women reported that participating in psychodrama therapy enhanced and escalated their recovery process, identifying the modality as being more impactful than other therapeutic interventions they had tried previously.

- They liked the benefit of having the opportunity to become familiar with their group members before engaging in valuable parts of the process.

- The most impactful healing took place when playing roles in another's drama or watching. Although all the women had been protagonists in dramas, they were highly sensitive about their bodies feeling on "display" and greater self-consciousness would tend to be associated with defense mechanisms rooted in the eating disorder. As auxiliaries or audience members they did not imagine that they were scrutinized or judged and therefore felt less pressure to show themselves as perfect.

- All participants identified a sense of an internal shift, allowing them to feel a connection not only to others in their group but also in their relationship with themselves. This shift allowed them to feel less alone in their diagnosis and more engaged in the recovery process.

Ways to investigate and heal

Action methods are particularly useful in addressing the educational necessities, clinical challenges and developmental milestones of eating disorders recovery. The sociometric standards of observing group relationships and connections, and the psychodramatic techniques of soliloquy, doubling, mirroring, concretization, role reversal and others offer an immense range of ways to investigate and heal:

- Action methods provide valuable tools to assess, build and strengthen the therapeutic alliance at the beginning of treatment and evaluate progress as treatment continues.

- Enactments engage physical, emotional, psychological and spiritual aspects of the person, when the protagonist's truth is put into action, sparking action insight.

- Rather than being drawn into a power struggle with the protagonist's defenses, the defenses are acknowledged and concretized as having served a useful purpose while recognizing that they now stand in the way of recovery.

- The roles of the eating disorder may be enacted so they do not remain covert and expressed through the body with eating disorder symptoms. Here the psychodramatist and protagonist discover that the eating disorder has more roles than the individual, such as friend, comforter, empowerer, punisher and more.

- Protagonists may work through developmental tasks that were detoured at the onset of the eating disorder. For example, role reversal can facilitate expression of the adolescent's struggle for identity and separation versus the need to stay connected. This may be acted out, revealing the adolescent's projections of those in parental roles and providing safe expression of intense and ambivalent feelings.

- Action methods provide an opportunity to practice making choices for new roles in developing a self with a voice. For example, the "good-girl-eager-to-please" role may be transformed into the "assertive woman" role; the "caregiver" role may be transformed into the "self-caretaker" role.

The warm up to create openness and safety

Action methods are powerful because they introduce and sustain a gradually evolving process of healing and change. If we are able to give ourselves to the process, we can not only experience new aspects of ourselves but also integrate these experiences into the activities of daily living. The key is becoming open, flexible and safe enough to have these therapeutic experiences.

The way to accomplish this sense of flexibility and safety, according to Dr. Daniel Siegel (2010a) is to work within the "Window of Tolerance" (pp.137–139). When this window is expanded, we will maintain equilibrium in the face of stresses that would once have thrown us off kilter. Siegel describes this window as the band of arousal within which an individual can function well. If an experience pushes us beyond our window of tolerance, we may fall either into a pattern of rigidity and depression or a space of free-falling uncontrolled chaos.

This optimal window offers sufficient stimulation of the brain's limbic system to access the material in need of healing while supporting balance with the necessary containment by keeping the brain's frontal cortex engaged. Experiential methods accomplish this delicate balance, as we will demonstrate in later chapters, because we can travel slowly into the process and adjust our experiences according to different kinds of dramas as necessary.

The process of psychodrama

Psychodrama gives us the warm up, the activity that prepares us for fully experiencing the drama to come. The best warm up is designed according to the goal of the therapy session and the relationships between people in the group. The director will take time to create or select the type of warm-up activity that will enliven clients—bringing them to states of spontaneity, readiness and creativity so that the experience can be accepted and taken in, rather than defended against.

33

This book intersperses warm-up suggestions with therapeutic action structures so the helping professional can adapt to individual needs, group process, time constraints and spontaneous and unexpected happenings within the unfolding process. Because these action structures are organized with a beginning, middle and end, they maximize therapeutic interventions rather than serving as stand-alone activities that are not as effective.

In addition, we offer what we call "projects of integration" for our protagonists to pursue after the drama concludes; these incorporate the experiential learning into the brain and body.

Assessment and evaluation

The spectrogram, the sociometric test that measures a range of behaviors, beliefs, roles or feelings, is useful for both assessment and evaluation. The spectrogram is an imaginary line drawn on the floor between opposite poles, marked by pillows, chairs, mats or other objects. The director may assign one statement at one end:

I think about food 100 percent of the time.

and assign a differing statement at the other end, such as:

I think about food zero percent of the time.

The protagonist or group members place themselves on the spectrogram accordingly. Having the client place his or her body on the line—rather than just talking about his or her preference—has a powerful impact because it allows the client to physically acknowledge how much energy is spent there. Conversely, if the client stands at the "zero" pole, that presents an action opportunity for challenging denial, or, at the very least, dissociation from experience. In addition to non-verbal disclosure by body placement, the director may ask for verbal sharing, having participants explain why they chose their places.

Repeating the spectrogram as therapy progresses provides the opportunity to assess change and to examine a future projection—as a future scene is called in psychodrama—of where the client will stand on the spectrogram at the completion of recovery.

The locogram

The locogram, another sociometric activity, designates locations on the floor that represent certain roles or preferences about specific questions in any given moment. Participants step to the place that most closely identifies their feelings, thoughts, preferences or choices in the moment. This technique can be used as a check in, a warm up, an assessment or part of the sharing process.

We have found that the locogram can help group members and individuals to identify their most troublesome obsessions. The obsessive thought patterns that plague eating disorder clients may vary, with some people more focused on food, others on weight, shape or different aspects of appearance.

In a group, for instance, we may place scarves, mats or pieces of paper with words on the floor to indicate topics of obsession: body shape, weight, food, exercise, purging. We always add "other," giving a choice to those who do not identify with the major categories.

After participants make their choices, each is invited to share the reason for taking the place. This sharing helps the director to learn the central concerns of the group, at least for that session. When used during an individual session, the director will have a greater sense of which therapeutic action structures are best for an appropriate intervention. For instance, if a client identifies an obsession about a particular body part, perhaps thighs, the director may introduce the "String Thing," explained in Chapter 10, as a way of addressing what may be a body image distortion.

■ **VARIATION**

Food could be separated into categories of obsession: carbohydrates, sweets, salty foods and fats.

■ **VARIATION**

Feelings may be identified generally: angry, sad, glad, lonely, scared—giving participants a way to consider feelings in the moment and disclose them in a safe group setting. A "don't know" or "unsure" category may be added.

■ **VARIATION**
Recovery pathways: attending a support group, keeping psychotherapy or nutrition appointments, mindful eating or movement, appropriate rest, supportive relationships, journaling and meditation.

Concretization, especially with the social atom

Concretization takes abstract concepts and makes them immediately real. For example, the "social atom," first done with pencil and paper, identifies important interpersonal relationships from the client's perspective. The client draws himself or herself on the page surrounded by circles for significant females in his or her life, triangles for significant males, and rectangles for significant groups, institutions and the like, such as school and church. The closeness or distance of each significant person or item is also noted in the diagram. The diagram may be concretized using sand tray figures, stuffed animals, puppets, chairs, mats or sheets of paper during a private session or with the participation of other members in the group. By enacting the social atom, the protagonist gains insight into how relationships with particular persons or even with particular places—such as school, restaurant, work place, holiday locations—contribute to the eating disorder.

Concretization permits direct relationship to these absent people and abstract qualities with physical representation. Concretization may involve the use of people to portray roles of humans or abstractions; at other times we include props to add to the dramatic action.

For example, instead of a human helper, known as an auxiliary, who has been trained to play roles, the client may choose a "furry auxiliary," Linda's name for a plush puppet, stuffed animal or small figure that warms up the client's spontaneity, to represent defenses. For instance, if the protagonist appears unusually emotionally defended, the director may ask him or her to choose a stuffed animal to represent defenses—an elephant for denial, an owl for intellectualization, and so on—and place them in another part of the room during the therapy session.

The director can make a playful game of being on the same team as the protagonist and look for evidence that one of the "furry defenses" may be creeping back into the recovery space during the session. This activity facilitates self-awareness so the protagonist will consciously choose when to pick up the defenses—it role trains the protagonist to use the Witness role, the part of the self that can observe thoughts and feelings without judgment. Giving the client conscious choice acknowledges his or her power and establishes a playfully serious therapeutic alliance in which client-protagonist and clinician-director work together.

The eating disorder as the double

Often, the eating disorder has more active roles than the person who "chooses" it. When the individual is rigid in his or her behavior, the eating disorder remains persistent and defended. In fact, the disorder serves as a maladaptive double function, representing the other parts of self that reflect and take care of the self, doing what the person cannot do. In other words, the eating disorder is an attempt to meet the needs that were unmet due to insecure attachment in childhood.

From the therapeutic perspective, the director can strengthen the therapeutic alliance and begin to create secure attachment through the use of doubling, a basic psychodramatic technique, whereby the director or group member stands or sits shoulder to shoulder with the protagonist and speaks as the protagonist's inner voice, expressing thoughts and feelings that the protagonist may be unable to verbalize. Doubling is a flexible tool used not only to create an empathetic connection between the director and the protagonist but also to gain valuable information about the protagonist's life and habits. For instance, a director may wish to introduce doubling to help the protagonist reveal what transpired during the 24 hours prior to the therapy appointment; it is particularly useful in helping to identify triggers for and consequences of eating disorder behaviors. At other stages of treatment, the double's voice can slowly be internalized in the protagonist as a voice of strength, cognitive reasoning or another important part of self.

See Chapter 9 for specific discussion about the Double and its uses along with modifications of the Double.

Mirroring as a tool for attachment repair

Mirroring is a psychodramatic technique in which the protagonist steps out of the scene and watches the scene enacted by auxiliaries taking the roles of the protagonist and important others. It creates distance so the protagonist can safely see the bigger picture.

For example, we are learning that children with insecure attachment had parents or caregivers who were not able to accurately reflect to the child the child's feelings and behaviors. The toddler—whose developmental task is to attain a sense of self while feeling bonded to the parent or caregiver—learns to experience himself or herself not as a distinct individual but as an extension of the parent. Psychodramatic mirroring creates the opportunity for the adult protagonist to observe his or her reality with his or her own eyes, rather than through the eyes of the parent.

Action insight by role reversal

Role reversal, an interaction or exchange of roles, facilitates a vibrant kind of action insight that cannot be discovered by intellectual exploration alone. When we exchange roles with the "other," we have a fresh and immediate experience of the "other" that is beyond the intellectual grasp.

As we step into the role of the "other," we are able to explore, feeling its form, speaking its language and learning its secrets. This experience helps the protagonist know the roles the eating disorder holds and the limitations of those roles. The knowing is action insight; the fact is that we often unconsciously role reverse with others. A prime example is the parentified child who unconsciously role reverses with the helpless or demanding parent; when we use psychodrama, our role reversals become conscious.

For example, the protagonist may identify that the eating disorder is her friend. The director may ask the protagonist to take on the role of the eating disorder as friend by moving to another chair or space in the room, then taking on the role and speaking from that role to herself in the empty chair or space. In a group, the protagonist may choose another group member to take the role of the eating disorder as friend. The action insight engages both the physical and psychological aspects of the self and allows the protagonist to feel the insight *in* the body, not just to intellectualize it.

We may role reverse with a part of the self—the self who wants to recover, for example—and let this part of us have its say. Or we can role reverse with the part of self that is resistant—wanting to stay sick, not wanting to take action, being fearful to take risks, etc.—and discover its existence as a real force in our life, rather than denying it.

We may role reverse with the other person—the mother who criticizes our body shape, the prospective boyfriend who thinks we would be just a little more beautiful with plunging necklines and a tighter dress, the waitress at the neighborhood restaurant who teasingly insists that we must have dessert after a meal, even if we are already full.

Finally, we may role reverse with "things"—the mirror, the scale, food, a particular kind of food, a binge food, the diet, the food plan, the eating disorder, the body, a part of the body, the bodybuilder muscles, "fat" clothing, the closet, the refrigerator, the pantry, the exercise machine, the gym, the personal trainer, the breast implant, the plastic surgeon, perfectionism, treatment, the Barbie doll, the G.I. Joe action figure… The list is endless, only determined by the director's alertness to the roles or "things" significant to the protagonist. Some of these roles are roles with which a person struggles; others are strengths and gifts such as courage, compassion, the willingness to be willing. These roles create inner conflicts within the self that may be enacted and externalized so that the roles may become conscious.

When the protagonist takes the role of "other," the director may ask for a soliloquy—the "other" simply has its say—or the protagonist may step into a role and the director may use the technique of interview, asking specific questions to tease out the attitude, meaning and significance of the relationship.

For instance, Lucy shared, "I love cheese, but I won't eat it—I can't let myself." When asked why she couldn't eat cheese, she gave the typical response of, "It has too much fat."

However, this answer seemed to limit, rather than expand, her knowledge of her cravings and eating patterns. She was asked to "be the cheese," and there was a series of role reversals with Lucy speaking in her voice and the voice of the cheese. Finally, Lucy stated, as the cheese: "I'm just like your mother. You love me and you want me, but I make you feel bad. You're never good enough and no matter how much of me you eat you'll never feel good enough so don't eat me at all."

Lucy started sobbing, saying she couldn't believe how much a single food meant to her and how much meaning the food held. Through her tears, she asked, "Will all of my foods be a person?" Of course, we do not know if her foods will represent a specific individual, but we can say she has a relationship with each food that could be helpful to explore. She left the group thinking that she would not always feel trapped in a cycle of restricting, binge eating and purging—the first time she felt hopeful.

In another group, Gina struggled with the reason she did not eat her mother's tomato sauce. She loved the sauce and loved her mother, but through role reversal she was able to own the anger she has felt for much of her life, an anger that translated to: "I will not eat your homemade Italian food because it makes you happy and I'm too mad at you to make you happy."

Scene setting

Scene setting, a common element of psychodrama, supports the warm up of the protagonist. If the vignette is to focus on an encounter between the protagonist and his or her binge food, the director may ask the protagonist to set the scene. Are you:

- Standing in the kitchen next to the cupboards?

- Idling with a co-worker in front of the vending machine at work?

- Talking in the buffet line at a holiday party?

The scene is usually set by the protagonist walking the space and noting pertinent imaginary items in the area, making the scene as real as possible. Pillows, scarves and other props may be used to identify certain objects or places, and the director may role reverse the protagonist into an object to further the drama.

For instance, Millie identified her internal conflict during her weekly shopping trip to the supermarket, when she invariably stood for a long time at the potato chip aisle, mentally debating whether to purchase a bag of spicy potato chips, a favorite binge food. Millie knew that she would gobble the entire package minutes after she returned home.

Karen began the vignette by requesting that Millie mark out the sections in the supermarket in the group room while speaking a soliloquy—having her walk in the front door, select an invisible shopping cart, notice the various sections of produce, bulk foods and canned foods before she arrives at the potato chip aisle. As she stands in front of the shelves holding the bags of chips—the shelves portrayed by a line of group members standing shoulder to shoulder—she did a soliloquy before facing a chip package. When she mentioned that there was a clerk watching from the deli section nearby, Karen asked her to role reverse with the clerk and back again to herself.

Finally, Millie role reverses with the potato chip package; by this time, she is fully in the moment and the drama unfolds, meaningful to Millie and the whole group. Millie discovers that the chips were holding the role of the part of herself that is "spicy"—the part that she described as daring, adventurous and willing to take risks.

■ VARIATION: FLOOR PLAN IN ACTION

We also like the floor plan activity by Cynthia M. Bulik in her 2012 book *The Woman in the Mirror: How to Stop Confusing What You Look Like with Who You Are* where she suggests that women draw a floor plan of their houses and analyze the places where their self-esteem is negative, neutral or positive. A second activity analyzes body esteem. With psychodrama, this activity will become more powerful because the protagonist is actually able to experience the floor plan by walking in the "rooms" and stopping at significant places when the director recommends a soliloquy, role reversal or mirror technique.

Adapting talk therapy interventions: CBT Chairs

Many classic talk therapy interventions translate well into action structures. For instance, the five-step cognitive behavioral chart—which supports clients looking at the situation, the emotions and automatic thoughts that emerge, contrasted with objective reality and options for new feelings and behaviors—can be easily adapted with a series of empty chairs.

In this action structure, the director places five chairs on stage, labeled with signs for the specific steps of the chart:

Chair 1: Situation. (What is going on?)

Chair 2: Emotion. (What are you feeling?)

Chair 3: Automatic thought. (What is the first thought that comes to your mind?)

Chair 4: Objective reality. (The truth of the situation.)

Chair 5: Different feelings and behaviors. (How do you feel once you have had time to think about the objective reality?)

The director or client(s) can choose the scenario or problem to be explored or that needs resolution. Clients can take turns in each chair, voicing responses to the corresponding section of the chart. Other clients or the director may double, and in a group setting everyone can take the opportunity to sit in the different chairs. Process the experience, results and provide feedback.

Here is a sample scenario, in this case, beginning with the first statement on Chair 1:

Chair 1: My sister refuses to be part of my treatment.

Chair 2: I feel rejected.

Chair 3: She hates me.

Chair 4: I don't know why she has made this decision.

Chair 5: I can feel sad that she's not going to be involved and I can continue to focus on my treatment and my personal goals.

Projects of integration

Trauma hardwires the brain and body to cling to a particular belief–feeling–behavior system: ways of reacting, ways of being with self, ways of relating to others, much like a mosaic whose pieces have been put together in a particular configuration. Psychodrama takes apart the old mosaic configuration and puts the components together in a new way. However, the newly configured pieces are up in the air for a while—not yet "glued" together. These projects of integration firmly glue the pieces together in a new design and help them settle into the brain and body.

Projects of integration arose from the desire to educate clients and trainees about the basic neuroscience of healing and give them a vital role in that process. We describe the projects of integration in the following way:

Psychodrama helps integrate the limbic brain—which holds pictures, fragmented body sensations and feelings—with the cortex of the brain, which has words and makes meaning. To maximize this integration, we ask that you take the parts of the drama you find most important—both images and words—and concretize them. This might include a journal of pictures (drawn by hand or cut from magazines) and words, which can be important lines from the drama that seem essential to your new way of being. It can be as simple as a single page with a doodle and a word or as complex as a PowerPoint presentation.

We suggest that your project takes place within 48 hours of the drama. We recommend this time frame because the brain tends to revert back to its previous pattern unless the new one gets "glued in." The protagonist returns to the individual or group session with his or her project and shares it or shows it—so that the learning continues to be anchored within the person. The project is also useful when reviewing the history of treatment and setting future goals. In future chapters, we will continue to demonstrate how these projects may be used during sessions and as homework.

What's in the psychodrama room?

Professionals who use action methods always look to concretize concepts and experiences so the protagonist has a participatory, sensory, emotional and embodied learning of the knowledge rather than simply intellectualization. The room of a practitioner of action methods will have props to stimulate imagination, spontaneity and creativity.

In psychodrama, the biggest prop is not really a prop at all but a space: the stage where the action takes place. When the protagonist steps on stage, he or she is also making a non-verbal statement about bringing his or her truth forward to share with others. Today, clinicians, educators and others may not have the means to construct an actual tiered stage like J.L. Moreno's original design, which remains in use at Boughton Place in Highland, New York. However, the stage can be concretized by using a large rug or outlining part of the room so that the stage space is evident.

Props increase warm-up options for the group and the protagonist and offer options to experiment with spontaneity and creativity. In addition, the presence and use of objects keep the brain's right hemisphere engaged, and adding visual symbols to the verbal conversation can stimulate bilateral integration of the brain (Badenoch, 2008).

The empty chair is the classic psychodrama prop. Other useful objects are pillows, scarves, stuffed animals, puppets and dolls. Linda uses her "furry auxiliaries" to concretize various aspects of an eating disorder, such as defenses, rationalizations, secrets, longings and the like. Karen uses a sand tray and a wide array of small figures on shelves to create vignettes in the sand, using the small figures as substitutes for auxiliaries.

It is helpful to have a range of plastic, paper mache or cloth objects of food, especially for children, that might include fruits, vegetables, eggs and fast food items like cheeseburgers and French fries. These may be found in toy stores, hobby stores, cookware and decor shops and in sand tray catalogs online.

Chapter 4

Multi-dimensional Illnesses, Multiple Healing Choices

Capabilities are clearly manifested only when they have been realized.

Simone de Beauvior

The feminist perspective

Women have traditionally been taught to be silent and pretty, so it's not surprising that the majority of people with eating disorders and body image struggles are girls and women.

Because women have been taught "Don't talk," or "What you say is wrong," or "What you say doesn't matter," finding and using their voices to speak their truth is the primary goal of treatment. In addition, lessons are learned that restricting food means giving up the power to choose due to the inevitability of overeating: binge eating follows restriction. Action methods provide the opportunity for gaining insight and learning and practicing new roles—in other words, having a voice.

Learning to accurately label feelings and speak the truth about feelings and needs advances recovery. Psychodrama provides embodied role training for speaking up and speaking truth, which is at the core of healing eating disorders.

The self-soothing voice, based upon neurobiology and object relations theory, is a musical role that uses the elements of sound, rhythm, tone, melody and lyrics to calm the limbic system, facilitate developmental repair and lay the groundwork for making meaning of experience. Created by psychodramatist, musician and clinical social worker Kathy Amsden, this helpful intervention develops the self-soothing role and the truthful voice role.

The developmental perspective

Recovery involves moving from denial to reality, alienation to connection, and passivity to personal power. Clients can learn new roles in action to replace the roles the eating disorder symptoms have been holding. When we explore the roles in greater depth, we will quickly realize that the roles arise from layers of behaviors and experiences, beginning from our very birth.

Eating disorders, like addictions, can develop as part of the struggle to complete the tasks of one or more of the stages of life development. The person with an eating disorder often becomes stuck in the developmental stage in which the eating disorder began. The action techniques derived from psychodrama help clients work through these developmental tasks. Because various kinds of eating disorders appear to reflect various stages of development, we identify the psychodramatic techniques that should help the client move through these developmental stages.

The technique of doubling creates a "felt" connection with another. As a child grows older, the parent's mirroring allows the toddler to learn how to observe, literally establishing skills to see the whole picture. The table lists life developmental stages as identified by Erik Erikson in his classic 1959 book, *Identity and the Life Cycle*, and shows the action techniques that we have found helpful.

Table 4.1 Developmental Action Interventions for Eating Disorder Treatment

Psycho-dramatic technique	Developmental stage	Developmental challenges	Correlation with healthy relationship with eating and food
Double and Body Double	Infancy (The child takes in food and nurturing and learns the difference between hunger and other feeling states.)	Bonding and trust, creating limbic resonance and empathetic attunement.	Infant–mother bond creates connection with food and nurturing. The warm milk and the parental bond helps tone the vagus nerve, preparing the infant to develop the capacity to self-soothe and self-regulate.

cont.

Psycho-dramatic technique	Developmental stage	Developmental challenges	Correlation with healthy relationship with eating and food
Mirror	Toddler (The child begins to feed himself or herself with simple finger foods, sometimes needing assistance.)	Accurate reflection of the child's external world and ambivalent feelings: "I can do some things myself and need help with other things."	The child learns to have preferences, both with food and people, and tests limits and boundaries. The child also develops attunement with hunger and fullness cues. Attentive listening by the primary caregiver further tones the vagus nerve.
Role play	Latency (The child is likely to focus on safety and predictability, developing "food jags," such as eating the same foods for weeks at a time.)	Giving voice to a sense of self in a rule-oriented world that seems divided into right and wrong: "I'm on the right side of things."	The child learns to experiment with other realities and possibilities when trying new foods and new relationships.
Role play and role reversal	Puberty (The young person is concerned with body changes and the need to "fit" with peers. This is the most likely time for onset of anorexia.)	Struggle for separation and need for control versus dependency and belonging.	The young person experiments with conflicting roles and changing needs in action and developing spontaneity rather than rigidity in both food and relationships.
Role play, role reversal and soliloquy	Later adolescence (The young person is faced with opportunities to make decisions about what to take in and what to let go of. This is the most likely time for binge eating or binge eating and purging.)	Struggle for identity and separation versus the need to stay connected.	The young person is developing spontaneity, a purposeful and creative response to new situations, rather than impulsivity. Also, the ability to speak one's truth regarding food choices, self-care, emotional needs and behaviors.

Rebecca M. Ridge (2012), a psychodramatist and body worker, has identified how these psychodramatic techniques not only support life stage development but also the development of the vagus nerve and emotional regulation:

- The first phase involves the psychodramatic technique of doubling, along with soothing sound, gentle touch, higher frequency sounds and soft eye contact, and placing no demands on the infant.

- The second phase is the psychodramatic technique of mirroring, which is seen as a higher engagement because we are seen and acknowledged by another who gives us feedback about our behavior and teaches us social cues in the world. Mirroring offers recognition of the person's external world, giving appropriate neural feedback and facilitating the ability to regulate affect.

- Finally, there is the psychodramatic technique of role reversal, which involves a high level of social engagement—the ability to step out of the self and being able to reflect how another might feel or behave. Role reversal is not possible unless there has been adequate toning of the vagus through empathic attunement and social engagement.

Feed the Baby: A vignette designed for the developmental task

With the awareness of the developmental tasks and the accompanying psychodramatic tools, we can assess our protagonists and design vignettes that address these developmental stages. One fun—and revealing—activity is what Karen calls Feed the Baby. The warm up starts with bringing a tray of jars of commercial baby food into the group setting, explaining to the group that we will revisit the participants' experience of being fed by their parents. Spoons are provided, as are paper napkins in case of spills.

Using sociometric choice, each participant selects the person he or she wishes to pair with during this activity. Once paired, one person agrees to act as the Parent and the other as the Baby. The director suggests that the person in each role pays attention to his or her experiences, whatever they may be, for later sharing.

The tray of containers of baby food—a variety of fruit purees is recommended—is presented by the Parent to the Baby, and the Baby chooses by pointing because as Karen explains, babies don't yet know how to talk. The Parent makes a show of opening the jar and taking a spoon and then beginning to feed the Baby. The Baby is able to communicate with hands, facial expressions and gestures if necessary.

Time is given to feed the Baby, attuning the Baby's rhythm of accepting food from the spoon, eating and swallowing. Parent may look into the Baby's eyes, smile and talk and use the paper napkin to dab at the mouth if necessary. When the Baby signals "fullness," the roles are reversed, and Baby now takes the Parent role and the Parent becomes the Baby.

After both in the dyad have the experience of playing both roles, there is verbal sharing first within the pair, then in the whole group.

This simple exercise, which relates to trust and mistrust, is rich for sharing. In one group, Monica noticed that her legs began swinging happily when her caregiver approached her with food and she was eager to eat. By contrast, Jillian noticed that her caregiver appeared to be feeding her perfunctorily—almost absentmindedly—without eye contact; she noticed that she began to feel anxiety as the activity progressed. Michael reported feeling very hungry and recalled that the parent spooned the food slowly, appearing not to realize his level of hunger. Daniella noticed that her parent did not recognize when she signaled "full" by turning her face away, and instead tried to spoon more food into her mouth.

The food and sex connection

Eating disorder clients are often disconnected from their bodies and, therefore, the experiences and pleasures of having a body. The condition of anorexia suggests the prohibition of bodily experience, because food, eating, digestion and elimination certainly remind the person that he or she has a body. Extreme thinness disguises gender-specific features, such as breasts, buttocks and hips for women, and muscle wasting minimizes typical male body features for men. Rigid boundaries reflected in food rituals, such as cutting food into small separate pieces and not letting one food touch another food on the plate, sometimes are a metaphor for the fear of contact with others.

According to the fact sheet *Males and Eating Disorders: Research* compiled by Tom Shiltz and published by the National Eating Disorders Association in 2005, males with anorexia displayed a considerable degree of anxiety about sexual activity, and eating disordered men were significantly less likely to have had sexual relationships. Another study that Shiltz cites found that as many as 80 percent of men with eating disorders reported they grew up in families that regarded sex as a taboo subject.

In contrast to some studies, which reported a higher incidence of eating disorders among gay men due to the stereotype that a trim physique is highly valued in gay male culture, other studies found no relationship between eating disorders and homosexuality. In *The New York Times* article (Goode, 2000), "Thinner: The male battle with anorexia," Dr. Arnold Andersen is quoted as saying, "There is nothing about gayness itself that increases eating disorders" (ibid).

Weight gain may protect men and women from being romantically and sexually involved—or serve as some kind of test to see if the prospective partner is genuinely interested in them as a person, not as a sex object. Men and women have also gained weight to repel any sexual interest on the part of others; they often discover this unconscious motivation when they begin to lose weight—and are overwhelmed by flirtation, suggestive comments and requests for dates and sex. Women in particular may have difficulty saying "no" to men when they don't want involvement.

Body image fears are related to dating as well as initiating or participating in sexual activity, especially with women concerned about the size of breasts (too small), the size of hips (too big) and the bulges and hollows that come with overeating and aging, or simply one's genetics. Men have their own worries about their bodies, noticing the size of their paunch, the "love handles" at their waist, their muscles and their aging process.

Our clients have told us that binge eating is a safe way to enjoy the sensuality of food and eating and to feel comfort and connection without having to deal with an actual human being and the risks of physical intimacy. Purging may force up what the client can't "stomach," and becomes a metaphor for abuse, trauma or anger.

The pregnancy complication

Pregnancy may push women in either direction of the eating disorders spectrum. The very best of responses may inspire the pregnant woman to consider, "I have another life to care for inside me, and I owe it to that life to take care of myself." However, many women consider pregnancy as "permission to eat whatever I want and as much as I want," leading to binge eating; others misinterpret the normal weight gain of pregnancy as "fat" and restrict or purge. In addition, some women may become obsessed with post-partum weight loss and body image, sometimes resorting to compulsive exercise, harsh diets and weight loss pills.

CASE STUDY: DIANE AND THE SOCIAL ATOM

Diane consulted Linda's lifestyle counseling practice because she wanted to have a child, but her doctor was concerned about her digestive issues and possible complications for fetal development should she become pregnant. Her food intake varied significantly even within a single day—in quantity and quality—causing abdominal pain and bloating followed by bouts of constipation or diarrhea. Although she was tall and slender at the age of 30, she expressed intense fear of weight gain, weighing herself multiple times each day and frequently overexercising and abusing laxatives, especially after episodes of binge eating. She mentioned stressful events that contributed to her inconsistent eating patterns.

Linda provided education about the connection between food, exercise and stress, and reviewed Diane's food diary assignment. It was clear that Diane's stress related directly to people and places and had an impact on her intake of food and alcohol, an additional concern because her social history revealed a family history of alcoholism. It was clear that she needed friends to support healthy eating practices and moderate exercise in order to heal her digestive system and nutritionally prepare her body for pregnancy. She also needed to address the binge drinking issue, not only for herself but also for her future child.

Inspection of Diane's social network with the social atom revealed a problematic relationship with a certain friend. She met this friend weekly for dinner and drinks at a local restaurant, and this meeting consistently involved binge drinking and binge eating. She felt guilty about this pattern but said the dinner with the friend was her one chance during the week to "unwind."

Diane decided that she would not be able to return to that restaurant if she wanted to recover her health. She realized she would have to choose the company of supportive friends who understood her need to change behaviors. Hearing Diane's desire to relax after her work week, it occurred to Linda that she would benefit from a regular activity that eased her stress, and where she could move her body in a gentle way and meet people likely to support her well-being. Linda suggested that she enroll in a weekly tai chi class to substitute for the evening when she met her friend at the restaurant.

When Diane followed this suggestion, her episodes of binge drinking and binge eating reduced significantly. Linda continued to examine Diane's social network to identify relationships that needed attention, and they continued sessions through Diane's subsequent pregnancy and the delivery of a healthy baby. During Diane's pregnancy, Linda frequently used role reversal, letting Diane take the role of her unborn child expressing concern when Diane was struggling, and gratitude when Diane was appropriately caring for herself and her unborn child.

The addiction perspective

Addiction and substance abuse often intersect with eating disorders. Many people admit they use nicotine as a diet aid—having a cigarette to calm their nerves rather than a snack—and fear stopping the use of nicotine because they don't want to gain weight. People in recovery from alcohol and drug use often find themselves lured to the mind-numbing qualities of the overuse of food, especially foods that contain high amounts of sugar or carbohydrates, which mimic the ingredients of alcohol.

Kimmy stopped smoking marijuana easily—she was worried about failing a drug test for employment—but soon found herself waking in the middle of the night to clear out sleeves of cookies and crackers from boxes in her cupboards and chunks of cheese and slices of bread from her refrigerator shelves. Jim, a heavy-set man in his middle 50s, became sober through Alcoholics Anonymous (AA) and was proud of his nine years of recovery. However, he began eating the doughnuts at the AA meetings, went out with his AA friends for large breakfasts and binged with second and third helpings at home; his weight tilted the scale more heavily and he arrived in therapy when his doctor warned that heart bypass surgery was imminent.

Addictive substances that are often under-recognized are the high use of caffeine, ephedra-like herbs and energy drinks. People who complain about chronic exhaustion, gaining weight easily, being frequently constipated, suffering with headaches and low mood should be evaluated for conditons related to thyroid and educated about the relationship between chronic stress and adrenal hormones. We have found naturopathic physicians to be especially helpful in these matters.

Chapter 5

Men and Eating Disorders

All the appetites and anxieties of man, his eating habits, his
sexuality, his friendships, are one single appetite and one single
anxiety to achieve union with one another and with the cosmos.

Ernesto Cardenal

Although women comprise nearly 90 percent of the diagnoses of eating disorders, men are not immune. In fact, professionals are noting an increase in males with the diagnosis of an eating disorder with an accompanying distortion in body image, often perceiving the body as smaller than actuality, a perception that may contribute to steroid abuse and excessive exercise to build muscles. A presentation to the 2012 conference of the International Association of Eating Disorder Professionals (Lemberg and Stanford, 2012) revealed that eating disorders in men have increased an astonishing 250 percent during the last ten years.

The same media that glorify the superwoman—the idea that women can be super-achievers at work and nurturing mothers, sexy wives, perfect housekeepers and gourmet cooks at home while looking fresh and super-thin everywhere—also glorify the superman.

Our culture presents the superman as the invincible warrior who is in control of every situation, powerful in the work place and admired by both men and women. He displays a body that is youthful, athletic, lean and muscular; when he takes off his shirt, he shows a chiseled torso, six-pack abdominal muscles and well-developed pectorals.

Men who have been typically concerned about the thickness of their hair and the size of their penis now worry about their weight, muscles and body image. It is no wonder that many men are turning to cosmetic surgery—liposuction to reduce fat at the waist and implants for biceps and calves—to reshape their bodies, along with dieting, excessive exercise and, in some cases, anabolic steroids.

Special issues for men

Men—who by various studies comprise 10 to 40 percent of all eating disorders and 40 percent of those with binge eating disorder—are often invisible. They are less likely to seek treatment because of the perception that these ailments are "woman's diseases." They do not relate to the website and brochure pictures of treatment centers geared to girls and women. And they are socially conditioned, more so than women, to hide their feelings and struggles, and they typically do not talk openly about their body problems or concerns.

Both men and women suffer body dysmorphic disorder, a separate condition from eating disorders diagnoses. This disorder is characterized by preoccupation with one or more perceived defects in physical appearance that are not observable or appear insignificant to others. However, men tend to experience more muscle dysmorphia, which has been popularly dubbed "bigorexia."

Men who want bigger and more muscles and men who seek a trimmer physique are often involved in excessive exercise and awarded respect and praise for long and intense workouts. Men who are overweight are often given a quick recommendation by their doctors to follow a diet. They—plus their family and their doctors and other health care providers—often do not identify certain behavioral and thought patterns as indicators that their relationship with food, diets and body image is skewed and problematic. For example:

- When the retired pastry chef at the White House revealed in *The Washingtonian* that former president Bill Clinton ate five to six pork chops at one sitting for an evening meal, followed by half of a strawberry cake for dessert—and yelling that he wanted the other half of the cake for the next morning—much of the media response considered these anecdotes entertaining rather than signs of an eating disorder. Later, Clinton suffered a serious heart attack and underwent two surgical procedures.

- When Steve Jobs, the brilliant entrepreneur and Apple computer founder, periodically focused on fasting or eating only fruits or vegetables for weeks, many people considered these habits associated with the hippie scene of the early 1970s, along with taking drugs and writing poetry. As years passed, the adult Jobs, always the perfectionist, continued his highly restricted diets, extreme picky eating and compulsive use of certain foods.

• When actor Dennis Quaid shed 40 pounds to capture the gaunt look of his character of Doc Holliday who was dying from tuberculosis in the film *Wyatt Earp*, even he was surprised how the weight loss affected him. "My arms were so skinny that I couldn't pull myself out of a pool," Quaid told a reporter from *The New York Post* in 2006, saying that he suffered from what he called "manorexia." "I wasn't bulimic, but I could understand what people go through with that." But, like other people who suffer from the disease, he couldn't see himself clearly. "I'd look in the mirror and still see a 180-pound guy, even though I was 138 pounds," he says.

The Keys study

Such body distortion aligns with research from a study by Ancel Keys in the 1940s, retold in depth in the book *Rethinking Thin: The New Science of Weight Loss—and the Myths and Realities of Dieting* by Gina Kolata published in 2007. This fascinating research project observed young men who were conscientious objectors imprisoned during World War II. The men who took part in the study, sometimes known as the Minnesota Starvation Study, were of normal weight and considered physically and psychologically healthy. They were restricted to 1500 calories per day, well below the average recommended intake of 2500 to 3000 calories per day for men, depending on age and activity. After just one month of participation in this diet, the men began to obsess about food and weight and suffered anxiety, depression and mood swings. When the study concluded, many men had problems including binge eating. It took nearly two years of normalized eating for the men's perception of their body size to return to normal.

Ordinary men

In ordinary life, men who are obsessed about weight or appearance may be involved in occupations and avocations that value a certain weight or body shape, such as wrestlers, gymnasts, body builders, bicyclists, musicians, dancers, skaters, jockeys and models. Many participate in sports where a certain kind of body weight determines their class, such as wrestlers. Other men succumb to the cultural pressure that women have felt for decades: recent surveys show that male body dissatisfaction has increased dramatically during the past 30 years, from 15 percent to 43 percent, a rate comparable to those found in women. Interestingly enough, in the past two decades, the industry of men's health, fitness and grooming magazines has tremendously increased.

In our practices, we have not discovered a single profile of the man who suffers from an eating disorder. There are many:

- Allen grew up as a small and frail child who was brutally bullied throughout his school years, with much of the teasing related to his sexual orientation as homosexual. His career choice of dance reinforced the necessity of the need to look thin. He frequently talked about wanting to become what he called a "breath-a-tarian"—wanting to live on air, as some highly evolved spiritual masters are reported able to do. He habitually returned to his favorite fantasy—about wanting to be so light, so ethereal and untouchable that no one could hurt him.

- George came to Karen's office as a recovering alcoholic, with nine years of sobriety. However, George was dangerously obese, tipping the scales to approach 400 pounds. The doctor told him that his heavy weight contributed to heart problems and advised a diet. Since George was familiar with the model of addiction, he realized that he was addicted to eating, just as he had been addicted to alcohol. He wanted help to arrest the addiction since he believed he could not stop eating compulsively on his own.

- Luke and his fiancée Sophie started couples counseling because Sophie felt unloved and neglected. In an individual assessment session, Karen learned that Luke was constantly training for triathalon competitions and had won several medals. His travels to triathlon events combined with 20 hours per week of training placed a strain on the relationship. Further investigation revealed that Luke had several male cousins who were diagnosed with hypertension, diabetes and other serious health conditions complicated by their weight, and he saw excessive exercise as a way to prove that he was healthy and to avoid succumbing to these conditions.

Compulsive eating

Of course, many men simply overeat—enabled by a society that endorses and advertises cholesterol-laden and high-calorie foods as hearty "men foods"—huge triple burgers, fatty steaks, piles of chicken wings and sides of French fries. These foods, along with beer and liquor—are synonymous with the watching of sports events, hunting parties and men's nights out—in other words, identifying what it means to be a man. Few will challenge the man with a large appetite—overeating is seen as a sign of a person with a healthy appetite—only to be detoured by doctors' orders that recommend reducing fat, salt and sugar.

Similarities and differences

Boys often become aware of body dissatisfaction as puberty approaches. Their bodies do not look like the plastic figures of the action heroes that have been their childhood playthings. Studies (Andersen, 1992) show that men tend to start diets because they are actually overweight; women tend to diet because they "feel" fat, even if they are not overweight. Women tend to diet to enhance physical attractiveness, and men tend to demonstrate more goal-oriented behaviors—to achieve sports-related goals, to reap health benefits and to avoid future medical problems. Finally, many men feel more masculine and in control when they can maintain a thin and toned body and are exercising. They believe their reward for working out will be greater admiration and respect from others.

Professionals specializing in work with men with eating disorders have developed a specialized assessment tool known as EDAM, an acronym for Eating Disorder Assessment for Men. It states the common issues that men with eating disorders share, which have some differences from the issues that women typically face. The four essentials as mentioned by EDAM's founders (2012) are: muscle dysmorphia, binge eating, preoccupation with weight and weight issues, and disordered eating. We use action methods, including circle sociometry and other sociometric tools, to make the assessment more engaging and to reveal commonalities to increase bonding among men.

Step to the Line

In addition to circle sociometry, we may use "Step to the Line" to uncover issues in action. In this structure, we lay a length of masking tape on the floor of the group room that is the "line." The men are directed to "step to the line" if the stated criteria applies to them.

We may say, "Step to the line if you...

- have a history of weight issues...

- are involved in a sport...

- have a history of sexual abuse...

- have a history of other kinds of trauma...

- have struggled with addictions...

- believe your muscles are never defined well enough...

- think about gaining muscle when considering what foods to eat...

- feel out of control if you are not able to exercise...

- have injured yourself due to exercise...

- find yourself eating very quickly...

- have gone for days at a time without eating...

- have used water pills, laxatives or enemas as a way to control your weight...

• check your body several times a day for fatness..."

Because these EDAM assessment criteria are very specific and may feel intrusive, we will intersperse additional criteria, such as:

"Step to the line if you...

- have a pet...

- like music...

- are the oldest child in your family... (or the youngest or the middle)

- enjoy the outdoors...

- are in a relationship...

- have children..."

The men are also given the opportunity to present criteria they feel are important in order to become acquainted and more comfortable with one another.

Hidden disorders

Men may not arrive in the psychotherapy room with the presenting problem of an eating disorder or dissatisfaction with body image. Except in extreme cases, the problem of overeating, overexercising or restricting may be buried, with the man instead speaking of depression, anxiety, low self-esteem or problems finding and keeping relationships.

In the physician's exam room, they may pat their bellies and speak of "liking food too much" or confess that they can't keep to a diet. Even physicians themselves may not easily identify or diagnose the man who overeats as a binge eater. Doctors are more likely to refer men to a personal trainer or dietician for weight loss and are often not aware of the psychological underpinnings relating to boundary issues, trauma and why the men have not been able to take care of themselves to address heart problems, diabetes and hypertension, and cannot seem to follow doctors' instructions.

Slow disclosure: Two case studies

As men reveal their inner world, however, we learn their concerns about weight, appearance and how they feel about their bodies. Henry, for instance, is one such man.

CASE STUDY: HENRY

Henry arrived in the therapy room with loose blue jeans and an extra-large polo shirt and expressed anxiety about his finances and job prospects, since his home-based business as a software designer had been slowing down. In later sessions, he spoke eloquently and quietly, confessed his loneliness after a divorce and problems of socializing, followed by sessions exploring how he could identify opportunities for socializing and building new friendships after divorce.

Karen helped Henry diagram his social atom, showing few current friendships. He was asked to add to the diagram symbols for prospective friendships with both men and women, and discussed places to find friends. Karen and Henry role played how to say hello and make appropriate social contact. Only later, when Henry felt comfortable in the therapy sessions, did he reveal that he was unhappy with his weight and that his feelings about his weight played a large part in avoiding social events, including church, visits to coffee shops, concerts and other events where he had been invited. It was here that the real work could start.

CASE STUDY: BRENDAN

When working with Brendan, information about Brendan's eating habits emerged after conversation to explore issues of communication. Brendan sought out psychotherapy to discuss a troubled marriage. He had suffered abuse as a child growing up with a chronically mentally ill father—his mother abandoned the family shortly after his birth—and spent much of his time after work watching television, a habit that dissatisfied his wife, who wanted more time with him. He made an appointment with Karen to satisfy what he called her "pushing."

Brendan appeared to have difficulty speaking, explaining that his mind was blank and that he did not know what to say. Karen, mindful that people cannot benefit from even cognitive therapy because their brains aren't getting enough fuel, asked about his food consumption. She wondered if he was exhausted, dissociative, had cognitive difficulties or was malnourished.

Brendan reported that he ate just one meal a day, skipping breakfast as a way to save time and trying to control his weight. He consumed multiple cans of energy drinks and diet soda throughout the day to stave off hunger. He admitted that when he did eat breakfast he felt hungry later, a fact that disturbed him because hunger related to eating, and he did not want to gain weight. He admitted that he had been body conscious since his middle school years, remembering that he hated playing "skins and shirts" basketball and always held his breath hoping to be chosen for the "shirts" team so he could cover his body with a T-shirt.

Karen began with education, providing information that his body and brain needed well-balanced meals to function. In addition to paper handouts, she offered a referral to a nutritionist; Karen also used the psychodramatic technique of doubling to develop the voice of a "caring self" that Brendan could begin to reference within himself.

Action techniques

Action methods well serve this population in particular. Because men are conditioned to take action rather than spend hours talking about their problems, they can easily warm up to action for a number of themes. Soliloquy, doubling and role reversing with the body may be used to explore the meaning attached to body size and shape and how stress or fear contribute to overeating, restricting and compulsive exercise. Many like the quiet meditation exercises that help them quiet their minds and find their inner observer.

Circle of Chairs

In this action structure, we begin with our group of men seated in chairs that are placed in a circle. The director may discuss how men are not conditioned to talk openly about their problems but nevertheless have an inner voice that is active in the "back of the brain" with thoughts about themselves, their bodies and the capabilities of their bodies.

The men are encouraged to be their own doubles and stand behind their chairs, and then invited to silently consider "the way you think about your body."

Time for adequate quiet reflection is allowed. Then the director may say: "Share out loud what you have not dared to share about the way you think about your body."

CASE STUDY: A DRAMA OF GRIEF

Ryan, a successful vice president of a corporation in his late thirties, arrived in Linda's consultation room because his wife and his doctor were "nagging" him about his health. His parents died in a car accident when he was a toddler, and he was raised as an only child by his maternal aunt and uncle. His aunt died suddenly at the age of 38; he remembered watching with horror at the age of ten when she collapsed in the dining room and died of a stroke. There was a quick funeral, with no acknowledgement of Ryan's sorrow. Ryan's uncle shortly remarried, and Ryan, who had been close to his aunt, saw the marriage as a betrayal. As an adult, he began to act out, compulsively overspending and overeating and pursuing risk-taking behaviors that put his job and his health in jeopardy. In fact, his physician told him that his eating habits were shortening his life expectancy and recommended serious changes to improve his health. His wife was distraught about his visits to pornography web sites and their marriage was fragile.

When exploring his unhealthy behaviors with Linda, Ryan realized that his defiance of medical orders was a way to defy death and feel powerful in a way that he never felt since his parents and aunt died. His hidden anger was rooted in the fact that he was powerless to save his parents and his aunt and equally powerless about his uncle's quick remarriage. He did not like the feeling of being helpless as a child, unable to make a difference in his life.

Linda first set up the strengths that Ryan identified for himself—his love of his children, his determination and his appreciation of music. The contract for the drama was to express and resolve grief and anger about the loss of his aunt and his uncle's remarriage.

In the next scene, Linda directed Ryan to set up the scene in the dining room of his childhood home, the same room where his aunt had died. He used chairs to show the dining-room table and pillows to mark other items of furniture.

Thinking that Ryan, a first-time protagonist, would feel stronger in the observer role, Linda directed Ryan to the side of the group to watch the upcoming scene in the role of his adult self. As Ryan watched, group members enacted the scene of his aunt collapsing in the dining room while a trained auxiliary in the role of Ryan as a child grew large-eyed and panicked when he could not revive her.

When the scene closed, with the aunt auxiliary sprawled on the floor, Ryan moved to the next scene, speaking as an adult to his child self, acknowledging the shock and horror the child was feeling.

Linda directed an exchange between his adult self and his younger self in a series of role reversals, with Ryan giving validating messages to his younger self about his deep grief and loss.

A trained auxiliary for his uncle was brought into the scene, and, with his child self at his side, Ryan spoke to his uncle, telling his truth about how painful his aunt's death had been and how sad and helpless he had felt during his growing-up years.

After these scenes of emotional repair, Linda directed the closing scene, with Ryan speaking to his children, telling them he loved them and promising to attend to their feelings.

He understood through action insight that his self-destructive behaviors were an attempt to feel more powerful than death. He wanted to feel the kind of power that he hadn't felt since his parents and aunt died.

CASE STUDY: SECOND AND THIRD HELPINGS

Bill grew up on a large farm in the Midwest where there was always lots of work to do—loading hay, cleaning animal stalls, shoveling feed, driving the tractor—from morning to night. The meals placed on the family table were generously large. Bill's father, a stern and hardworking man, ate silently at the head of the table, and his mother looked approvingly upon the men as they ate, offering second and third helpings.

Bill watched other group members work during a weeklong group intensive, which warmed him up to his childhood and youth experiences. Remembering that he shoveled grain for the cattle to eat, followed by giant pitches of hay, he sobbed as he realized that he was fed "like a work animal" as a child. He had been told that eating would make him big and strong, and the pattern of heavy eating continued for years until Bill weighed 320 pounds.

In the group, Bill spoke to his parents, telling them what he wished he could have told them as a child. "I needed to be seen as a human being, a human being!" he said, expressing anger and pain through his tears, "Not just an animal. I'm not a commodity—I'm a person! A person!"

He continued to speak to the parent auxiliaries, claiming his love for them but acknowledging that the pattern of overeating had been unhealthy for him and that he needed to take responsibility to change it.

Food atom

The food atom, which diagrams the foods in a person's world and is explained in depth in Chapter 8, aids in the exploration of food and relationships. The diagramming of the food atom gives men something to "do," rather than talking about their feelings, which some men have been conditioned to avoid. Yet the feelings and insights that emerge with food atoms can be profound, as we see here.

CASE STUDY: FOOD ATOM AND BARIATRIC SURGERY

When Frank was preparing for bariatric surgery, he made a food atom to learn about his relationship with his current foods. As he inspected the finished diagram, crowded edge to edge with magazine pictures of food, Frank realized that he ate a "huge amount" of food. It was almost surprising to him that he had reached nearly 400 pounds and didn't realize the amount of food that he was eating. The food atom led to investigations as to how his overuse of food attempted to fill the void of empty relationships and how he was disconnected from his emotional and physical selves. Frank went on to have surgery and after several years has not regained the weight; he returns to his atom when he finds himself abusing sugar.

In social atoms, men may become aware that they have learned to depend on women to shop for, prepare and provide their food since childhood. Many men do not know how to cook or have knowledge of basic nutrition, having lived in an atmosphere where the kitchen was the women's domain. Sam's social atom revealed that he had never learned to be responsible for his food habits because his mother, stepmother, girlfriend and wife prepared food that he ate without question. With this new awareness, Sam decided to take cooking lessons to discover, expand and enjoy his creativity in the kitchen.

Male-friendly techniques

Professionals working with men must attune to the language and images that men consider familiar. Linda uses a collection of professional photographs, which she calls the "Work Deck," showing construction equipment and other male-friendly themes with evocative titles of change and transformation. Some photographs show construction sites; one photograph of a partially built building is titled "Far from Finished." A photo of a tall crane is called "Stretching," and a landscape of a construction scene with earth-moving equipment is titled "Organized for Work." Other photos show rugged nature scenes: a rocky cliff with small bushes growing between the rocks is called "Persisting on a Rocky Hillside."

Linda uses the cards to concretize the Observing Ego role, the Witness role, or in lieu of the scarves in the Circle of Strengths. Male facilitators have creatively used substitutes to concretize strengths, like Kevin Fullin (Carnabucci and Fullin, 2013) who has adapted the Therapeutic Spiral Model's strengths for men, using colorful bandanas and small stones to represent strengths rather than the usual scarves.

Men often appear able to talk easily when they have objects that assist in disclosure. Karen has found the use of the sand tray, with a large variety of small figures available on shelves, helpful when working with men—a man may feel comfortable and more in control as he looks at the small objects or directs them to talk, or picks them up.

The sensitive director will be mindful of language and pick words that are amenable to men. For instance, "coach" might be substituted for "inner healer." Men may feel more comfortable with words like "team" or "tribe" or "posse" than "support network." These terms are then translated into roles that can be embodied on stage. We know of one group session where the protagonist, Alvin, who had been somewhat isolated in his daily life, was surprised and gratified when group members showed up for the session wearing T-shirts saying "Team Alvin."

Sometimes the setting for men's groups also makes a difference. Lights may be dimmed on the stage to metaphorically reflect going into the unconscious part of self. The low level of light may provide safety to more fully express emotion or revelations of difficult sharing. Other options to support the sharing of sensitive material might be to have the group agree to look away while a group member talks.

In addition, Linda has found that yoga classes and specific yoga poses can assist in making men feel more connected to their bodies. Since men consider exercise an activity for which they have previous references, they often are willing to experiment with using their bodies in this way. Sometimes a single yoga pose, taken at a crucial point in the drama, is the turning point to healing and health.

CASE STUDY: YOGA AND PSYCHODRAMA

Marc, a middle-aged social studies high school teacher, found himself gaining weight as he grew older. After a day at school, he developed the pattern of coming home, eating dinner and sitting in his over-sized chair, watching television and eating ice cream and cookies. In sessions with Linda, he realized that he punished himself and soothed himself with food. He felt "battered" by the students' demands and enjoyed what he called "peace and quiet" in the evening; the sweet food comforted him.

One of two men in Linda's group, Marc attended the warm-up yoga that Linda offered before the weekly group session. In one session, he realized that he experienced the students' demands as a "wave," a tsunami that he could not control. In another drama, which involved an enactment of how Marc felt overwhelmed by the students' demands, Linda directed him to take the classic Warrior II pose as he faced the group members role playing the students. Linda asked him to hold the pose and say: "I am strong, centered and able to hold my ground."

The Warrior II pose which involves the person standing with a bended front knee and the back leg nearly straight, with arms extended out from the shoulders—has both feet rooted on the floor. In this confident and grounding stance, Marc was able to not only say the words but also experience his body as strong and powerful.

After this session, Marc was able to set boundaries more effectively with his students. In the evening, when he wanted comfort from the challenges of the day, he talked to his wife, a minister with good listening skills, instead of isolating. He continued to practice yoga as a way of centering and grounding himself in his strengths and managing his stress at work.

Chapter 6

Education in Action

The great aim of education is not knowledge but action.

Herbert Spencer

Many people, even health professionals, have misinformation and misconceptions about the nature of eating disorders. With the use of action methods for experiential learning, we can actually *feel* what is happening in our bodies and brains when we watch or participate—making action-oriented educational programs highly dynamic learning experiences. We have found sculpture, dramatic storytelling and music essential teaching tools; this show-and-tell learning is engaging, even mesmerizing, and remains with people longer than the common classroom types of lectures.

Action learning is suitable for all ages, from very young children to older adults, in schools, treatment centers, hospitals, clinics, community presentations and other settings. Unlike many action structures in this book, which are designed for persons with training in psychodrama and sociometry, many of the action structures in this chapter may be used easily by professionals who do not have extensive training. They may be employed as stand-alone structures for educational purposes; for those who have clinical experience and work in a clinical setting, they are great warm-up activities to move into a personal drama with the group's protagonist.

Education has a profoundly healing effect in itself. Participants often report feelings of relief and increasing self-acceptance when they learn that their inner experiences are normal, or at least in common with others. Family members also report a greater understanding about the nature of eating disorders and the recovery process, and may begin to alter their behaviors with the eating disorder client.

For instance, a little-known contributor to weight issues is polycystic ovary syndrome, known as PCOS, an endocrine disorder that is often misdiagnosed. Women with PCOS are often instructed by their physician to lose weight due to the increased risk of Type

2 diabetes associated with PCOS, but they are often given little, if any, guidance on safe and effective practices to balance nutrition and exercise, or referrals for psychotherapy to address the complex and multiple challenges such as mood, fertility issues, body image and discouragement.

It is also helpful to know that body fat distribution is due, at least in part, to the location of fat-burning and fat-storing enzymes. For example, where there are a greater number of fat-storing enzymes, there will be a propensity for accumulating fat in those locations, such as stomach or thighs. Where a high number of fat-burning enzymes are located, there is a likelihood of less fat storage in those areas. The number and location of these enzymes are genetically determined. We have learned that sharing this kind of information with clients, even at intake, serves to ease their self-criticism regarding body shape, and educational action vignettes often bring laughter and lightness to what are often painful issues.

We believe that educators are obligated to be thoughtful about the messages that they deliver. The current anti-obesity school programs are often misinterpreted by youth who become fearful of normal developmental changes with their bodies and may restrict food, behaviors that tend to encourage dieting and body dissatisfaction. In addition, when educational materials are not thoughtfully created and presented, the resulting risk is that mean-spirited messages will promote prejudice, shaming and lack of acceptance of body diversity. The organization Health at Every Size advocates for respect for body size diversity and the Binge Eating Disorder Association is educating the legislative communities and others about how anti-obesity campaigns unwittingly contribute to an increase in eating disorders and weight discrimination.

The range of eating disorders (Eating Disorders Spectrum)

Educational sculptures and other action structures use visual images, rhythms and words that allow us to see, feel and hear information that we may understand intellectually but have difficulty grasping emotionally. In this simple sculpture, we demonstrate that there is no single eating disorder, but rather a range of behaviors when people focus excessively on their appearance, weight or intake of food. You may wish to have certain props ready, such as a hand mirror, a tape measure, a small dumbbell weight, extra chairs, cardboard shapes made to look like a bathroom scale, a diet plan or diet foods.

We begin with a spectrogram, the line on the floor that represents a progression of attitudes and behaviors. Part of the warm up may include an explanation about the fact that, although modern psychiatry considers three specific eating disorders—anorexia, bulimia and binge eating—as significant, there are many ways that people are troubled with relationship to food and body.

To ease the willingness to volunteer and increase group involvement, make sure that you have selected a suitable warm up to stimulate group energy and interest. For instance, you might ask group members to share in dyads or triads about a non-threatening but appropriate topic, such as three things that you know about eating disorders or three related themes that you have noticed in popular magazines.

Begin with a row of chairs that represent this range. At the far left, the first chair represents a person concerned about his or her appearance. We give that person a hand mirror to hold to accentuate the role. As the person takes the role, the chair is removed. The next chairs might show:

- weight, with a cardboard scale on the chair

- size, with a tape measure on the chair

- diet, with a diet plan or packaged diet food on the chair

- exercise, with a dumbbell weight on the chair.

Participants can talk to the chair that represents their primary focus, with doubling from director, group members or both.

At the extreme right, we show the life-threatening results of an eating disorder, a person who is sitting in the chair, quite ill, with the chair representing a wheelchair. Then have group members take turns sitting in the wheelchair with other members speaking in soliloquy from roles of family and friends about what it is like for them to have their dear one in a wheelchair and so weak and ill.

■ VARIATION

Keep the chairs in the line, allowing the participants to sit in the chairs, rather than stand. For various reasons, including weight and physical problems such as back distress and weak knees or ankles, they may have difficulty standing for a lengthy period of time.

Learning, Seeking, Getting Hooked

This action structure shows how people learn to depend on food to solve emotional problems and conflicts. In setting up this sculpture, we clarify that we are not telling one person's story but rather taking part in a group learning process where all are contributing and witnessing. Explain that this sculpture will demonstrate how we gradually change our relationship with food from nourishing to compulsive and unhealthy.

For the warm up, we might ask group members to share in dyads or triads about three life goals that they have; three things that they know about eating disorders; a memory of a time that they used food or another consumable item to soothe or change their feelings.

After all have shared and there is a palpable energy change within the group, ask for a volunteer who is willing to portray a generic "person" for our group story. Have the volunteer and others identify at least three goals that this person might have regarding self (e.g. losing weight, increasing self-esteem, reducing obsessive thoughts about food, wanting positive relationships).

People who may volunteer to portray these goals should stand a distance from the protagonist with their hands reaching out toward the protagonist.

Identify feelings that the protagonist might have (angry, sad, glad, lonely, scared, worried, confused, tired) and what has helped in dealing with these feelings. Ask the protagonist and the group what food or foods might help to soothe these feelings. Pick someone to portray that food, standing next to the protagonist, holding on. Identify the message that food might have, such as, "I'll help you feel better," or "It's not so bad."

Discuss the "learning" stage—when we discover that a food, or a group of foods, will help us change our mood when we're feeling unhappy, overwhelmed or exhausted.

73

Next is the "seeking" stage. Have the group pick another food and ask for a volunteer to play that food—where the protagonist is now actively seeking relief, becoming preoccupied, planning to eat or binge. Identify messages from the second food, such as "I'm always here for you" or "You know I can help you forget your upset feelings" or "You're tired, and I can perk you up."

Finally, there is the "hooked" stage, concretized by another group member hooked to and firmly holding the protagonist. Note that, when we lose our ability to choose a food and our control over that food, it now controls us. Ask the group, the protagonist and the role players: what is the message from this control?

Suggest that the protagonist try to actually move forward to reach goals when held back by the foods, compulsive eating and binge eating.

Have all group members de-role and return to their seats and discuss the following:

- "What did it feel like to play a particular role?"

- "What role did you most identify with?"

- "What role did you least identify with?"

- "What parts of the vignette did you each identify with?"

Exploring other metaphorical roles

In addition to the Learning, Seeking, Getting Hooked sculpture, we may vary our presentations with metaphors illustrating the various roles linked with dieting regimens, body image struggles or eating disorders. One role that we have borrowed and adapted is the "salesperson" from the writings of Tony Paulson who co-wrote the book *Why She Feels Fat: Understanding Your Loved One's Eating Disorder and How You Can Help* with Johanna McShane.

Diet Salesperson

This "salesperson" structure shows clients, family members and students how the disorder or diet "sells" itself. The typical scene has two characters. One is the person struggling with feelings of vulnerability, pain, fear or stress, who is seeking a way to effectively cope in his or her daily life. The other is the salesperson who has a "product" that bolsters feelings of confidence, power and invulnerability. In this presentation, group members may be enlisted to play roles or the director may have trained auxiliaries to act out the roles. The director takes the role of the narrator, explaining the progression of behaviors.

The struggling person voices his or her desire to cope with his or her life. In return for minor changes in behavior—such as eating less fat or exercising an hour every day—the salesperson promises he or she will feel terrific.

Soon, however, the salesperson returns with a new and improved product. To receive this good-feeling product, our client must make more changes—maybe skipping a meal, exercising an extra hour or using a laxative. Each time the salesperson returns, our client responds, this time telling a little lie about eating (when he or she didn't) or starting to take diet pills, focusing more obsessively on counting calories and carbohydrates...

At some point, these behaviors begin to exact a toll. As time passes, dependence on these behaviors escalates to the point where our client is reluctant to let them go, probably because he or she believes they are the only way of coping.

The narrator explains that the salesperson is not a bad character— simply one who believes in the efficacy of the product that is offered.

We have chosen this salesperson metaphor but any metaphor or story may be externalized when you have the knowledge of how to identify pertinent roles, concretize them and narrate the story. We also have purposely kept the "salesperson" without gender so that our listeners and clients can identify for themselves the gender. In a therapeutic setting, we will be able to explore who in the immediate or intergenerational family may be playing this role.

Dramatizing a well-known story

The director may select a current event that is commonly known to participants, a variation of the Living Newspaper, which we discuss in greater depth later in Chapter 7. Here is an example of an educational structure that uses the story of the late singer Karen Carpenter, which Linda directed to benefit the National Eating Disorders Association.

It contains elements related to sociodrama (Garcia and Sternberg, 2000) and drama therapy (Landy, 2008) in that participants collaborate to enact a story that is not personal to them but relates to one or more of their personal or interpersonal roles.

The participants in this enactment were members of an ongoing psychodrama training group. Linda brought music from Karen and Richard Carpenter, known as The Carpenters, a popular brother–sister music duo in the 1970s. Karen Carpenter died in 1983 of heart failure due to anorexia.

Linda first conducted action explorations to learn:

- who in the group has heard of the Carpenters?

- who knows their music?

- who knows the story of Karen Carpenter?

Linda read a brief article about Karen Carpenter and group members volunteered to play roles: Karen Carpenter, her brother Richard, her agent, her mother, her father, her psychotherapist. Others played her young fans who looked up to her.

In the director role, Linda made doubling statements to deepen the understanding of the various roles. At the drama's conclusion, when the character Karen Carpenter died from her eating disorder, Linda asked the fans to say how they felt, after which the Karen character returned from the other side of death to speak to her fans. The Karen character told her fans to honor themselves and their talents by accepting their bodies and not giving in to external pressures but rather valuing their gifts and talents. It was a powerful program, with some participants emotionally moved; others shared about having body issues and talked about becoming politically active with this social issue—even though several participants were too young to remember Karen Carpenter.

The gifts of music

Music and rhythm are invaluable for educational and treatment purposes when working with people with eating disorders. Brain imaging and brain mapping (Campbell, 1992) show that music has a great impact on the neurobiology of the brain. Music travels between the brain's right and left hemispheres throughout the limbic system and within the temporal lobe; while background music activates the right hemisphere, the lyrics activate the left.

Music is yet another way to define the "voices" that we contain within ourselves, such as the critical voice, and experiment with new and healthy voices, such as the truth-telling voice, the self-soothing voice or the spontaneous voice.

When we have worked with music by ourselves or with a colleague with a high level of musical skills, we emphasize that the focus is not on performance but rather activating the musical ear to access and open pathways in the brain and the body, plus finding one's voice and regaining the internal rhythm that has been disrupted by disordered eating. We have learned a great deal from Kathy Amsden, a musician and certified psychodramatist who uses a series of warm-up exercises to awaken the strengths of the musical brain and rhythmic body while decreasing anxiety about working with music, movement and instruments.

Self-soothing voice

She introduces the role she calls the self-soothing voice to safely release emotions while calming the internal chaos. In its basic form, this self-soothing voice does not require words but uses only the breath, sound, tones, melody and rhythm. She may later assign "buddy groups," using the role of what she calls the inner musician to create meaning through improvised melodies, song, poetry readings and dance.

She often sings during workshops, using her music and music written by others. When first singing by herself, Kathy brings attention to breathing, tone, rhythm and melody. She might say, "This first time through, let's just listen to the music… Allow your breathing…to connect…with the movement, rhythm and flow of the song… Feel the tones…and the melody…wash and ease your mind…"

She invites group members to notice their emotional connection to the music: "See how your body wants to or even begins to move naturally in time to the music's rhythm." When the refrain comes, Kathy draws people to join the song if they wish. She sings:

"Ahhhh…
I have a voice…
I have a choice…"

"OOOOooooo
Loud and clear…
Without fear…"

After the group learns to sing the background, Kathy sings her song, "I've Found My Voice Again," which clearly captures a main goal of recovery.

Explore self-expression

We have used the elements of music to discuss pertinent points: women have been taught that their voices don't matter or what they say is not important. For both genders, there may be shame and embarrassment about singing or using the body as self-expression.

Here we might use safe circle sociometry to explore how group members experience their self-expression. Using the step in sociometry activity, we ask people to stand in a circle and step in if:

- they have at any time experienced shame and embarrassment in using their voice in words or song to express themselves

- they have at any time experienced shame and embarrassment in using their body to express themselves

- they have felt intimidated about singing or expressing themselves musically

- they have an inner self-critical voice that prevents them from singing or playing music.

From an educational perspective, we discuss how we have played roles of feeling inferior due to feeling intimidated or criticized. Then, with hands-on sociometry, we ask group members to place a hand on the shoulder of the person who could best play:

- the role of their truthful voice

- the role of their self-soothing voice

- the role of their creative voice.

These selections warm group members to transform the painful roles into behaviors that are healthier, more whole, more expressive. When one group member is chosen by another to hold the transformed role, he or she practices the transformed role, using the voice not only on behalf of the person who chose him or her but also for themselves.

In sharing, we purposely share from our experience. Linda, for instance, might talk about finding her speaking and singing voices, and note that her voice works well when she teaches yoga. Karen, who sometimes identifies as a "recovering shy person," might share about finding her spontaneous voice after playing dozens of unruly and rebellious children on the original Moreno stage during her training with Zerka Moreno, so that she is comfortable with acting silly or childlike.

Songs as fun

Music also brings fun to educational and treatment settings while disseminating important information. As every advertising jingle writer knows, repetition and rhyme make concepts memorable. One of Linda's favorite songs—sung to the tune of Rodgers and Hammerstein's "Getting to Know You" from *The King and I*—demonstrates the wonders of the human body and is well received by women in middle age. Professionals with younger populations can use their creativity by using current music or having the group create a rap song, jingle or poem with positive appreciations for various muscle functions. We have also provided handheld musical instruments to accompany the songs.

Body rhythms

The rhythms of music help with another educational point: how the natural rhythms of the body have been disrupted by disordered eating. All body systems—circulation, respiration, digestion, elimination—have rhythms of their own.

Using a drum or an inverted five-gallon water jug, we drum out the rhythm of the heartbeat, then alter the pattern to demonstrate a heart that is arrhythmic due to starving or high restricting. We may request small groups to select a body system—verbally or by picking an index card with a name—and create a simple movement and sound sculpture to demonstrate the original natural rhythm, then the disrupted rhythm and then, as healing occurs, the return to the original natural rhythm. In this way, participants discover what natural and disrupted body rhythms *look* like, *feel* like and *sound* like, which provides deeper embodied learning.

As with other action structures, this structure may stand alone or serve as a warm up for a drama.

Support System Sculpture

Ask for a volunteer willing to create an action exploration of the task of a support system. Place a paper plate and plastic spoon on a chair in front of the volunteer and identify the need for support to stay balanced in relationship to food. Brainstorm about elements that support recovery. Although everyone's support network may look different, here are common elements of a support network:

- Psychotherapist.

- Psychotherapy group.

- Healthy friends.

- Self-help group like Overeaters Anonymous.

- Sponsor or friend in self-help group.

- Higher power or religious faith.

- Individualized nutrition plan.

- Nutritionist.

- Yoga or movement group.

- Telephone or online help group.

The director enlists group members to take these roles and stand behind the protagonist. If the protagonist is willing, the auxiliaries can place their hands lightly on his or her back to signify support that can be felt in the body. Have the protagonist lean back slightly to feel support, then stand. Ask the supporters to take two steps away so the protagonist is alone with the temptations of the eating disorder. Finally, have the supporters return so the protagonist can experience the difference.

As we see, there are tremendous opportunities to use action for diverse educational topics. Creative directors can use imagination, spontaneity and knowledge to teach complex body processes such as metabolism, the relationship of nutrition to brain chemistry, the connection between food and mood, and the multiple effects of stress on the brain and body.

Chapter 7

History of Diets, Timelines and the Pull of Popular Culture

When we are no longer able to change a situation,
we are challenged to change ourselves.

Victor Frankl

Eating disorders often begin with a diet—a four-letter word with the first three letters spelling "die."

Our cultural images present unrealistic images of bodies—the ubiquitous Barbie doll that is a popular toy for toddlers and young girls, celebrities who are cosmetically and surgically altered, dressed by designers and enhanced by cosmetics experts. Women's and men's magazines alternate pictures of calorie-laden treats with instructions for new diets and photos of six-pack abdominals. Advertisements encourage eating to deal with emotional issues, so we have "happy meals" and invitations to "treat yourself—you deserve it." Add to the mix the Western traditions of mindless consumption with junk food as acceptable "meals" and we have a society that grows larger while feeling the need to slim down. Hence, the paradoxical message: "Eat to excess—and be thin."

Our society judges people by appearance—as esthetic objects rather than human beings. People make frequent comments about the appearance of others rather than focusing on character, personality, well-being or social contributions—for instance, "rating" a person's appearance on a scale of one to ten. Commercials, ads using sex appeal, beauty pageants, body building competitions, sexist films and pornography objectify the body.

Diet and exercise are promoted as the solution to remedying the problems of fat while promoting fear of fat. The goal is to attain a perfect body—and exercise is the way to work off extra calories. The undertone of this approach is that exercise is punishment for having eaten "bad" food or for having "ugly" fat. It is ironic that fit-appearing and smiling people, rather than a diverse representation of shapes and sizes, are the typical models in advertisements and videos for exercise classes. Although there is acknowledgment of the health benefits of regular moderate exercise, they are often presented as secondary to the benefits of appearance. The idea of physical activity as fun and as healthful recreation is often ignored.

A person with low self-esteem begins dieting to look slimmer, perhaps to feel better by conforming to the current societal ideal— slender for women, lean and muscular for men. Sometimes habits of dieting spiral out of control and the dieter believes that "thin" is never thin enough and continues restricting food intake, firmly convinced that he or she is fat, even at low body weight.

Diet timeline

Creating a timeline of significant events that relate to health, diets and body experience is a simple and useful action structure that offers multiple possibilities not only for psychotherapy but also education, consciousness-raising and personal growth. Begin by placing a line on the floor from one end of the room to the other with scarves, masking tape, yarn or whatever is appropriate.

The timeline below illustrates the history of diets, which can be put into action by the director accompanied by the protagonist. At each point along the timeline, the director asks the protagonist to voice his or her soliloquy upon hearing the various historical events.

- 1087—William the Conqueror is unable to mount his horse and is placed on a liquid diet by his doctor.

- 1800s—Early ideas about weight loss regimens are discussed as people in the Western nations start to eat more sugar, drink beer and wine and other distilled beverages, and obesity becomes an issue for the first time.

- 1850—William Banting, an English undertaker, is told his obesity is incurable. Dr. Harvey suggests a change in diet, eliminating sugar and starch. He loses 50 pounds and writes the first known booklet on weight loss, *Letter on Corpulence, Addressed to the Public.*

- 1879—Saccharin, the artificial sweetener, is invented.

- 1894—The medical profession believes obesity is caused by lack of thyroid function so doctors begin prescribing animal-based thyroid compounds for weight loss.

- Late 1890s—Corsets help women achieve an hourglass-type figure.

- 1896—Advertisements for weight loss products appear. Some ingredients in these products include laxatives, arsenic, strychnine, washing soda and Epsom salts.

- Early 1900s—Upton Sinclair, the muckraking journalist writes *The Jungle,* the exposé of the meatpacking industry, and declares fasting as the route to weight loss and emancipation.

- 1912—Spiritualist and magician Hereward Carrington advocates eating only raw fruits and vegetables in his book, *The Natural Food of Man.*

- 1918—Dr. Lulu Hunt Peters publishes *Diet and Health: With Key to the Calories,* the first book to tout calorie counting and to suggest that successful dieting must be paired with exercise and lifelong commitment. She sells two million books, making hers the first best-selling diet book in the United States.

- 1930s—Food combining becomes popular until the Great Depression causes a setback for the dieting industry—many poverty-stricken people are hungry and can hardly afford food.

- 1961—Joe Weider and his wife Betty, a former pin-up girl, found the International Federation of Bodybuilders.

- 1960s—Weight Watchers starts, followed by a long line of diet and weight loss programs.

Depending on the age, the director may ask the client to add more information to the timeline, such as the use of commercial diet aids or examples of overexercising, fasting, cosmetic surgery and excessive laxative use.

After the protagonist completes the diet timeline—by writing, drawing, collage making or using the sand tray—the director may ask for a soliloquy and double as necessary.

This activity may be used in individual or group sessions. It also serves as a warm up for protagonists to do their personal histories of dieting in a timeline.

■ **VARIATION**

Use index cards to write significant events of the evolution of diets, with one event per card. Shuffle the cards and have each group member pick one. Each person in the group may read aloud the information on the card to the group as a whole or share more extensively in dyads or triads.

CASE STUDY: MOLLIE'S TIMELINE

Mollie, a 17-year-old girl in her senior year of high school, was referred to Linda by her psychotherapist following hospitalization for cardiac arrhythmia and collapse during one of Mollie's running competitions. She was the youngest of three children, with two older brothers; both brothers were scholar-athletes and considered stars. Her mother worked in a profession that was appearance related—and was a frequent dieter—and her father was a businessman. Mollie noticed at an early age that her mother often looked at herself in the mirror, making comments about her body, her need to lose weight to wear her swimsuit, or remarking that she had gained weight during the holiday season.

Here is Mollie's personal dieting history timeline, which she completed for a homework assignment for her weekly group:

- 1995—At age five, teased about being "chubby" in kindergarten and she asked to "go on a diet like mommy."

- 2000—Tried Slim-Fast® for first time.

- 2002—Heard a classmate vomiting in the bathroom after lunch and learned about purging as a substitute for dieting.

- 2005—Began to use diuretics and diet pills.

- 2006—Joined track team at school in hopes that extreme running would contribute to weight loss.

- 2007—First hospitalization following cardiac arrhythmia and collapse during a running competition.

- 2007—Continuing with a diet after discharge from hospital.

In group, Linda asked Mollie to explore her history in action. She made available a number of scarves and other objects on the psychodrama stage to create the timeline on the floor. Mollie, warming up quickly, set several scarves on the carpet and began a soliloquy:

"I'm five years old. I'm very excited about going to kindergarten. I want to be a big girl. My brothers are big boys and they go to school. Now I get to go to school. I go to school and somebody says 'Aw, there's that chubby kid, she can't play with us on the see-saw.' I cried and went home and told my Mommy, 'Mommy, I'm going on a diet just like you.'

"I feel like something is the matter with my body. I feel like I'm not going to have any friends because my body isn't OK. I feel like I've got to do something about my body to make it smaller so that other kids will like me."

Here, Linda notices that Mollie is using the word "feeling" but is really talking about thoughts. She makes a doubling statement, naming the feeling:

"I feel so sad."

"Yes," says Mollie, "I feel really sad. I feel like hiding."

As Mollie reaches the 2002 mark in her timeline, she says: "I'm in the bathroom in my middle school. It's after lunch. I'm still unhappy about my body. Everybody, it seems, is talking about their bodies all the time and comparing themselves to various music stars, or movie stars, or TV personalities. When I go to the bathroom after lunch, I hear somebody vomiting in the stall next to me. When she comes out, I ask, 'Are you OK?' And she tells me she's perfectly fine, that she's doing that so she doesn't have to worry about her weight, that she can have all the lunch she wants and get rid of it, and still wear the cutest clothes."

Linda makes another doubling statement: "I feel hopeful that there's a way for me to get the body that I want, and I begin purging. At last, I can finally do something to get my body to do what I want it to do."

Three years in on the timeline, Mollie is in high school. "It's 2005, and I'm using diuretics and diet pills," says Mollie. "I'm shaking all the time. I'm running to the bathroom, my hands shake, I don't feel good. I have trouble concentrating. I don't know what else to do. I'm afraid. I'm really afraid that if I don't use diet pills and diuretics I'm going to be fat; nobody is going to like me."

Doubling statement: "I'm afraid. I'm beginning to feel trapped by my eating disorder. I don't know what to do."

"Yes," Mollie says. "I'm trapped."

Mollie takes another step on the timeline. "I decide to join the track team at school. I had been running on my mother's treadmill at home, and I figure if I join a team and I could be running all the time I might be able to get my weight where I want it without using diuretic or diet pills, and I always have purging as a backup."

Doubling statement: "My worry about my weight and my body still consume most of my life."

"Yes," says Mollie. "That's it, that's all I think about—my body and my weight. I keep running. I keep trying to be successful on the track team. To keep my grades up, to keep my body slim. It's a constant battle. One day in the middle of the competition, I collapse, and I end up in the hospital and—well, here I am."

Doubling statement: "I'm here now, and I still worry about the size of my body, and I also know that I want something else in my life besides this constant worry about my body."

Mollie says, "Yes, that's right. I feel really scared, and really worried, and I don't want to keep living like this."

This was the beginning of Mollie's decision to recover.

Cultural changes timeline

The diet timeline can be adapted for an action-oriented presentation to demonstrate how our culture has changed its ideal body image during the past century. This educational presentation warms up the group to the fact that the "glamorized body type" has drastically changed due to socio-cultural-economic factors.

- 1890s—The famous stage actress Lillian Russell weighs 200 pounds and has 32-inch thighs; the best-selling beauty product is thigh cream advertised to increase thigh size so "You, too, can look like Lillian." Stoutness in men is associated with prosperity and positions of power.

- 1920s—The "flapper" is popular as women enter higher education and the world of work. Breast binding and hair bobbing are encouraged to present a boyish look.

- 1930s—The Great Depression results in food deprivation for thousands of people. Florenz Ziegfeld requires his Broadway dancers to maintain a curvy 5-feet 3-inch figure of 135 pounds.

- 1936—Joe Weider publishes the first issue of *Your Physique* magazine, extolling the virtues of body building.

- 1940s—Men go to war, and women take factory jobs. The women watch movies and wear broad-shouldered padded suits like Joan Crawford and try to look like flirty and curvy Betty Grable.

- 1953—*Your Physique* magazine is renamed *Body Builder*.

- 1950s—The White Rock Girl, the advertising icon promoting soft drinks, stands 5 feet 4 inches tall and weighs 140 pounds. (Today she is 5 feet 10 inches and 110 pounds!) With men back from war and women returning to their homes, women are again valued as traditional girlfriends, wives and mothers.

- 1950s—Marilyn Monroe, the sexy movie star icon, has a weight that fluctuates between 115 and 150 pounds.

- 1959—The Barbie doll phenomenon begins, glamorizing large breasts, very long legs and tiny waists. Her dimensions, if they were human, would be 38-18-28, and her feet are in the permanent "high heel" position.

- 1964—Toymaker Hasbro introduces the G.I. Joe action figure, setting up a strong and lean model for boys.

- Late 1960s—The very thin Twiggy becomes a fashion model sensation, and the "baby doll" look counters the second wave of feminism.

- 1972—Arnold Schwarzenegger is associated with products promoting an increase in body mass for men. He wins the Mr. Olympia contest seven times, along with other body building titles.

- 1970s—The women's fitness craze emerges with emphasis on large breasts, an increase in breast augmentation and defined musculature, and an increased use of airbrushed photographs.

- 1980—*Body Builder* magazine is renamed again, this time to *Muscle and Fitness*.

- 1980s—Lingerie advertisements emphasize the sexiness of the Barbie doll look.

- 1991—The G.I. Joe action figure bulks up with more muscles while staying lean.

- 2000 to today—Gossip and fitness magazines compare body, breasts and clothing of celebrities; widespread computer-enhanced photography prevails; more photographs of undressed men start appearing in women's magazines. Hairless chests become fashionable for men, exposing defined pectorals. Reality television shows like *Toddlers and Tiaras* are aired as acceptable mother–daughter activities. A condition dubbed "pregorexia" is attributed to the glamorization of celebrities who hardly appear to be pregnant with limited weight gain. Body piercings and tattoos are increasingly common.

Linda presents this timeline in a sociodramatic fashion, taking the role of a woman of the time, talking about the type of body that was glamorized and the contributing social and cultural factors.

In the "typical woman" role, she may also refer to the kind of male body type attractive at the time. Directors with mixed-gender or male-only groups may adapt the timeline in different ways for their male clients.

Apart from the presentation's educational value, the timeline serves as a unique assessment tool. We can learn what kinds of behaviors, activities and beliefs are important to our clients and what preferences, interpretations and experiences may require further exploration. For example, a person may decide to get a tattoo or body piercing to fit in with a social trend or a particular crowd—following a fad—or they may decide to inflict physical pain on themselves to deflect their emotional pain. Or the tattoo or piercing may serve another purpose, such as a statement to the world about the body, a belief about the body or as part of a struggle with the body. All become material for future dramas—perhaps role reversal with the body part that was pierced or with the tattooed image.

Timeline as warm up

The personal history of dieting timeline is an ideal warm up for a protagonist-centered psychodrama. As the protagonist walks the timeline, certain points will elicit greater emotional response. The director may ask if a particular scene comes to mind. The protagonist may wish to revisit a scene psychodramatically to gain insight into what happened at that time that reinforced the development of the dieting pattern that led to an eating disorder.

CASE STUDY: KARLA AND TIMELINE

Karla was admitted to a hospital-based treatment program at 19, suffering with bulimia that alternated with bouts of purging-type anorexia. She was a gymnast in high school and received a scholarship to college. Linda gave Karla the option of doing the timeline starting in the present and going backward, or starting at the beginning and going forward.

Starting in the present felt safer for Karla, who identified that just prior to entering the hospital she had committed to a strict diet to lose weight and improve performance in her sport:

Once again I convinced myself that this time starving would not lead to binge eating and once again, I was wrong. Two weeks into the diet, I binged for several hours, with each binge episode followed by purging. Eventually I passed out and ended up here in the hospital.

At 17, Karla was a star on the school's gymnastics team, winning multiple awards in competitions.

I should have been happy, but I was heartbroken because my brother ran away from home. He just couldn't take the chaos any more. I decided I would feel better if I just lost weight. This time I tried the Atkins diet, and once again I ended up binge eating and purging.

The timeline continued backwards until Karla reached the age of 12. She took a deep breath and sighed:

I'm involved in gymnastics. I'm 12 years old and my body is changing. I'm beginning to develop breasts, and I've gained a little weight, just a little weight. I'm self-conscious about my body. My mother decides to motivate me to slim down by purchasing a new leotard that is too small for me. She told me to "Fit into this by the competition date or forget gymnastics— looking good is a big part of this!"

Linda asked if Karla was willing to revisit this scene in a psychodrama vignette and Karla agreed. After establishing the contract for the work—she wanted to tell her mother how angry and hurt she had been about the humiliation—Linda set the scene and Karla was able to tell her mother the truth about how that incident was the beginning of her eating disorder. She later expressed her disappointment to her father in role play about not intervening.

Timeline as future projection

The timeline may be extended into the future, as a surplus reality scene, to help the client visualize his or her healthy self.

The protagonist may step to that future place and speak from the role of the Future Recovered Self to the Present Self. The role of the Present Self may be taken by another group member, or an empty chair in an individual session. The chair is placed on the timeline at the place indicating the present day. This gives the protagonist an experience of "trying on" the role of her Future Recovered Self. The director can assist by doubling: "I never thought I'd be here, but here I am."

Sociodrama

Sociodrama, which dramatizes a social issue rather than a personal one, is a good choice to educate and provoke awareness when group members may not feel able or ready to disclose personal details.

The history of dieting timeline can be a warm up for a sociodrama in which group members enact roles like the Teen Dieter, the Adult Dieter, the Advertising Executive, the Fashion Magazine Editor, the Concerned Parent, the Dieting Buddy and so on. The director helps the group decide the theme of the drama, such as the current issue of a teen fashion magazine.

Pairs

Magazines show recipes for fancy desserts next to articles on how to lose weight with extreme dieting. Television shows very thin people eating very large amounts of food. Advertisements suggest eating to soothe emotional issues, to provide a respite from a hard day's work and as the most important part of celebrating.

To identify the feelings stimulated by such mixed messages, we like the activity known as Pairs, which comes from Playback Theater, a derivative of psychodrama. With Pairs, two people stand front to back – with each expressing an opposite emotion or response to the same experience (Salas, 1996). They may use sound, physical movement and words in verbal and physical interaction as they improvise. A scene with a pair is typically short—from 30 seconds to a minute.

Group members may call out feelings or situations or the two players may decide on feelings and present them to the group. At the beginning of each enacted pair, the scene is set with a brief statement.

For example, the situation is walking into your office on Monday morning and finding an array of sugar-frosted doughnuts:

- "Umm—yum!"

- "Oh, no—should I break my diet?"

Or being served a plate of food at a restaurant:

- "This plate is beautiful…"

- "It's not enough!"

Or watching a three-year-old girl play with a Barbie doll:

- "So cute—she wants to be grown up!"

- "I want *my* legs to be that long!"

It is important to let the group members identify the situations and the emotions to heighten spontaneity and creativity.

Mixed messages

Messages come from our teachers, families and schools starting in early childhood, when food is used as enticement to good behavior, reward or punishment:

- "Be good until we finish shopping and I'll buy you an ice cream."

- "Stop crying—here's a cookie."

- "If you don't stop fussing, you won't get dessert."

- "Have some more—I made this special, just for you."

The messages continue in adulthood; we have office traditions of bringing cupcakes to celebrate a birthday, having doughnuts and coffee at a club meeting and celebrating a business milestone with pizza for everyone. Food is considered a reasonable solution to deal with boredom, loneliness, frustration, disappointment, grief, celebration and other situations.

The warm up for this mini-sociodrama might begin with group members sharing in dyads or triads messages that they heard while growing up—or continue to observe and hear with their families, friends and other social groups. The director places an empty chair in the center of the group, with the chair representing a "generic" person. Group members are then invited to circle around the chair (use clockwise direction to avoid bumping into each other) speaking the messages.

Sharing follows—how did it feel to speak the words?

■ VARIATION

Have half of the group speaking the messages, the other half standing with the empty chair. Then role reverse the groups, with the speaking group hearing the messages and the listening group speaking the messages. Now share—which group role felt more comfortable or more familiar?

■ VARIATION

Have the group brainstorm positive messages they have heard or wish they had heard at any point in their lives. The director places an empty chair in the center of the group, with the chair representing a "generic" person. Group members are invited to circle around the chair (use clockwise direction to avoid bumping into each other) speaking the positive messages. Role reverse with half of the group as you wish. This variation is a good ending after a drama or before concluding the session so that participants leave with the new positive messages reasonating in their ears.

The Living Newspaper

The popular press is full of news and information about diets and recipes as well as breathless stories about celebrities who are back at their "bikini bodies" just six weeks after delivering a baby.

The Living Newspaper is a classic psychodramatic structure that originated when participants in J.L. Moreno's groups in Vienna, Austria, would peruse a copy of the day's newspaper, select articles that were of interest and then improvise the scenes of the story (Marineau, 1989). Modern psychodramatists have employed this structure to address all kinds of news events for personal growth, political awareness and social activism.

We suggest the Living Newspaper to raise consciousness about the media's influence with food, nourishment and bodies and to encourage group members to become critical thinkers about what they read in newspapers, gossip magazines and on the internet.

Newspapers, both print and online, are ideal for articles that relate to body image, abuse and other related issues. Useful news topics might include parents starving or limiting food to their children, famines in Third World countries, and anti-obesity programs in schools.

Celebrity magazines tell stories of cosmetic surgery, spotlight celebrities with cellulite and often mock or criticize entertainers who are not dressed perfectly while shopping for groceries, going out for coffee or swimming at the beach.

Women's magazines contain recipes for high-calorie dishes on one page and dieting plans on the next. There are accompanying advertisements for fat-burning diet aids, colon cleanses, exercise gadgets and body wraps. The counterpart men's magazines recycle stories about "Bigger arms, fast!" and "Your secret weight loss weapon!" along with advertisements for muscle-building programs and workout equipment.

To put the Living Newspaper into action, here are the basic steps we take:

- Find a variety of articles about the topics of your choice, clipping them from print newspapers or magazines or printing online versions.

- Post a selection (about six to eight) articles on the wall of the group room.

- Design a warm-up activity that allows group members to deepen into the topic. For instance, if the topic is celebrity magazines, the director may ask the group members to identify celebrities they admire, how often they read gossip magazines, whether they like gossip magazines or not. You may use spectrograms and other sociometric tests, such as the locogram, or other activities that bring focus on the impact of celebrity news regarding appearance and diets. In the locogram, the director assigns certain characteristics or ideas to locations within the group room, marking the locations with paper signs, pillows, chairs or other items. Each location indicates a particular role experience such as "I like reading celebrity magazines," "I like watching celebrity news on television," "I have a favorite celebrity that I wish I looked like" and "other." Group members are instructed to cluster at the location of their truth and share with others and the group as a whole.

- Have group members roam the room to read the articles on the wall. Ask group members to congregate next to the article that they find most interesting or that stirs their emotion.

- Have each small group create and enact a sculpture or simple vignette that puts into action the essence of the article. The sculpture or vignette may involve speaking or may be done in silence.

- Share about the experience with group members, either as a full group or in small groups.

■ VARIATION

Use vignette activity as a warm up for a full drama.

Chapter 8

The Three Faces
of Eating Disorders

We don't see things as they are, we see them as we are.

Anaïs Nin

People who suffer with eating disorders are disconnected from their feelings and their relationships. In other words, the unresolved relationship issues and the painful feelings become encoded and enacted in the relationship with food.

Helping the client connect the "dots" between food, feelings and relationships is the first step in helping the client to see that the real issue isn't the food; rather, it is the feelings that need recognition and the relationships that need tending. This does not mean that food issues are unimportant; in fact, the food issues must be addressed for the client to recover.

Therefore, we begin by looking at the foods that hold a powerful charge and our clients' readiness to change. Next, the feelings are brought in, then the relationships. Finally, the food, the feelings and the relationships are woven together, providing the client with an opportunity to experience their inter-relatedness and identify goals for change.

Experiencing how the food, feelings and relationships have become intertwined is the first step in untangling them. The directions for completing a food atom can be used for all disorders or modified when working with specific populations.

Social Atom

The social atom is a classic sociometric diagram that notes a person's significant social connections. In this exercise, a symbol for the individual is drawn in the center of a blank sheet of paper and important relationships are marked according to a nearness-to-distance perspective to show who the person feels close to and who he or she tends to distance from. This diagram essentially shows the patterns of our immediate social network and the "tele"—Moreno's name for the invisible energetic connections—between people whether positive, negative, neutral or ambivalent.

By diagramming a social atom on paper, the protagonist can see clearly how relationships contribute to the eating disorder. Putting the social atom into action allows protagonists to role reverse with the people and places in the social atom and acquire immediate experiencing of their impact on the eating disorder. You may want to have the protagonist sign and date the initial social atom; this activity may be repeated after several months as a method of identifying how the protagonist's shifting social atom is reflective of recovery, or how the "stuckness" of the social atom reflects the "stuckness" in the eating disorder.

Food Atom

Like the social atom, which diagrams connections to people or groups, the food atom identifies the person's connections to food. It is a safe way to explore relationships with food—whether the person has an eating disorder or is involved in a longtime dieting pattern—and is a versatile intervention for individuals or mixed groups with anorexics, bulimics and overeaters. It is also helpful when working with patients who are preparing for gastric bypass surgery, those who identify problems with dieting and those who are making efforts to keep a healthy food plan on doctors' orders.

When diagramming the food atom, we use a nearness-to-distance perspective to show which foods the person feels close to and which foods he or she tends to distance from. We also note which foods are included and excluded—this allows the identification of what motivates food choices: often "black and white" or "all or nothing" thinking will be concretized as "good" or "bad" foods. This helps the client, nutrition counselor and psychotherapist work together toward nutritional homeostasis—a varied and well-balanced diet. It also sets the stage for revealing the metaphoric meaning of the client's relationship with food, self and others.

We offer Linda's version of the food atom first and demonstrate its versatility by showing food atoms from other psychodramatists who specialize in eating disorder treatment.

Making a food atom

To begin, you will want to talk with clients about the food atom as a helpful tool to explore current relationships with foods.

Give the client(s) a blank sheet of paper, pencil with eraser, and invite him or her to place himself or herself somewhere on the page; and then to think about foods that are especially significant at the present time. Important foods may have either a positive (+) or a negative (-) connection, or both (+ and -) indicating ambivalence. The client may use circles, squares, triangles, rectangles or drawings of foods, labeling each one, to diagram its relationship to the self. When the client finishes the diagram, say: "Look this over and see if you've left out any significant food or beverage."

Next, give the client three different colored pens or markers and ask him or her to first outline the self in the atom with one color; with a second color, to outline the symbol for the food relationship they most want to change; and with the third color to outline the food relationship they feel most ready and capable of changing at the present time. This may be the same as the previous one or different.

Finally, have the client sign and date the food atom. Begin to notice the following:

- Is the food atom crowded or empty?

- What are the patterns that emerge as the client talks?

Invite the client to share his or her emotional responses and insights.

Moving the atom into action

Here, the director may have the protagonist choose an auxiliary to play the role of the food he or she is *most ready* to change the relationship with. In an individual setting, a chair can be designated as the food the client is most ready to change a relationship with—a sign with the name of the food can be placed on the chair.

The director says, "Role reverse with the food." During role reversal, feelings associated with each food will emerge. Have the protagonist choose a scarf or stuffed animal or puppet for that feeling and place it with the person or on the chair holding the role of food and feeling. There may be more than one feeling for each food. The director may double.

CASE STUDY: JESSICA

Jessica arrived for a nutritional counseling session with Linda because she had difficulty keeping to a balanced meal plan. Her meals were disorganized, and she had little variety in her menu. She usually skipped breakfast, ate a salad for lunch and stopped at a local ice cream shop after work for a triple scoop of peanut butter ice cream. Sometimes she'd binge on ice cream or spoon peanut butter out of the jar at night. She alternated between strict dieting and binge eating with some laxative overuse, fearing weight gain.

Through work with the food atom, Linda discovered that Jessica's mother behaved unpredictably when Jessica was a child due to the mother's untreated mental illness. The mother's only consistent behavior was her focus on physical appearance; she often warned Jessica to "Stay slender—otherwise, no man will want you." When Jessica visited her grandmother, who lived near an ice cream parlor, the grandmother gave Jessica money to buy ice cream and showed her affection. However, when the mother discovered that Jessica had eaten ice cream, she berated her about being "a little pig" and "getting fat."

Jessica's father avoided the home, preferring to stay late at the office. He was rarely present and did not protect Jessica from her mother's physical and emotional abuse. One exception to this pattern was Friday nights, when Jessica and her father watched a favorite television show together, without her mother present. During this time, the father ate peanut butter and crackers that he shared with his daughter.

Jessica's food atom

Here is the food atom that Jessica made during a group facilitated by Linda:

Most ready to change

Most want to change

Peanut butter + -

Ice cream + -

Salad +

Don't want to change

Figure 8.1 Jessica's first food atom

Ice cream, a favorite binge food, was marked with both a plus sign and a minus sign, indicating ambivalence. Peanut butter, also marked as ambivalent, was what Jessica was ready to change. Salad was identified with a plus sign, signaling a favorite food item that she accepted as healthy for her.

"Safe" and "unsafe" foods—feeling connection

In Figure 8.2 we see that Jessica placed "safe foods" closest to her, saying that when she eats these she feels "thin" and "in control." The foods she placed further away she identified as leading to "feeling fat" and "out of control." Eventually a story emerged from each food, providing a warm up for enactment.

Figure 8.2 Jessica's food atom of "safe" and "unsafe" foods

Jessica then identified the relationships with foods that she is most willing to change:

Figure 8.3 Jessica's food atom with feelings

Action vignette with Jessica

Jessica says she is most ready to change her relationship with Peanut Butter and chooses a brown scarf to hold the role of Peanut Butter and places it on a chair. An empty chair is placed across from the chair holding the scarf. Jessica is directed to sit in the empty chair, facing Peanut Butter.

Linda (as director): "Jessica, here is Peanut Butter. Peanut Butter plays a significant role in your life. What do you have to say to Peanut Butter?"

Jessica: "I love you and I hate you! You taste so good. I can't stop eating you. You make me fat!"

Linda, as director, calls for role reversal, placing Jessica in the role of Peanut Butter. Jessica is instructed to hold the brown scarf, deepening her connection to the Peanut Butter role. Jessica's original chair holds the plush stuffed hippo puppet that she chose to represent herself.

Jessica as Peanut Butter: "It's not my fault you have no self-control. Besides, you know you love me—I make you feel better."

Linda calls for role reversal.

Jessica as self, holding hippo puppet: "Yes, you do. I love your creamy thickness, and I can depend on you. I just wish you didn't make me fat!"

Linda calls for role reversal.

Jessica as Peanut Butter: "I'm a lot more reliable than the people in your life!"

Linda calls for role reversal.

Jessica as self: "You're right, you *are* more dependable than people! I just wish you didn't have calories or fat."

Linda calls for role reversal.

Jessica as Peanut Butter: "Then I wouldn't taste good. I wouldn't be able to distract you so well when you feel miserable."

Linda calls for role reversal.

Jessica as self: "I just can't get enough of you. I wish I could just eat a teaspoon of you and feel better!"

Linda calls for role reversal.

Jessica as Peanut Butter: "It's not my job to fix your feelings! I'm only Peanut Butter, after all!"

Linda calls for role reversal.

Jessica as self, starting to cry: "I wish I had you right now so I could stop feeling so mad and sad!"

Linda makes a doubling statement, as Jessica's double: "I'm overwhelmed and I just want to feel better."

Jessica as self: "I *am* overwhelmed and I want to feel better. I'm *so tired* of all this!"

Linda, giving direction: "Using auxiliaries, group members, or chairs and props, sculpt your food atom as it exists now and then re-sculpt your food atom as you'd like it to be."

Jessica created the two sculptures from the mirror position, with a group member playing her role, and observed the first scene and then the changed scene. Then she stepped into the new sculpture to feel this new relationship with her food choices.

To close, Linda gave further instructions to Jessica:

- "Make a statement to the one food item you are *most ready* to change your relationship with."

- "Make a statement to the food item you most *want* to change your relationship with (if different from above)."

- "Make a statement to the feeling that you're *most ready* to change your relationship with."

- "Make a statement to the feeling you most *want* to change your relationship with (if different from above)."

- "Add the feelings to the foods on the paper food atom."

Through use of the Three Faces of Eating Disorders and then putting it into action, Jessica gained insight into her disordered eating. She realized that, when she consumed the large serving of peanut butter ice cream, she was acting out her desire to have her father's love (peanut butter) and her grandmother's nurturing and approval (ice cream). She also saw that she was "biting back" at her mother—she reported that crunching the cone had "an angry feel"—and realized that she was both rebelling against and expressing her anger towards her mother. In contrast, she attempted to self-soothe by recreating the feelings of being with father and grandmother with her peanut butter ice cream.

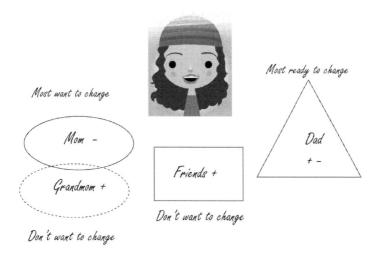

Figure 8.4 Jessica's food and relationship atom about what she wants to change, is most ready to change and is not ready to change

Jessica also realized that when she ate salad she was usually either alone or with safe colleagues, and since no one would criticize her for eating salad, it was a safe food. This laid the groundwork for her recovery from eating disorders.

Adding the social atom

After the food atom has been completed, create a social atom on the same paper as the food and feeling atom. Who in the social atom is connected to what food and what feeling?

Give the following instructions:

- "Role reverse with the person with whom you *most want* to change the relationship."

- "Role reverse with the person with whom you feel *most ready* to change the relationship."

- "Sculpt the current social atom using auxiliaries, group members or chairs. Re-sculpture the social atom as you'd like it to be."

- "Make a statement to the person with whom you feel *most ready* to change your relationship."

- "Make a statement to the person with whom you *most want* to change your relationship."

After putting the atoms together, sculpt the Three Faces of Eating Disorders, adding a prop or symbol for the food to be held by each person and placing a scarf (or scarves) identifying the feeling(s) associated with each person.

Figure 8.5 Putting it all together: Jessica's connections between food, feelings and relationships

Hatred of food leads to encounter

Favorite binge foods are not the only foods to be explored in the food atom; sometimes a repulsive food reveals information for exploration, insight and change. For instance, Pamela's food atom showed an extreme hatred of beets. The beet is not a food that appears often on the food atom, but she had such an emotional reaction we chose to have an encounter to learn about the emotions connected with this food.

During the encounter, Pamela remembered being forced to eat a bowl of beets because they "helped you lose weight." She had been labeled an overweight child, and her parents forced many diets on her. When she remembered the beet diet, she sculpted her food atom and realized that each food had either been force fed to help her lose weight or restricted from her; she chose to binge and purge in her disease. She felt drawn to a certain food but experienced so much guilt because she was breaking the rules to eat that food.

Although Pamela knew she had been forced on to diets in childhood, she was not conscious about her current food relationships until the food atom activity. After this exercise, she participated in role play to soothe and emotionally nourish her child self and learn to feed herself without punishment and fear.

■ VARIATION BY COLLEEN BARATKA

Give clients blank sheets of paper and ask them to place themselves on the paper using a circle (for female) or triangle (for male). They are requested to draw around their personal symbol the foods that seem to hold the most emotional energy—usually binge foods and foods that they fear.

They may represent the food in whatever way they like, with common geometric figures or more literal representations of the food. Attention to detail in the drawings can be telling; when there is much graphic detail, it usually indicates deeper obsessions with the food.

After the drawings are complete, ask the clients to label them with the following symbols:

- Mark any food that they like and allow themselves to eat with "+".

- Mark any food that they like but restrict or purge with "+ and -".

- Mark any food that they don't like and will not eat with "-".

- Mark any food that they dislike but force themselves to eat with "- and +".

- Mark any food that they dislike and eat for purging purposes with "-" and "-".

The marking of the diagram is specific to allow exploration of normal and pathological eating patterns. It is normal to eat the foods we like and to avoid the foods we don't like. It is not so normal to force ourselves to eat foods we don't like because our eating disorder tells us we have to eat them. Likewise, it is self-punishing to force feed ourselves food that we don't like just so we can further harm ourselves by purging. It may make sense that we binge on foods we like, but not so foods we don't like. In our diet-crazy world we understand forgoing what we like, but to the eating disorder person this is a deeper issue since the disorder is about restricting pleasure and feeling guilty for feeling good.

Once the food atom has been drawn, each person is invited to share his or her picture and answer two questions:

- "What does your food atom say about you?"

- "How do you feel when you look at the diagram?"

Have each person address the one food that brings up the most emotion for him or her. This allows each participant to realize that food has more issues than expected and permits them to explore their relationship with food at a different level.

■ VARIATION BY MARY BELLOFATTO
Give clients blank sheets of paper and ask them to place themselves on the paper using a personal symbol. Then:

- Place symbols for the foods that they crave or use as binge foods with the foods closest to their personal symbols.

- Place the foods they are fearful of or don't enjoy at a distance from their personal symbols.

- Have the clients remember the last time they binged or restricted each food and add an emotion they were feeling, if they can.

- Add the name of a person who is connected to that food.

When a client can put together all three—food, emotion and person—this activity is a powerful warm up to action when working in a group with a group member playing an auxiliary role of the food, the person, or the feeling.

■ **VARIATION WITH FUTURE PROJECTION**

Ask the client to draw what his or her food atom will look like in the future—perhaps two weeks, two months, 12 months from now—to gain information regarding his or her readiness for change, sense of hope or hopelessness.

■ **VARIATION WITH IDENTIFYING ENABLERS**

Many times people with eating disorders have enablers who support unhealthy behaviors. Here, we draw the social atom, with the client depicted in the center of the paper and others in the client's life depicted as close to or as far from the client symbol, according to the client's experience of the relationship. With a separate colored marker, have the client circle the symbols or names of the people who promote overeating, binge eating, purging, restricting, dieting, etc. Note those who ignore or explain away such behaviors or do not take them as serious life-threatening illnesses.

■ **VARIATION WITH SOCIAL OBSESSION OR CONNECTION WITH FOOD**

After including the people and other symbols on the social atom, take a different colored marker and mark those persons or symbols that may have a connection with food in some way: overeaters, undereaters, chronic dieters, persons with health conditions relating to food choices, working in food-related businesses and occupations, persons obsessed or constantly talking about food or those very interested in physical appearance.

■ VARIATION WITH IDENTIFYING SUPPORTERS

When diagramming the social atom, identify people and groups who are supportive of a person's recovery. These people and groups may include helping professionals, a therapy group, a support group and those the client can trust to respect boundaries and encourage healthy eating and healthy behaviors with body, exercise and the like.

■ VARIATION WITH COLLAGE

Rather than have the client draw the food items, provide glue and an assortment of magazine pictures and ask the client to bring a picture of himself or herself. Clients often find that making collages with magazine pictures, photos or computer printouts of clip art are easier to make if they become anxious with art-making projects.

■ VARIATION WITH "SAFE" AND "UNSAFE" FOODS

Ask the client to draw himself or herself on the page, surrounded with by inner circle of "safe" foods and an outer circle of "unsafe" foods. Then ask the client to add feelings in the "safe" and "unsafe" circles as they relate to individual foods. Explore the connections between foods and feelings.

■ VARIATION WITH PUBLIC AND PRIVATE FOODS

It is not unusual to have people eat in a certain way in public (restaurants, parties, holiday meals) and eat in a different way when they are alone or at home. With this food atom, two different colored pens are used to identify public and private eating patterns. For instance, fatty foods, desserts and breads may be turned away or not ordered in public; when alone, the person may binge on cookies, ice cream, pizza and other dessert or high-carbohydrate foods.

■ VARIATION WITH ENABLERS IN ACTION

Have group members mill about the room, at first simply being aware of their bodies and movements. Now ask each to "be" a person who enables his or her overeating, chronic dieting or excessive exercising as the walking continues. As the enabler, identify what message you give. Pair with another, with each taking a turn to speak as the enabler and the self. Give each person the opportunity to say "no" to the enabler. Process in dyad and in large group.

These diagrams and their action portrayals are extremely helpful ways to reveal the connections among foods, feelings and relationships, moving our clients forward to the next step of their recovery journeys. Later vignettes and full dramas will address necessary aspects of deeper healing.

Chapter 9

The Triple Powers
of Doubling

There is more wisdom in your body than in your deepest philosophy.

Friedrich Nietzche

The Double is a special auxiliary role with the function of supporting the protagonist during a drama. Although the Double originated as a psychodramatic role, later research has shown that there are multiple powers to doubling, including safety and enhancement of the therapeutic alliance.

The Double gives voice to the protagonist's inner experience, verbalizing what may be beneath the surface, what is unsaid or merely hinted at, and speaks in the "I." The director always gives the protagonist the option to correct or modify what the Double is saying so that the statements accurately represent the protagonist's experience. Even when the doubling statement is inaccurate, it helps the protagonist clarify his or her feelings, thoughts, desires and longings.

For instance, if the protagonist appears anxious—or verbalizes anxiety—the Double may stand or sit next to the protagonist and, after taking a similar body posture, say, "I'm anxious because I'm in a new situation and I'm not sure how to respond."

The Double works towards establishing empathetic attunement, paying close attention to the protagonist's breathing, posture, facial expression, gestures, verbalization and voice tone. In many ways, sitting next to the protagonist is a natural posture for talking and people find it quite comforting after a few of these experiences.

The classic Double

The director, when taking the classic Double role, sits or stands beside the protagonist and speaks as the protagonist's "inner voice," expressing feelings and thoughts that the protagonist may be unable to verbalize. If the statement is correct, the protagonist repeats the statement and perhaps embellishes it; if not, the protagonist corrects it.

Some psychodramatists have adapted the position of doubling to be standing or seated slightly behind the protagonist. Either way, when the director is serving as the protagonist's Double, the therapeutic alliance is strengthened because, as the Double, the director speaks in the first person as the inner voice of the protagonist. Research has shown doubling to have value at intake with greater self-disclosure and a deeper level of experiencing by the client (Hudgins, 1987) and to helpfully contain overwhelming feelings in the client (McVea, 2009, 2013).

Double in individual psychotherapy

In individual psychotherapy and coaching, the director may take the Double role by first explaining to the protagonist what the Double role is and asking permission to sit next to the protagonist.

Karen refers to the Double as the "inner voice." After rising from her chair and while still standing, she may say: "Let's imagine that Karen is still listening in her chair, as I sit here as your inner voice." She sits beside the protagonist, taking his or her posture as closely as possible so the protagonist senses that the Double is joining him or her physically, mentally and emotionally. If the protagonist is standing, the Double stands, approximating the protagonist's stance with legs, arms and posture.

This kind of doubling—to identify, clarify and help the protagonist get in touch with feelings—is classic doubling. It is particularly helpful with people who have alexithymia—difficulty in understanding, processing and describing feelings—who intellectualize as a defense, or who are reluctant to state their feelings.

CASE STUDY: TESS ACKNOWLEDGES HER FEELINGS

Tess was recalling a binge that took place after she ended a phone call with her older sister, who accused her of being selfish and self-centered when she declined a weekend invitation.

Tess: "I felt upset when my sister said that to me, but I didn't really let it bother me."

Karen (as Double): "I felt angry and insulted when my sister spoke to me like that!"

Tess: "Yes, I was angry and insulted, but I never let her know how bad she makes me feel."

Karen (as Double): "I don't let her know how badly I feel because..."

Karen pauses, allowing the client to speak and fill in the blank.

Tess: "I don't ever let her know how badly I feel because I don't want her to gloat over hurting my feelings."

Karen (as Double): "The whole thing makes me feel sad."

Tess (begins to cry and nods her head): "So sad..."

The director may continue the Double role as long as it appears helpful to the protagonist. To assist the protagonist with role transition as the director takes the Double role in individual sessions, it is often helpful to place a scarf or a stuffed animal in the director's chair to hold that role before taking a seat next to the protagonist. When the doubling is finished, the director returns to his or her chair; the movement and prop keep roles clear. When working with a protagonist who is familiar with psychodrama, the director may find it unnecessary to use a prop and a complicated explanation.

Containing Double

While doubling, watch for signs that the client is becoming overwhelmed or flooded with feelings. If this occurs, we use the Therapeutic Spiral Model's Containing Double, which reduces dissociation. We use the Containing Double when we notice that expanding the inner reality of the trauma survivor is not useful—since a survivor easily expands from fear into terror, from anxiety into dissociation, from annoyance into rage.

The Containing Double, then, puts a framework and context to the experience as well as the affect. We describe it this way to a client:

This is the role inside of you that knows your strengths, no matter what level of distress you are experiencing. It is the part of you that knows your body sensations, thoughts, feelings and whatever else you are experiencing. This role can put words to what is happening in your inner world, and let people know what is going on for you. If your Containing Double is wrong, please say what is right for you.

The Containing Double identifies three segments that assist containment: a reflecting statement, a statement to promote containment and a here-and-now statement to anchor the protagonist in the reality of the moment. It is unconditional in its support and stability. It contains unprocessed trauma material by building a holding space with flexible psychological boundaries so that internal experiences can be labeled and expressed. Not a formula but a structure, the three segments are adapted to the needs of the moment and are flexible in a number of settings, situations and feelings.

First, there is a statement showing a reflection of the process, content, affect, intensity or defense structures that the protagonist is showing in the moment. "I'm feeling scared right now—like I'm about five years old. I don't want to eat in front of people."

Then, a statement labels the ability to contain the reflected process, content, affect, intensity or defense structure into conscious awareness. "I know that I'm really scared right now and feel like a child. And I know that I can take a deep breath AND get curious about why this is happening now."

Finally, anchor the reflection and containment in the moment with time references, sensory information or interpersonal connections. "I can look at the other members of my group and know that I'm an adult having feelings from my past. I can feel my fear in this room AND know that nothing bad is going to happen to me now."

Group therapy

In group, the director may periodically take the role of Double to teach the other group members how to act in the Double role. This second option keeps group members involved and allows them to speak words that they may not yet be able to voice on their own. Again, the protagonist has the option to change the doubling statement if it is not correct.

The director, acting as the Double, may also double the group when sensing that the group as a whole is struggling with a common issue.

The Body Double

The Body Double is a newer psychodramatic adaption of the classic Double and was created as part of the Therapeutic Spiral Model. This experiential intervention for trauma that is useful for teaching people with eating disorders how to experience their bodies with pleasure and appreciation.

The Body Double is a clinically based experiential intervention that teaches self-soothing at the physical level (Burden and Ciotola, 2002; Hudgins, 2002; Hudgins and Ciotola, 2003). Through non-verbal empathy and labeling of feelings, the director helps the protagonist find words to express what he or she is experiencing in the body and to calm the internal sensations, images and compulsive urges related to eating disorders. It approximates what Bonnie Badenoch calls right-brain to right-brain bodily based regulatory experiences that unfold between parent and child in the first two years of life (2008).

Use of the Body Double

To use the Body Double intervention, the director sits or stands next to the protagonist and speaks in the first person. As the Body Double, the director tunes in to the non-verbal nuances of the protagonist and attunes to the breathing and patterns of tension.

By speaking in the "I," the director is able to begin to identify and label sensations of distress and to increase awareness of positive bodily states. The three steps of the Body Double are to:

- put words to uncomfortable or painful non-verbal symptoms to contain them

- reflect non-verbal awareness of comfortable states

- anchor the senses in the here and now.

The Body Double puts words to a healthy state of body awareness—breathing to open the lungs, feet that are grounded on the floor, movement that is calming—and gently leads the protagonist into a state of self-soothing. The Body Double speaks slowly and breathes slowly, modeling awareness and mindfulness, which sends a calming message to the parasympathetic nervous system—an activity that tones the vagus nerve.

The process involves noticing where the protagonist is and then leading him or her to a healthier, safer place. If you are playing the role of the Body Double and you notice your protagonist is picking at a thumbnail and one foot is off the floor, a useful statement might be: "I can notice that my right foot is off the floor and resting behind my calf, and I can slowly allow that foot to come down to the floor. And I can notice that my thumb can release from the other finger, and my other hand can gently stroke my thumb rather than picking it."

CASE STUDY: JAMIE SAYS "I WANT TO PURGE..."

In this scene, Linda takes the role of Body Double with Janney, a young adult who has been purging since the age of 11:

Janney: "I feel gross and disgusting and I want to purge."

Linda (as Body Double): "My stomach is queasy, and I can put all four corners of my feet on the floor, connected to the support of the ground under me." (Janney places both feet on the floor. Previously, one foot was off the floor with the ankle rotating.)

Janney: "I feel my feet on the floor and I feel queasy. I want relief—I hate this."

Linda (as Body Double): "My stomach and throat feel queasy, and I can take a deep breath in through my nose and to the bottom of my lungs." (Janney rolls her eyes but begins breathing through her nose. Body Double breathes in through the nose and slowly exhales through the nose. Janney's breathing deepens.)

Linda (as Body Double): "I can focus my eyes on the tree outside the window and notice my heart slowing down as I slow my breathing." (Body Double chose the tree as a visual anchor based upon knowledge of Janney's love of the woods and nature.)

Janney: "I still feel this lump."

Linda (as Body Double): "I can notice the lump in my throat and allow my breath to wash over the lump, slowly dissolving it."

Janney continues with breathing, and is now twisting a strand of her hair.

Linda (as Body Double): "I can continue my breathing (pause), and feel my feet on the floor (pause), focus on the tree (pause), and release my fingers from my hair (pause), and slowly and gently stroke my hair." (Linda as Body Double models these actions as she speaks.)

Janney's breathing is slower now; she is stroking her hair rather than twisting it, and she is gazing at the tree.

Janney: "I feel less queasy and my throat is less tight. Everything has slowed down now—I feel more in control and less frantic. Thanks."

When you become familiar with the art of doubling, your clinical skills will allow you to move among the three types of doubling—classic Double, Containing Double and Body Double—in the same session. Linda has combined the three types of doubling in what she calls the "Triple Double," providing moment-to-moment application as the protagonist's needs demand. In addition, the Containing Double and Body Double may be used with group members, who appear to be dissociating while watching a drama, to keep them grounded and present.

Chapter 10

Building Body Empathy

*Everything we need to know about life can
be found in the fathom-long body.*

Buddha

The Body Dialogue

The body that has been the battleground is frequently viewed as "the enemy" and the source of pain, shame and struggle. Body dissatisfaction can lead to blaming the body for emotional distress and attempts to punish the body or force it into a particular size, shape, or weight.

The Body Dialogue, a conversation between the self and the body, is an action structure designed to create a positive connection to the body. It transforms feelings of criticism and distrust into compassion and connection.

Trauma survivors have an especially troubled relationship with the body because the body is the holder of pain and trauma. Often there is a history of addictions, eating disorders, self-harm practices and habits that attempt to provide escape from the body; the person does not want to feel *in* the body. Intrusive memories, flashbacks, emotional flooding and body memories result in dissociation and disconnection from the body. There is an antagonistic relationship with the body because it is the vehicle through which the abuse occurred.

The Body Dialogue is a versatile action structure for individuals and groups. With individuals, Body can be concretized with an empty chair. With groups, the protagonist can choose a group member to play the role of Body or opt for the empty chair. This structure may be facilitated with the addition of a role player portraying a strength—courage, or truth teller, or an interpersonal strength like a best friend—so that the protagonist can role reverse into the strength role if additional support is needed to continue with the Body Dialogue.

The six steps for the Body Dialogue

The protagonist and Body sit in chairs facing one another:

> **Step 1**: The director says, "Here is your Body. How long have you had this relationship with your Body?" (Protagonist says how many years). "Tell your Body how you feel about your Body now." Protagonist makes a statement to the Body.

> **Step 2**: Role reverse with Body to discover what Body says, wants, needs.

> **Step 3**: Role reverse to learn if protagonist can do what Body is asking and make a commitment. Director: "Look into the eyes of your Body and make the commitment to do what you said." (Looking into the eyes without blinking is crucial for developing limbic resonance between the body and the self.)

> **Step 4**: Continue role reversing between Self and Body until there is some agreement and a new relationship between Body and Self.

> **Step 5**: Director looks for non-verbal cues for information about a possible new relationship. Body positions can be exchanged to facilitate the new connection—for example, from face to face to side by side. Encourage physical connection between Body and Self if it doesn't occur spontaneously—for example, holding hands, hugging, etc.

> **Step 6**: Director says: "Make a final statement to your Body to close the scene."

CASE STUDY: KRISTA'S DIALOGUE WITH HER BODY

Krista struggled with anorexia and compulsive exercise in high school and college as a scholar-athlete. She worked hard on her recovery but had a pattern of pushing herself in all areas of her life, resulting in insufficient rest, sleep and renewal.

She had taken great responsibility in her family, helping to raise her younger siblings, while her emotional and developmental needs went unmet.

Step 1: In group, Krista chooses Missy for the role of Body.

Linda asks, "What do you want to say to your Body?"

Krista moves closer, holds Body's hands and begins to cry. "You are sick right now, and I feel sad that I haven't been taking good care of you. I know I've gotten better, but I'm still not good at letting you rest, rest for no reason, not just when I am sick."

Step 2: Role reverse.

Director to Krista in role of Body, "What do you want Krista to do *before* you get sick?"

Body answers, "I need to go slow sometimes and it's hard for you, for your mind to go slow. You forget it's important to go slow with me and when we rest we have time to be together. I need more rest than you. Sometimes you try to make my needs match yours, and we aren't always in tune."

Step 3: Role reverse.

Krista admits to Body that she doesn't pay attention to Body's needs.

Body repeats, "We are together when we rest, that's our time together."

Krista says, "I have heard the teenage part, but I forget about the baby—that's the part that needs to rest. That's the part I forget because I didn't even know you were there for a long time."

Here Krista is referring to an earlier dramatic session when Krista discovered her inner child who had been lost in the parentified child role and gained an understanding of developmental phases that had been neglected during her growing-up years.

Step 4: Role reverse.

Krista speaks in role of Body, "I'm really cute and I need to rest. Babies need to go slow and to rest. I'm good at the later years, but I need more rest."

Self (Missy as auxiliary in role): "You are cute!"

Linda calls for role reversal.

Krista (as self): "I will let you rest more, hear your needs and be attuned. I'm not going to wait till you cry. I'm just going to know what you need."

Step 5: Linda calls for role reversal, so Krista as Body can hear the promise.

Krista (as Body) says, "I do trust you."

Linda calls for role reversal so Krista returns to own role.

Step 6: Final statement to Body.

Krista (in self role): "You are a gift from God and I am grateful you didn't die despite my hurting you."

Body says, "I stuck with you and I'm still here."

Krista (as self) says, "I don't feel like you're holding it against me, and I'm grateful for that as well. I'm going to listen to the baby better. I can do that."

Krista and her auxiliary as Body hug. The director gently facilitates a rocking motion and labels it "Rock the baby."

Body Tracing

Body Tracing is an intervention with applications to challenge body size distortion, notice feelings and thoughts about the body, identify specific body parts that may hold trauma and anchor forgotten strengths and inner resources. It may be a stand-alone activity or a warm up for a dramatic vignette or full drama. It may be a one-time event or it may be repeated over time to assess changes in feelings and perceptions.

For this activity you will need large rolls of paper purchased at an art store or printing company. As you begin, it is important to prepare the client for this activity, which will likely cause some discomfort. Explaining the process to the client in detail and allowing time for questions and concerns are crucial to the warm up for this activity. Allowing the client to choose what materials are used (pen, pastel crayon, marker, pencil and the like) and permission to take breathing breaks will provide safety and autonomy.

If body image distortion is an issue, the director can ask the protagonist to draw an outline of how he or she experiences his or her body before doing the actual tracing of the body, and then compare the two and process the feelings that emerge.

The paper can be taped to the wall and the protagonist can stand against the paper for the tracing, or it can be done with paper on the floor and the protagonist lying on the paper. Again, let the protagonist choose.

If the person is too large for one sheet of paper, have him or her tape two sheets together. If anyone has a disability or has difficulty moving easily, have him or her draw his or her body on paper taped to the wall and later stand against the paper on the wall for Body Tracing. For those in wheelchairs, the director may have to improvise: drawing part of the body while seated; supporting the person to stand briefly for the drawing with supports or help from group members; or having the wheelchair-bound person select another group member whom he or she believes is similar for the tracing. Another option may be to draw body parts, such as arms and legs, and tape them together as a collage.

When feelings surface as the protagonist hears the assignment and progresses through the process, affirm that all feelings are acceptable and encourage participants to be aware of their emotions and body responses, because there will be an opportunity to share as the process continues.

When the tracing is complete, ask the protagonist what the process felt like and if he or she is surprised by what is discovered.

After the bodies are traced, have participants add any other marks, symbols, colors, shapes or doodles to identify physical or emotional pain that is carried, as well as feelings about body parts, memories or observations about relationships of the body or body parts to others in their families.

Allow ample time to share, with one group member sharing while others listen. Be sure to include the identification of feelings that emerged during the process. Affirm the representations as appropriate; for instance, affirm the importance and presence of feelings if the person includes a heart on his or her Body Tracing.

■ VARIATION

Ask the client to write on the tracing of various body parts any strengths that can be claimed; for instance, "strong legs" or "arms for hugging" or "eyes that are perceptive." You can also ask the person to label body parts that hold trauma. This activity can be a warm up to the Body Dialogue.

■ VARIATION

When the Body Tracing is complete, have the protagonist stand near or in front of the tracing when it is posted on the wall. Ask the protagonist to speak as the body.

■ VARIATION

Have each protagonist draw a word balloon above the head of the tracing. In that word balloon, have the person write what the body is saying. Emphasize that the message comes from the body speaking to the person, not the person speaking. If people have difficulty with this assignment, ask them to focus on the image itself until the words emerge.

■ VARIATION

After the tracing is completed, ask participants to journal about their feelings, thoughts and experiences. They may also dialogue with their body in writing, which might involve writing with the dominant hand only or with the dominant hand for self and non-dominant hand for body.

■ VARIATION

If a drama, or dramas, follows the Body Tracing activity, have the participants return to the tracings and add new healing images, colors, shapes and symbols to the figures.

The String Thing

This activity to address body distortion was originally developed by psychotherapists Ron A. Thompson and Roberta Trattner Sherman (1993) who work with athletes with eating disorders. Linda's clients have labeled this activity the "String Thing," and it is obvious that it is useful as well for clients who are not athletes.

Linda uses two colors of yarn and has the client make a circle of one color of yarn, indicating on the floor the circumference of the body part that he or she feels most obsessed about—such as the waist, thighs or upper arms. Then she asks the client to take a length of the second color of yarn and actually wrap it around that body part and then lay that circle on the floor inside the original circle.

In anorexics and bulimics, the imagined circle is always bigger, often by double, than the actual measurement. Of course, the clients are typically baffled and we often repeat this several times in one session because they cannot believe they are the size of the second yarn strand rather than the first (imagined) one.

This is a warm up for action—they can role reverse with the yarns, with the body part, with the part of themselves that makes choices based on illusion, denial, delusion and the like.

CASE STUDY: SUSAN AND THE STRING THING

Susan came to Linda's lifestyle counseling practice at the age of 18. She had relapsed following discharge from an inpatient treatment center where she had been treated for anorexia. At five feet tall, she was extremely thin, weighing 65 pounds and repeatedly expressed disdain for her "fat thighs." She would frequently touch her thighs, bemoaning the fact that no matter what she did she could not get them any smaller.

Linda confronts the distortion using the String Thing. First, she gives Susan a ball of peach-colored yarn and asks her to make a circle on the floor with the yarn, representing what she believes to be the circumference of her thighs. Next, Linda gives Susan a length of purple yarn and instructs her to wrap it around her actual thigh. Linda then instructs Susan to place the purple circle inside the peach circle on the floor. The peach circle was three times the size of the purple circle.

Susan declares with astonishment, "This can't be right!"

Linda responds, "OK, let's circle your thigh again."

Susan looks skeptical as she again wraps her thigh with the purple yarn. The length is the same; Susan still looks at Linda with disbelief. Linda explains that body image distortion is one of the most insidious effects of starvation and briefly describes the Keys study (1950), which involved conscientious objectors imprisoned during World War II who were restricted to 1500 calories per day. After just one month, the men began to obsess about food and weight.

Next, Linda holds the two pieces of yarn side by side in the air and uses a ruler to show the numerical difference between the actual size of Susan's thighs and her perceived size.

"I see it but I can't believe it," Susan says, still shaking her head.

Linda assigns Susan to take the two pieces of yarn home and tape them to her mirror and to make a note to paste on her mirror that says, "Pay no attention to the imposter in the mirror." This intervention was a turning point in Susan's recovery and one that Linda revisited from time to time throughout the recovery process. As Susan's healing progressed, there was less discrepancy between her perceived size and her actual size as demonstrated by the String Thing.

Dear Body

As we have observed, people who overeat have difficulty with self-soothing. This activity, which Karen teaches to overeaters, trauma survivors and others with high levels of anxiety, involves identifying a part of the body that is feeling wounded, scared or tense.

Karen suggests that clients place one or both hands on the area of the body that is tense—frequently the heart or stomach—and asks the client to breathe deeply and say aloud, "Dear Body, we are safe."

Clients typically report that saying and hearing the words aloud, along with feeling the gentle touch of their hands on their body is calming. Karen explains that the "we" recognizes that the mind, body and spirit are joining to create the safe feeling. This short activity may be used as part of the warm up to create safety and grounding, during a vignette to establish soothing when fear arises, or at the conclusion of a drama to support the calm feeling that has been generated as a result of the work. It also is one of Karen's frequent homework assignments to people who demonstrate anxiety or obsessive thoughts about their body.

The Body Book

The Body Book is an art activity that explores the strengths of the body, the way the body has been wounded by trauma and the evolution of the recovery process for the body, mind and spirit. In other words, the Body Book begins by finding and showing strengths that the body has; it acknowledges the body-based trauma, and finally celebrates the healing of the body. This activity was developed as an art project at a Therapeutic Spiral Model workshop when Linda collaborated with dance movement therapist and psychodramatist Kim Burden, and it has evolved through the years for use with individuals and groups during sessions and as client homework.

For this activity, the director will have blank paper (various colors or white or both), a plentiful supply of magazines, glue, glitter, stickers, pastel crayons, markers, pens and other materials, including commercial scrap book items. Participants are also welcome to bring personal photos and other items. A three-hole punch should be available so that the pages can be punched and inserted into a three-ring binder enabling participants to use it as an ongoing project throughout the recovery process.

The first section focuses on identifying strengths regarding the body. For example, if a person has positive associations with holding her children, she may include a photo of herself cuddling her children, or a representative photo cut from a magazine, or she may choose to draw a picture. She may add a caption that says, "Strong gentle arms protect and comfort my children." Gregory was proud of his shoulders, which were strong enough for him to carry his young son in piggyback style. Upon reflection, he realized that his shoulders were "good enough" even though he had wished for bigger muscles for decades.

The next section of the Body Book expresses the trauma-based body parts. For example, there may be a picture of a little girl with a round belly and an adult next to her saying, "You're too fat—no man will ever want you!" In this section, we have participants add what the body really needs; for instance, "What my body needs is acceptance and compassion."

The last section of the book focuses on the transformational body-based roles that the person is developing during the recovery process.

For example, if the person has begun a yoga practice, she may have a picture of a favorite yoga pose with the words "calm breather" or "peaceful warrior." Or perhaps he has begun nature walks, or kayaking or massage, and he can show these and label the feelings and roles that accompany these activities such as "nature lover," "rhythmic paddler" and "relaxed receiver."

Adding psychodramatic methods

The value of the Body Book can be further expanded with action, including doubling and other techniques.

For instance:

- The protagonist may dialogue with the arms that comfort her children (similar to the Body Dialogue) whereby she can discover ways in which the arms that comfort her children can also help her.

- Voice can be given to the traumatized body part or parts to speak truth and ask for needs to be met. For example, Gregory, who was rudely told by a coach that he wasn't strong enough to join the middle school wrestling team, confronts the coach in a psychodramatic vignette saying, "My shoulders are strong enough for what matters to me now," and speaks to his shoulders with appreciation.

- A future projection of the transformational body-based roles can be enacted to inspire the protagonist to continue the recovery process.

■ VARIATION

To save time, the director may have blank comb-bound books ready for participants; such books may be obtained at an office supply store. Alternatively, the participants can bring blank sheets of paper and a three-ring binder to the session.

Feelings Sculptures

A big part of recovery involves the understanding that the body is the container of feelings; emotions reside in the body and not only in the brain.

Linda uses a set of nine clay sculptures, each about eight inches tall with no facial features or distinguishable age, gender or ethic group, that show a variety of poses and gestures relating to feeling states. She places them randomly on the floor in a locogram arrangement and asks the person or group member to walk to the sculpture that best represents his or her feelings in the moment. They are directed to take that position or posture; in other words, to sculpt themselves, "doubling" the inanimate clay sculpture. Invariably, putting the body into the posture brings feelings to the surface. Linda asks for a soliloquy from that posture, which serves as a warm up for a drama.

■ VARIATION

Have the protagonist make one small change in his or her first posture and speak from the part of the body that moved. For example, if the hand moved, have the hand tell why: "I want to reach out more…"

■ VARIATION

Have the participant choose another group member to take the posture and have the protagonist stand in the mirror position, first observing, then sculpting the auxiliary into a posture the protagonist wishes for. Then reverse roles and have the protagonist say what feels different.

■ VARIATION

Have group members create a moving sculpture that has each member evolving in slow motion into the "hoped-for feeling self," with each interacting with the others to co-create a moving sculpture of hope.

■ VARIATION

Direct the group members to be intuitively drawn to a particular sculpture and location rather than having a rational "reason" for their choice. For instance, rather than saying to themselves, "I feel sad," and then walking to the sculpture that most accurately presents an image of sadness, they are directed to slowly walk around the space, being aware of all body sensations and feelings. Note that certain locations may bring up more body sensations than others, such as tingling, heaviness, stiffness or heart pounding. They are to stand at the place that most resonates with their bodies. When all have found a place, have time for sharing.

Making Peace with the Body

The power of concretization can again be used with our Making Peace with the Body action structure, where we employ objects, this time weights, to show the connection between weight and hurtful messages.

CASE STUDY: KATERINA AND THE POWER OF CONCRETIZING

Katerina came to Linda's lifestyle counseling practice at the age of 32 to request help "to lose 65 pounds." When Linda explained that she does not focus on weight loss but rather on education and support for self-care, Katerina initially seemed disappointed. However, after discussion, Katerina acknowledged that she had been on more diets than she could remember, always regaining what was lost, and she agreed that she needed to make peace with her body.

Linda asked Katerina to recall the negative messages that she heard from others, messages that prompted her to want to lose weight. A few of several that she named are:

- "You have such a pretty face..."
- "I am not attracted to women with fat legs."
- "Your hair is sexy—too bad the body doesn't match."
- "You will never get and keep a boyfriend at this weight."

To increase the experiential message about various kinds of "weight" that we carry, Linda pulled out a set of dumbbells that she uses to teach clients about the body's muscle groups (see the Mind to the Muscle section in Chapter 15). She directed Katerina as follows:

See these weights—imagine they are any variety of poundage that you wish—1, 2, 3, 5, 8, 10 and 20 and so on. As you recall each of the negative messages, choose a weight to represent how many pounds that message carries to weigh down your self-esteem.

Katerina chose a series of dumbbells, assigning each with the body-hating message and the corresponding number of pounds, which Linda wrote on a sticky note and attached to the weight. When finished, Linda suggested, "Let's add these numbers to find out how these messages weigh you down…"

Katerina added the numbers and exclaimed, "Sixty-five pounds!" Linda affirmed that the weight of the messages was problematic rather than Katerina's body. Through a combination of nutrition education, personal training, mindful and enjoyable movement, stress management, body appreciation and action methods to deal with the negative messages and their sources, Katerina was able to develop her self-care role and make true peace with her body.

The Caring Observer

The Caring Observer, developed in action by Connie Lawrence James (2012), is designed to cultivate the trait of self-compassion, or the ability to treat one's self with warmth and positive regard. It is based on the work of Bonnie Badenoch (2008) and is the protective factor that guards against the ravages of the self-critic, often the feed monster in depression, anxiety and a variety of self-harming cycles. Instead, self-compassion offers a kinder internal environment, a soft place to land in difficult times and safe enough to learn, grow and flourish.

The Caring Observer is a complex role that may require small action structures to lay the groundwork for the more dimensional role to emerge. Just as J.L. Moreno said the smallest unit is two, the Caring Observer is relational: it is built through interpersonal relations rather than just "made up" solely through spontaneity.

These two components are helpful: First, most often people can show compassion and caring toward others and often lack the ability to show it to themselves. This is well illustrated in cases of caregiver burnout and compassion fatigue. Second, the sense of "being seen" or "felt with" comes first from an attuned person and can be internalized, rather than the reverse. It is important to give participants the experience of attunement through small action structures and warm ups, so they can draw from the "other" in the exercise.

An ideal warm up is the spectrogram, which allows group building through a shared inner world. Here, we create a spectrogram on the floor from zero to 100 and ask the group: "How critical are you about your body?" Allow members to share in the group or in subgroups.

You may continue to explore with a second question: "Where would you *like* to be on this line?" allowing members to experience a different state, speaking in the present: "Wow, I have a lot of freedom..."

To move into action and have clients meet the Caring Observer— and develop inner attachment and words of comfort—place two chairs on stage, one slightly behind and to the side of the first—similar to the Double position. In the second chair goes a soft object, such as a blanket, scarf or cloth that is comforting to the touch.

- In the first chair (the chair in front) we imagine the self. In the second chair (behind with the soft fabric), is the Caring Observer.

- Invite participants to come up one at a time, sitting for a moment in the Caring Observer chair, breathing and soaking in the feeling of love and support. From that role, offer any words to "yourself" that you have been longing to hear. The director may offer feeder lines, like "I am the only one who really knows..." Or closing sentences like "...no matter what happens, I am with you."

After all members of the group have taken the opportunity to experience a vignette with the Caring Observer, we offer time for sharing.

Chapter 11

The Link to Trauma

*The most beautiful people we have known are those
who have known defeat...suffering...struggle...
loss and have found their way out of the depths.*

Elisabeth Kubler-Ross

Professionals who treat people with eating disorders and body distress are likely to encounter a history of trauma.

Although many researchers have focused primarily on eating disorders as related to the aftermath of sexual abuse, other forms of childhood maltreatment and post-traumatic stress disorder are frequently seen among people with eating disorders, as well as those with early disruptions in attachment to caregivers, such as separation from mother due to premature birth, early illness and death of mother. In *Traumatic Relationships and Serious Mental Disorders* published in 2001, Jon G. Allen notes that because self-awareness is painful and difficult to control, binge eating is a common strategy to distract from feelings of anxiety, depression and generalized distress.

Bypassing defenses of trauma

People who have suffered trauma show a range of defenses to protect them from contacting long-held painful feelings. Linda's puppets and stuffed animals are a playful and effective way to bypass defenses; when she asks a client who is a survivor of abuse to take the role of his or her pet via the puppet, she learns information that the protagonist may otherwise feel uncomfortable to reveal. Such information might include childhood or adult abuse, other trauma such as a car accident, a crime or war.

Here is an example about how a dog puppet became an important ally in the healing of Lydia:

CASE STUDY: LYDIA BYPASSES HER DEFENSES

Lydia came to Linda's lifestyle counseling practice at the age of 35 with a long history of yo-yo dieting and was seeking help with practical aspects of self-care. A recovering alcoholic, Lydia had several years of sobriety and a stable job and marriage. However, she had suffered for many years with nightmares and flashbacks resulting from a long and complex history of childhood sexual abuse. She had never revealed this abuse to any professional. Linda referred Lydia to a colleague for in-depth psychotherapy and worked closely with the psychotherapist and later with an acupuncturist for a team approach while she offered periodic adjunctive psychodramatic sessions.

One of Lydia's strengths was her positive relationship with her dogs and cats. However, she was flooded with shame around issues related to her body and food, which made it difficult to accurately report her feelings and behaviors. Linda decided to use a furry auxiliary to help; because Lydia had shared photographs of her pets, Linda chose a soft dog puppet, which closely resembled one of Lydia's favorite dogs. She had earlier talked about this pet, saying the dog was constantly at her side every minute that she was home.

Linda placed the puppet on the back of the sofa in her office. When Lydia arrived, she immediately picked up the puppet and started to pet it, calling it by her dog's name, Bandit. This evidence of spontaneity affirmed that bringing Bandit into the psychodrama room would help bypass Lydia's defenses and help her to open up about her hidden life.

Linda began to interview Bandit, asking how long he had known Lydia, what life was like for him at Lydia's house, what his favorite activities were to do with Lydia and what he loved best about her. These questions helped Lydia really take the role of Bandit. As Lydia warmed up, Linda gradually turned to more sensitive questions like, "Is there anything that you notice Lydia doing that concerns you?"

The answer revealed Bandit's concern about Lydia's alternating episodes of binge eating and starving as well as episodes of other self-harming behaviors such as hair pulling and self-mutilation in the form of cutting her arms. Once the behavior was aired, Linda continued to periodically interview Bandit; the dog puppet became an ongoing "team member," playing an essential role in Lydia's recovery process.

The Trauma Triangle

The Trauma Triangle, taken from Hudgins' Therapeutic Spiral Model, is a helpful way to concretize what happens when trauma invades our lives, and also the roles that are the natural responses that we use to protect ourselves from feeling the full pain of the traumatic experience.

Although this action structure as described by Hudgins in *Experiential Treatment for PTSD: The Therapeutic Spiral Model* (2002) has many applications, the purpose here is to show how it may be enacted with people with eating disorders. The Therapeutic Spiral Model Trauma Triangle is adapted from the well-known Karpman (1968) Drama Triangle, which was inspired by Eric Berne's (1978) Transactional Analysis and delineates the roles of Victim, Persecutor and Rescuer as the three main characters. In the Therapeutic Spiral Model version, the altered roles are:

- Victim

- Perpetrator

- Abandoning Authority.

The Abandoning Authority role is experienced when a trauma occurs. In the original trauma, there is no one to "help"—there are only the Victim and the Perpetrator in the scenario. The person experiences abandonment, and the internal personality structure learns to abandon the self, that the self is not worthy of help, rescue or even basic connection. In the Therapeutic Spiral Model, the identification of this voice of self-abandonment is the key to change with people who have experienced trauma, and a new role must be developed as an antidote to the self-abandonment.

The new role is the Appropriate Authority and it must be developed as a role toward self. Its task is to take the right actions toward self without shaming or blaming the self, moving toward health. In the Therapeutic Spiral Model, the protagonist is never role reversed into a Victim or Perpetrator role until he or she has experienced self-rescue from the adult protagonist role, surrounded by the strengths and containment of other chosen roles for healthy spontaneity.

When trauma survivors have broken the "trance"—where they stay frozen in an internally helpless state—they have begun to develop their own Appropriate Authority internally. After self-rescue, the protagonist further develops the role from that of the wounded part of self by actually experiencing the self-rescue that *should* have been done at the time of the original trauma.

Then it is a role development task to move from taking the role once in a drama, to playing with the role of taking responsibility for one's self. As time passes, the transformative role of the Ultimate Authority (Hudgins and Toscani, 2013) becomes fully created and is spontaneously available in the person's daily life.

Strong caution

As we have noted earlier in this book, psychodrama is a powerful modality in which training is necessary for effective and safe use. This Trauma Triangle structure, in particular, is extremely powerful and should be undertaken in action only by highly experienced directors.

Less experienced directors should consider using this view of trauma roles and eating disorders as a psycho-educational tool rather than as part of an enactment. In such cases we suggest, as a paper and pencil activity, drawing the diagram and identifying each of the roles. This diagram-making activity may be followed by art making and journaling about new awareness and new roles.

Working with clients

When working with the Trauma Triangle, we first ask our protagonists to identify who or what outside of themselves holds each of the three roles of Victim, Perpetrator and Abandoning Authority. This approach is less threatening than beginning with the internalized roles; in group settings this activity aids group cohesion as members see the similarities in their responses.

In the world of eating disorders, we can find each of these three roles quite active, as shown in the following table:

Table 11.1 The Therapeutic Spiral Model Trauma
Triangle Adapted for Eating Disorder Treatment

Victim	Perpetrator	Abandoning Authority
Children whose caregivers "push food" or preach thinness.	Caregivers who "push food" and "preach" thinness.	Any adult (teacher, coach, family member, health professional, etc.) who observes this behavior and does not intervene.
Employees who are surrounded by nutrient-poor food choices in their work places.	Work places with vending machines that carry only junk food and cafeterias that serve dishes that mimic fast food.	Bosses, supervisors and other decision makers in the organization who see this and do nothing.
Children, teens or adults who are teased or bullied due to weight, appearance or underdeveloped physical skills.	Anyone who teases or bullies.	Any adult, especially teachers, teachers' aides, principals, coaches and school bus drivers, who observe this behavior and do not intervene.
Anyone who views or hears visual or auditory messages that promote unrealistic body types, certain physical features as ideal and/or promote dieting.	Media, movies, magazines, diet industry, fitness industry, internet sites that promote eating disorders and body dissatisfaction.	Producers, directors, editors, publishers, website designers, toymakers, diet and fitness industry executives and employees who participate in creating and distributing these images.
Anyone who views or hears messages promoting nutrient-poor choices for meals or in place of meals, such as soda for breakfast and the continuous use of processed foods.	The processed food industry that promotes highly processed foods for use on a regular basis.	Employers, food designers and other decision makers in the processed food companies who participate in making and distributing these products, and parents who unwittingly purchase and give these foods to their children on a regular basis.

In a group, the interaction of roles can be enacted by designating each side of the Trauma Triangle on the floor using large scarves, pillows, mats or masking tape.

The director can begin by asking group members to place themselves on the side of the triangle they feel most warmed up to play. The director also asks who is warmed up to take additional roles, such as:

- the Witness (or Observing Ego) role

- the Appropriate Authority role

- the Client role.

The auxiliary in the Witness role records observations, noting which roles are resistant to change, what the Appropriate Authority role does that successfully breaks stuck patterns, and so on. The goal of the Appropriate Authority role is to stop the Perpetrator if possible, or at least diminish the perpetrator's power. The Appropriate Authority also helps by strengthening the Victim—bringing in strengths like courage or "truthful voice." In action, these strengths can be concretized by having the Victim choose a scarf to hold the role of the strength and then place the scarf on his or her body.

Alternative warm up: Circle Sociometry

Instead of having participants write down commonly identified roles, use circle sociometry. This is a good warm up not only for the Trauma Triangle but also for many other activities, vignettes and dramas. Circle sociometry helps the director to assess the relationships within the group and to create a deeper level of safety. Members stand in a circle and make a statement about what is true for them and that they want to know if others share.

For example:

- "Anyone who had parents who enforced the 'clean plate rule', step into the circle."

Here are some common step-in criteria that we use, although each director will be wise to fit the questions to match the particular group and to ask group members to join in with their own questions:

- "Anyone who ever teased anyone else about their appearance..."

- "Anyone who overheard someone tell a 'fat joke' and remained silent..."

- "Anyone who had a Barbie doll while growing up..."

- "Anyone who reads gossip magazines..."

- "Anyone who collects cookbooks or recipes..."

- "Anyone who has purchased junk food from a vending machine..."

- "Anyone who has admired the appearance of a thin actress, actor or model in the media..."

- "Anyone who had a G.I. Joe action figure when growing up..."

- "Anyone who has criticized his or her own body..."

This structure builds group cohesion and warms people up for action. Once the group is suitably warmed, we can put the Trauma Triangle into action. Here is what the eating disorders Trauma Triangle might look like:

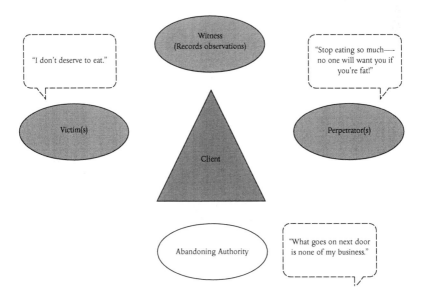

Figure 11.1 The Therapeutic Spiral Model Trauma Triangle for eating disorders

Putting the Trauma Triangle into action

When setting up this structure, it is crucial that the director assess the strengths of the protagonist and the group according to knowledge of the participants and the strengths demonstrated in the Circle of Strengths activity in Chapter 14.

The director can clinically assess if a trained auxiliary—a therapist or intern—should hold the Client role in the center of the triangle or if the protagonist can comfortably take the Client role. The director should be alert to determine the following:

- Is the protagonist able to stay grounded and present?

- Is the protagonist showing signs of dissociation that might require the use of Body Double, Containing Double, or role reversal into the mirror position of the Observer self, also know as the Observing Ego or Witness role?

If the protagonist and group have resources that are adequate to the roles, the protagonist and group members may take those roles. If it is a less well-resourced group, trained auxiliaries or empty chairs may be employed.

We have worked with the group to connect with their strengths and their resources to prepare them for this work and deepen their connections with each other. The director asks the protagonist to select group members to take the Victim, Perpetrator, Abandoning Authority and Witness roles.

Each role player (with the exception of the Witness who is recording) is given lines by assignment or with role reversal. A crucial element is the transformation that occurs when the protagonist, watching from the side, assumes the Appropriate Authority role, steps into the triangle and intervenes. For example:

- To the Perpetrator: "Stop! You are hurting him (or her) with this message."

- To the Victim: "It may seem like that's true, but it's not. You deserve better."

- To the Abandoning Authority: "It's not all right to stand by and see and hear this and to do nothing!"

It is important for the protagonist to role reverse with the Appropriate Authority role so that the protagonist experiences being in the Trauma Triangle *and* being in the empowered role of breaking the Trauma Triangle.

Clinical considerations

This is an advanced action structure, and it should be used with extreme care and thoughtful discernment by an experienced clinician. If an auxiliary holds the Client role, then the protagonist stays in the mirror position, in an observing role. This clinical discernment is particularly important if participants are enacting a personal Trauma Triangle rather than an archetypal one. For example, if a client were to identify the actual introjections of his or her own Trauma Triangle, it might look like this:

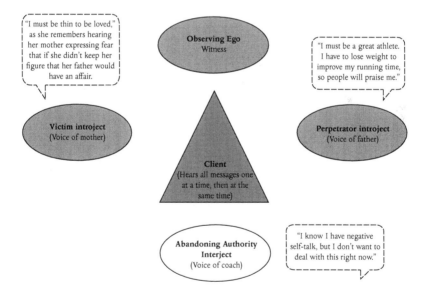

Figure 11.2 Trauma Triangle with introjected voices

141

De-roling the auxiliaries

In all cases, all auxiliaries should be clearly de-roled and plentiful sharing should follow the action. De-roling—stepping out of the role—separates the role player from the role and avoids confusion or transference about the role the auxiliary has played. De-roling is accomplished by having the auxiliary share with the protagonist and group about how it felt to play the role and then clearly state his or her personal experiences about how he or she related to the drama.

For example, the group member who played the role of Fast Food in a dramatic vignette might say:

> When playing the role of Fast Food, I felt very big and powerful and I was sure that I could get you to like me if I continued talking to you. However, as myself, I can remember how many times I promised to avoid fast food restaurants—and how many times I wasn't able to keep that promise.

Additionally, the director may use a scarf, rattle, fan, singing bowl or other object to touch or wave in front of or around the auxiliary to ceremonially de-role the person, especially if the role that was played was the role of a perpetrator or another difficult role.

■ VARIATION

In a group sociodrama, several group members may hold the Client role.

Ways to use the Trauma Triangle

The Trauma Triangle may be used as a warm up to a full protagonist-centered drama; as a warm up to a sociodramatic enactment; or as a vignette with each group member having an opportunity to participate. The director should monitor group members for signs of dissociation and pace the work appropriately. Reversing the protagonist with the Witness role and using the Containing Double and/or Body Double are useful ways to help protagonists stay grounded and present, which is crucial if the Appropriate Authority role is to be internalized.

To help the protagonist internalize and practice the Appropriate Authority role, it is necessary to facilitate the transformation of the

Abandoning Authority role into the Appropriate Authority role. As the protagonist, standing in the mirror position, observes the Client self trapped in the Trauma Triangle, all the roles speak at once. This scene often spurs the protagonist to rescue the Client self from inside the triangle—by spontaneously taking his or her by the hand and pulling him or her out.

The protagonist in the Client role will often say, "Thank goodness! I've waited so long to get out of here!" The director may then facilitate a conversation between the Client role and the protagonist—who has now assumed the Appropriate Authority role—to create intra-psychic bonding between the parts of self and to establish the Appropriate Authority role more securely.

■ VARIATION

Paper and pencil activity exploring the three roles may be used as a warm up before bringing the scene into action. Note that we suggest this structure in action only with a highly experienced director trained in both psychodrama and clinical issues related to trauma.

Recognizing and releasing anger

When we discuss trauma and perpetration, we must recognize that our clients have anger—which they have often turned on themselves or others—that must be metabolized and transformed. In role theory, the Perpetrator role has been introjected and acted out with the eating disorder with the Victim and Abandoning Authority roles. Anger must be acknowledged, addressed and expressed safely in the psychodrama room.

Zerka Moreno has admonished us that we must be careful about how psychodramatists warm up to the anger in case we get "stuck" there (Carnabucci, in press). Keeping this in mind, we prefer to use action techniques like doubling and concretizing to help the protagonist access and express the anger as a path to uncovering the underlying grief and pain. We also include the use of the Body Double and the Containing Double as needed to prevent dissociation.

Anger Release

Here is a way to safely express anger in a psychodrama setting. With an empty chair and a pile of pillows or a handful of small stones, we identify that the chair holds the role of the original perpetrator. The protagonist is invited to place a pillow or stone on the chair while revealing what was said or done by the perpetrator to hurt the protagonist, such as:

- "I'm so angry that you hurt me."

- "I'm so angry that you betrayed me."

- "I'm angry that you violated my body."

- "I'm angry that you told me was my body was not OK."

- "I'm angry that you gave me messages that hurt me."

One stone or pillow is placed on the chair for each statement, and the director may double as necessary, keeping the language clear, direct and respectful. Once the protagonist evidences a shift in energy through changes with the sound of the voice, posture and breathing patterns, the director continues doubling to uncover the underlying grief with statements like:

- "What I really needed from you was…"

- "What I really longed for was…"

Once the need or longing has been identified, we go to a scene where the longing can be enacted and the need met.

Other ways of supporting protagonists to release anger safely are by:

- feeling the anger, paying special attention to the body; the Body Double supports the protagonist to stay in the body

- moving the anger through the body with movement and breath, folding forward and inhaling while slowly beginning to stand, then exhaling vigorously while pushing the hands forward—clearing the system of the angry energy

- practicing the Lion pose of yoga

- stomping the feet in an alternate pattern for one to two minutes while sitting or standing

- making sound with musical instruments.

Chapter 12

The Age Spectrogram
Children and Older Adults

*The great thing about getting older is that you
don't lose all the other ages you've been.*

Madeleine L'Engle

As we sort through the realities of today's eating disorders, we see that the battleground has expanded to both sides of the age spectrum. One trend is that an increasing number of children, some as young as six, are developing eating disorders. Another trend relates to the fact that older adults, especially women in middle age and beyond, are seeking treatment for eating disorders.

Psychotherapists, treatment centers and programs are responding accordingly and developing specialized programs for both children and older women. As with other populations, we advocate the use of psychodrama and the creative arts when working with both sides of the spectrogram.

Children may begin diets due to suggestions from parents, coaches, pediatricians and other adults. They may seek popularity or want to avoid bullying or to find control of lives where there is otherwise little control. They may become entranced by cultural messages in a world where there are beauty pageants for toddlers who talk about starting a diet so they can fit into their pageant costumes, and advertisements of scanty clothing for pre-teen girls that show increasing amounts of skin, making children unusually body conscious. The processed food and restaurant industries have conspired to convince children and their parents that there is a category of "children's food" so many children consume a steady diet of chicken nuggets, macaroni and cheese and hot dogs—and often soda—which trains their taste buds to prefer nutrient-poor processed foods and encourages the adoption of unhealthy eating patterns very early.

Although every child goes through the "picky eater" phase, reports reveal a variety of unhealthy eating patterns that do not fit psychiatric criteria but nonetheless have significant health consequences for children's developing brains, bodies and teeth. Professionals have recently recognized a pattern discussed at the 2012 International Association of Eating Disorder Professionals conference, which involves children and teens eating only white foods—especially starchy foods like white rice, white pasta, white potatoes and white bread. This extremely restrictive preference does not seem to be associated with a classic eating disorder, fear of fat or body dissatisfaction, but these young people need treatment because this way of eating eliminates major nutrients and causes serious nutritional deficiencies and resulting health conditions.

Psychodrama and children

Dr. J.L. Moreno was inspired to develop the psychodramatic method as a young medical student when watching children play in the public gardens of Vienna. He began telling fairy tales to the children, often while sitting atop tree branches; he noticed that their play released their natural spontaneity and creativity and suggested that they be allowed to play to learn (Moreno, 2012).

Psychodrama is a natural and powerful method for helping children tell their stories, express feelings and experiment with new behaviors, and it has been used for treatment of grief, trauma, abuse, social anxiety and even stuttering. Many psychodrama techniques can be adapted for use with young people to teach social skills and problem solving and make learning engaging and memorable. Although the references for psychodramatic work with children are more limited than work with adults, there is *Who Calls the Tune? A Psychodramatic Approach to Child Therapy* by Bernadette Hoey in 1997 and *The Healing Drama: Psychodrama and Dramatherapy With Abused Children* by Anne Bannister in 1997.

Research with traumatized children

Research has shown that a multi-modal treatment style with maltreated and traumatized children that applies the principles of neurodevelopment (Perry, 2006) works effectively with the cognitive, emotional, behavioral and social consequences of trauma. Children who suffer trauma and neglect will function at age levels incongruent with their chronological age, and their functional ages may vary greatly according to the impact of the trauma. For instance, a 17-year-old youth may function like a ten-year-old child when learning in the school setting and like a four-year-old child in social settings and emotional development. Therefore, the teenager may be treated with a variety of interventions, each linked to a specific developmental stage.

Perry describes multi-modal treatment according to the needs and developmental stage of the child. This treatment might include dance, drumming, music, massage and body work—all patterned and repetitive sensory input that influences the brain stem to reorganize in ways that will lead to smoother functional regulation. Here is a sampling of Perry's recommendations:

- Birth to nine months: Massage, rhythm (such as drumming) Reiki, and Eye Movement Desensitization Reprocessing (EMDR).

- Six months to two years: Music and movement (with suggestions of specific beats per minute), Reiki, massage and animal therapy with horses and dogs.

- One to four years: Play and parallel play, play therapy, performing and creative arts and puppets.

- Three to six years: Storytelling, drama, exposure to performing arts; formal education, traditional psychotherapy.

(Perry, 2006)

These varied modalities that address each developmental stage are built into the theory and practice of psychodrama, which is a multi-modal method and one that is able to easily incorporate additional methods and techniques, as we shall see.

Drama, action and creative arts

To deal with attitudes and feelings about food, weight and appearance, a number of action and creative arts options are available. We have used games, music, puppets, sand tray and movement for education and to create a place where feelings can be contained, expressed and witnessed. Our psychodrama colleague Rebecca Walters suggests sociodrama, empty chair work, stories and fairy tales in her work with children plus sociometric group-building activities helpful when working in children's groups.

As with adults, these sociometric activities help children recognize commonalities with others, increasing comfort in a group setting. As always, the criteria must be carefully and thoughtfully identified. Spectrograms on what month of the year they have birthdays—from January to December—are more helpful than questions about who is younger or who is older or who is taller and who is shorter. Such questions might cause tensions or conflict within the group and create competition or hierarchy because such topics are just one step away from who is fatter and who is thinner.

Spectrograms may be constructed using polarities with food categories. Children stand on the line according to their preferences of a food category:

- Pizza or hamburgers?

- Ice cream or cake?

- Chocolate or vanilla?

- Fruits or vegetables?

Step-in circles might focus on statements like:

- "Something I like to do for fun outside…"

- "Something I like to do for fun inside…"

- "Something I like to do for fun by myself…"

- "Sometime I like to do for fun with others…"

These topics are enjoyable, and the children will notice who shares interests with them while the group leader will silently assess the moods, interests and preferences of the children to identify themes for later educational lessons or therapeutic work.

Music and play

For fun explorations of themes about food and movement with children, Linda uses music, movement and dramatic play, providing handheld musical instruments that the children play while singing and moving. Music warms the children to make songs about food likes and dislikes; Linda gives directions to "Be the food." Descriptions like "slippery spaghetti," "gooey cheese" and "sticky caramel" may emerge as children become involved. As the group warms, Linda suggests the children create a sculpture of "food friends" who might "hang out" together on their plate. If the sculpture appears lacking in nutrient density, Linda takes the role of a nutrient-dense food—such as an apple—and says, "I am an apple, crispy and sweet, some people eat me as a treat." She asks permission to join the others in the sculpture and allows the action to unfold as all foods interact with each other.

Locogram Food Game

We have created a locogram game that acquaints children with the variety of foods and tastes and supports exploration of new experiences with food. In this game, we create colorful locogram bowls, signs or pictures about the various characteristics of food tastes and textures, such as sweet, sour, salty, bitter, spicy and pungent, as well as a variety of textures like creamy, crunchy and chewy, and place them on the floor of the psychodrama room. After a warm up, the children are invited to stand on the place of the flavor and texture that:

- they most like

- they most dislike

- they have never tried

- they might want to try.

There is lots of conversation—and maybe some music—about various foods and tastes. If possible, the director may have a variety of actual foods available, naturally sweet fruit, sour pickles, crunchy corn chips, chewy popcorn, crisp green beans and tangy slices of lemon for children to touch and taste. The locogram activity may be incorporated into a cooking class where an adult guides the children in preparing foods like whole-grain pancakes, omelets, fruit smoothies and other dishes that represent the diversity of whole foods. For safety and to avoid choking and allergy hazards, directors will need to be mindful of the size, type and textures of foods they select.

Adapting psychodrama for children

The psychodrama director will have to adapt certain techniques and structures for children. Sometimes children fear speaking their truth to an adult, even in their imagination. Rebecca Walters suggests using the psychodramatic empty chair and has the child imagine the adult sitting in the chair. She gives the child a magic wand that will allow him or her to speak the truth to the person in the empty chair without repercussions. For instance, a child might want to speak to a parent who is still ordering a "happy meal" on behalf of the child; given the opportunity, Caitlin was able to emphatically tell her invisible mother in the empty chair, "I'm nine years old now—I don't like those kinds of meals any more! I can read the menu by myself and make my own decisions!"

Linda also may have children create "magic" shields from art supplies to use during dramatic enactments, a prop that is comforting when they feel scared. She may provide child-friendly shaking instruments to help children shake out or stomp out their anger. Because children may feel uncomfortable or self-conscious being the focus of a group or have limited attention spans, vignettes are brief and the director may opt for a sociodrama, sculptures or other group activities where all are included.

Children are quickly engaged with puppets of all sizes so the director may speak from the voice of the puppet in hand. The dialogues with the child and interviews with the child's significant others are conducted with the puppets rather than an adult professional, which creates a playful and inclusive atmosphere. Hoey (1997) points out that children, even as early as the age of three, are capable of taking the role of the significant other. Indeed, the child responds spontaneously from his or her new role position, which implies the capacity to empathize with the other. This method makes it possible to apply the principal psychodrama techniques such as role taking, doubling and mirroring.

Linda will bring out her furry auxiliaries so children can use puppets to accompany songs about animals. As director, she interviews each animal to learn what part of the song or dance the child liked best; this activity can warm up the children to using the puppets as role takers and they become a useful resource for the director who can interview the puppet to learn about the child in greater depth, and help him or her to express feelings and learn new behaviors.

Fruit Bowls

This fun educational structure focuses on appreciation of body diversity especially in elementary school children, but it can be adapted for youth, adults and families.

Linda brings two large bowls of fruit for this program. One bowl is filled with a variety of colorful fruits—apples, oranges, grapes, bananas, pears, strawberries, tangerines, pineapple and fruits that some children might not be familiar with, such as kiwi fruit and mangoes. In the other bowl, there are bananas. Linda asks which bowl is more "interesting"; invariably, the children reply the bowl with the fruit mixture. Linda explains that people come in a variety of sizes and shapes and colors, just like fruit, and points out that, although the "blonde" bananas, being tall and slender, are fine, life would be uninteresting if everyone looked alike, and that bananas would become boring if they were our only food.

■ **VARIATION**

Add a nutritional component. Have each child choose a fruit and become the fruit, taking a body position and even a colorful scarf or cloth that embellishes the enactment. Talk about the fruit's nutritional benefits and how each one helps the body grow and stay healthy; for instance: "I am an orange. I have Vitamin C to help fight germs." Each child in role is encouraged to show its taste appeal—"I am so juicy and sweet!"

Older children might be presented with a card to take home that has a simple statement on it about the health value of the fruit and its taste appeal.

■ **VARIATION**
Add music, using the song "Yummy, Yummy" which is perfect for having children act it out, letting each child be a different fruit and putting it all together to make "fruit salad." Follow up by having the ingredients available to make an actual fruit salad for children to taste and eat.

The use of fairy tales

Thanks to today's animation, children are familiar with age-old fairy tales—like *The Little Mermaid* and *Snow White*—as well as several newer ones, like *Shrek*, that contain themes about characters' attitudes about beauty and body. Showing a film clip or reading from a picture book are warm-up options to explore these attitudes, at first from the safe distance of the film or book.

We like the scene from *The Little Mermaid* in which Ursula, the sea witch, bargains with Ariel, the teenage mermaid. Ariel wants human legs so she can walk on land with her newfound love Prince Eric. Ursula tries to convince Ariel to surrender her beautiful and expressive voice to her as the price for her turning Ariel's mermaid tail into human legs. Ursula says men don't care about a woman's voice and that "You'll have your looks! Your pretty face! Your body language!" Ariel signs the agreement, only to discover that Prince Eric first fell in love with her voice.

This scene can be enacted with group members taking roles as the director doubles and calls for role reversal. Sharing may warm up one or more in the group to take the protagonist role—an opportunity to explore how she has silenced her own voice, believing that appearance is the key to finding love.

Linda has children enact the story from *The Little Mermaid* and then make up and act out alternative scenarios that the children think would have been helpful to Ariel. One solution involved having Ariel enlist the support of her sisters in speaking to her father, Trident, about her feelings for Eric; in psychodramatic terms, we call this enlisting the aid of auxiliaries. Another option was the creation of a new character, a kind of mermaid fairy godmother, who wanted Ariel to speak and sing her truth and feelings into a magic shell which was carried to the rock near Prince Eric's castle. When Prince Eric meets Ariel, the children created dialogue in which he explained that he loved Ariel's "beautiful inside self" which he got to know through her voice, and that the sea witch has lied when she had told Ariel that her looks were the most important.

CASE STUDY: CINDY LEARNS THE FUN OF MOVEMENT

Eight-year-old Cindy came to see Linda with her mother who was concerned about Cindy's lack of physical activity as well as classmates' comments about her increasing weight. Cindy had several siblings, older and younger, and they showed both the naturally leaner body types inherited from the father's side of the family, and the naturally heavier body types inherited from the mother's side.

Linda decided to introduce Cindy to a variety of physical activities, to incorporate positive affirmations to improve Cindy's self-esteem and to use puppets to explore and express feelings. Cindy reported that art was her favorite activity, so Linda introduced a variety of art supplies to begin drawing. Before long, Cindy was drawing horses and making up stories about them. When each drawing was complete, Linda asked Cindy to show how the horses moved, creating a variety of imaginary places for the horses, such as the farm meadow, the old country lane and the forest.

As Cindy took on roles of horses in her drawings, Linda doubled and mirrored Cindy and labeled herself the horses' "inner selves." Pretending to speak as a horse, Cindy revealed her desire to "be fast and beautiful like a racehorse." Exploration revealed that Cindy's eldest sister, a long-distance runner, won praise and medals; Cindy, unable to compete with her athletic sister, decided to withdraw from physical activity. Linda continued to use Cindy's love of art as a starting point for their sessions and to introduce a variety of ways to move her body in ways unrelated to competition.

Linda engaged Cindy with the animal poses of yoga; up dog, down dog, cobra, eagle, cat, cow, lion and others. Linda would ask Cindy which animal she felt like in the moment and to show that animal with the pose and a sound. Before the hour closed, Linda brought out her collection of puppet animals, and Cindy would choose the puppet to give her a positive "take-home" message. In this concluding ritual for the session, Cindy would choose a puppet to hold her role while speaking as the puppet who would deliver the positive message. After the message was delivered, Linda called for role reversal and the positive puppet delivered the message.

The next session began with Cindy drawing how the positive message had helped her during the week and was reinforced in movement and words. Over time, Cindy explored a variety of non-competitive physical activities, continued her art making, and learned to enjoy moving her body. Through the work with animal puppets, she learned to accept diversity in body shapes and sizes and individual gifts and talents.

Working with parents

When working with children, it is essential that professionals work closely with parents. Even loving parents will present messages to their children about foods, meals, appearance and diets that are unhealthy or can be misinterpreted by the children. Many other parents believe it is their responsibility to control their child's weight. We believe that education for parents, as well as other authority figures in the child's daily life, is essential to counter these strong social messages about body and food. We advocate to parents, teachers, coaches and school administrators that children should be encouraged to enjoy a variety of foods, including fruits and vegetables, and to experiment and enjoy healthy movement and recreation.

The parent interview

Because parents are often unaware about how their messages are received by their children, Karen makes use of role reversal, role reversing the parent into the child who has been brought to psychotherapy.

Once the parent has changed chairs and moved into the child's role, Karen might say, "Please, take some time to sit like your child and become your child," and she might present a stuffed animal to the parent-as-child to hold. She makes use of the psychodramatic interview technique to learn about the child through the eyes of the parent.

She starts with simple questions, asking the parent-as-child about his or her age, her grade in school, her favorite school subject and other basic topics. As the parent-as-child becomes warmed up in the role, Karen begins to ask open-ended questions that relate to the reason the child is in psychotherapy. A sampling of questions might include:

- "Your mom and dad think you should come to see me about your worry about your body. What is happening so that your mom and dad think you should be here?"

- "Where did you learn about diets?"

- "How does your mom take care of her body?"

- "How does your dad take care of his body?"

- "What do your mom and dad say to you about going outside and playing?"

- "What kind of foods does your mom (or dad) buy when she or he goes shopping?"

- "What message would you like to hear from your mom (or dad) that would be important to you?"

The interview continues until the parent appears to arrive at new information and awareness about the child's experience, and as time allows. Parents are often surprised with new understanding about the messages that they have been inadvertently "feeding" their child, the ways they have enabled their child's eating disorder or body distress, or that their child has feelings that have been kept hidden from the parent. They may also become aware that they know very little about their child's friends and how their child tries to fit with his or her peer group; sometimes they share that they have not taken the time to learn about other aspects of their child's life. Often, they realize that they have been trying to control what their child is eating and their child's overeating or undereating is their attempt to take control of his or her own food intake. They also may become aware that they have their own issues with food, dieting and body dissatisfaction.

After the interview, Karen discusses how the parent, now with new information and empathy, might change communication and behaviors to support their child's recovery and health. She may direct the parent in role play to rehearse new communication styles and behaviors or use action methods to explore the parent's personal issues. At times, she may use other simple experiential lessons, such as enlisting the parent to participate in a tug of war—with Karen providing a rope or scarf and tugging in the role of the child while the parent tugs the other end. After this experience, the parents have the opportunity to discuss how it feels when there is a power struggle between parent and child and how some may passively give in while others may increase their desire to control.

Educating the parent

Many parents do not know how to present nutritious meals to their children or how to resist a child's demands for fast food, soda, candy or other unhealthy foods, or how to introduce more movement and free play into the family. We like to present supplementary materials, including books, handouts and online videos, as helpful resources. Again, parents may rehearse new behaviors by role play in parenting groups and other therapeutic or educational settings so they may feel confident in introducing and sustaining these new roles in their families.

Honoring the aging process

On the other end of our age spectrogram are older people. Many women and men struggle with body and appearance issues as they age. These struggles may contribute to depression and isolation and revive habits of unhealthy eating or restricting from earlier years. We have especially seen women in their forties, fifties and sixties who are concerned with body dissatisfaction, body image distortions and fear of food. Issues are often exacerbated by the aging process. Some may have suffered eating disorders during their younger years, and others may have struggled intermittently throughout their lives. A third category have developed eating disorders and body dissatisfaction as they have grown older and faced typical mid-life stressors such as marital discord, divorce or death of a spouse, children leaving home, career disappointments or changes and chronic illness.

From the psychodramatic point of view, advancing age is framed as a time for changes in significant roles. There may be role losses due to the death of a spouse, retirement or adult children moving out of the home. New roles—like grandmother and grandfather—may create a shift in perception. There are also significant changes due to the reorganization of hormones—perimenopause and menopause for women and hormonal shifts for men. These hormonal changes may contribute to weight gain, mood swings, changes in the level of sexual desire and "foggy brain."

In addition, advertising and the influence of friends and acquaintances who have had extensive appearance-altering procedures—such as botox injections, facelifts, liposuction and implants—present apparent solutions to those who are seeking ways to compensate for role losses. We have noticed a bonding that occurs with women who attend "botox parties" and similar events where keeping a youthful look is highly regarded. The societal focus on maintaining youthful appearance—no wrinkles, no cellulite and bragging about returning to one's "high school weight"—coupled with ads for diets and digitally altered photographs of faces and bodies collude to undermine self-acceptance. In short, life in general and one's own body in particular are perceived to be, as our clients say, "out of control."

Through the decades we have worked to explore and transform cultural messages that push a youth-oriented perspective. Here the tasks involve accepting the realities of aging while learning how to practice self-care; we focus on educational and therapeutic action vignettes that promote self-acceptance, safe physical activity, awareness of choices that encourage vitality and healthy social interaction.

The archetypes—symbolic and mythological holders of universal energies—are often related to transpersonal strengths. We have found Great Mother, Great Father, Wise Woman and Wise Old Man, among others, to be important archetypes in working with people, especially when they lack models about growing older. When working with women, we have found that honoring the Wise Woman role, called the Crone in mythology, is a way to embrace the gifts and challenges of aging, especially in a culture that glamorizes youth. In this ritual-like activity, each woman locates a tall stick or branch to serve as a staff and attaches meaningful items that symbolize various aspects of the Wise Woman role. These may include aspects of nature—for example, being a caretaker of nature is one of the typical symbolic roles of the Crone—as well as other items that honor life lessons earned through decades of living.

The corresponding archetype for men is the Senex (or Sage or Wise Old Man) who contains the wisdom of a lifetime, which may also be embodied by the ritual staff. There are also the mature male archetypes of king, warrior, magician and lover, as outlined in the 1991 book *King, Warrior, Magician, Lover: Rediscovering the Archetypes of the Mature Masculine* by Robert Moore and Douglas Gillette. These archetypes embody the benevolent use of power, the ability to have courage and bear pain, the mature use of knowledge and skill, and the ability to be emotionally connected to others and have empathy.

Inspired by the article, "Reiki Talking Stick" by Colleen Benelli in the Spring 2012 issue of *Reiki News Magazine*, Linda charged her Wise Woman staff with Reiki energy for psychodramatic use. As part of introducing the Wise Self role, Linda explains that each of us contains that part of self, even if we are not yet aware of it, which is accessible through the collective unconscious, mythology, literature, art, oral traditions and perhaps one or more of our ancestors. Linda explains that this part of the self sees into the future to the Recovered Self and can help the Present Self see the recovery path through the use of future projection and role reversal. Giving the protagonist the Reiki staff to hold in the role of the Wise Self helps the protagonist literally touch the energy of that role.

■ VARIATION

The Wise Self staff may be used as a talking stick during sharing; as each group member shares, he or she holds the Reiki staff and is supported with Reiki energy to share from the heart.

CASE STUDY: BONITA RECOVERS FROM LOSS AND TRANSFORMS ROLES

Bonita was a 50-year-old woman referred to Linda's lifestyle counseling practice by her acupuncturist, who described Bonita as struggling with a metal element challenge: perfectionism. This trait well served Bonita in her career as an expert consultant who restored antique stringed instruments for musicians and museums around the world. However, the meticulous demands of this detailed work eventually resulted in severe loss of vision and job loss. Although her extended family was able to support her financially, Bonita was devastated. Her loss of vision meant she could not easily cook for herself, and the loss of her job role plummeted her into a deep depression.

Trying to find a sense of control and "perfect" what she could, Bonita began to eliminate foods from her diet, declaring them not "pure" enough, even if they were organic and locally grown. A psychiatrist diagnosed her with anorexia nervosa although it is likely she was suffering from orthorexia, or "fixation on righteous eating." This condition often begins with an attempt to eat healthfully, but becomes an obsession with food quality and nutrition rather than weight or appearance.

Collaborating with Bonita's acupuncturist, Linda learned about the metal element (see Chapter 14 for more on the five-element philosophy) and its association with grief and the search for spiritual growth. With this knowledge as well as Bonita's love of art, Linda initiated two action interventions. The first was the use of the "feeling sculptures," a set of small clay sculptures showing various emotions. Although Bonita could not see the sculptures very well, she ascertained their qualities with touch. Bonita chose a figure slumped to the ground, hands covering eyes. Linda directed Bonita to assume the pose of the sculpture and followed with a soliloquy.

Bonita said, "I can't see."

Linda doubled, "I've lost my vision and so much more..."

"Yes," whispered Bonita, "so much more..."

Linda presented a basket holding items of various textures and directed Bonita to choose objects to represent each of her losses, placing the objects one by one in a metal box. Bonita identified loss of vision, ability to be self-sufficient, loss of job, income, esteem and status in the eyes of others and self-esteem. Linda doubled to expand feelings and asked, "If your eyes could look inward at your soul, what would they see?" At this, Bonita wept. After a long period of weeping, she admitted, "I am so empty. I cannot see my soul. I cannot even feel it."

Linda doubled, "I miss my soul." Bonita nodded, "Yes. I miss my soul." Next, Linda presented a box of stones and shells and asked her to select one that represented "the jewel within the jewel," a phrase from the five-element philosophy about the precious essence of the soul-self. "This is a reminder," Linda said, "that there is a part of yourself that is unseen and that is precious." As agreed, this session was immediately followed by an acupuncture treatment with the referring practitioner to energetically support the psychodramatic work and assess what may have shifted.

The following session with Bonita focused on her desire to reconnect with her spiritual self. Bonita was somewhat familiar with Reiki so Linda brought out her Reiki crone staff, inviting Bonita to touch the items attached to the staff and to speak about what she felt as she explored each item. As Bonita correctly identified items like the moon, stars, sun, a metal butterfly and various beads and feathers on the staff, her face brightened and it was clear that she was literally and figuratively feeling a new strength within herself.

As this strength was integrated, Bonita stood and held the staff to take the role of the Empowered Soul, speaking to herself in the empty chair, telling herself that she was able to sense her surroundings even with her vision loss. Linda invited her to place the staff aside and vigorously rub the palms of her hands together, then hold them apart and notice the sensations that emerged.

"I feel tingling and a little heat," Bonita announced, as she held her hands in front of her heart.

"That," said Linda, "is universal energy and you are connected to it." Bonita began to cry—and this time the tears were not tears of pain but of "action insight." Again, this session was followed by an acupuncture treatment.

As Bonita progressed, she decided to enroll in Reiki training to use her hands in a new role, one in which she could sense energy without the need for sight. She likened this newly discovered sensing to the way she could "tune in" to the lost musical instruments that needed restoration. Gradually the combination of acupuncture, Reiki, action methods and growing social support helped her recover from her role loss and to treasure "the jewel within the jewel."

Replacing cultural myths for older women

Linda created a workshop "Ageless Beauty—Replacing Cultural Myths With Timeless Truths" with colleagues Patti Desert and Rita Preller for women dealing with body issues related to aging.

Participants selected a card from a deck of Goddess cards to hold the role of the Witness, first sharing about the card in dyads and then placing the card in a safe place in the room to hold the Witness role for the day. After the regular introductions, group norms and spectrograms to assess experience with action methods, anxiety in the moment, and comfort level with safe touch, we moved on to circle sociometry designed to address the concerns of our population of mature women.

Participants were asked to step in the circle if they:

- "have a self-care practice of any kind"

- "practice self-care beyond the typical "basics" of showering, brushing teeth and the like"

- "are self-critical about their body"

- "are critical of others' bodies and/or appearance"

- "notice that they have neglected their body"

- "have felt worry about aging"

- "have been influenced by our youth-obsessed culture"

- "carry family messages that are anti-aging"

- "have ever felt angry about any of these youth-oriented messages"

- "have felt angry but were unable to express their anger"

- "have expressed their anger in the past and been ignored"
- "are able to identify something they appreciate about their body"
- "have ever laughed so hard tears ran down their face"
- "are able to name one thing about their body that brings a smile to your face right now."

Other criteria might include if they have:

- "dieted to feel better about themselves"
- "looked in the mirror to count their wrinkles"
- "practiced binge eating to soothe or to distract from their feelings about aging"
- "exercised to the point of injury or extreme fatigue"
- "completely neglected exercise"
- "invested heavily in clothes, cosmetics or anti-aging products to feel better about themselves"
- "an eating disorder."

Each participant was asked to choose a group member to hold her role in group and then take her Witness role by standing at the card's location in the room. From the Witness role she was invited to tell the Self "one sentence about what you observed about yourself this morning."

To recognize the developmental phases, the after-lunch warm up included movement designed to energize: move like your aging body, move like your adolescent body and move like your inner child body. After each movement, the group members mirrored the movement back to the original person.

More questions may be asked about who could:

- "play the role of your healthy body"
- "play the role of your aging body"
- "play the role of your wounded body."

After each choice, the chooser shares with the chosen person the reasons for the choice. The director may ask the chosen people how it felt to be selected for that role.

As this kind of group proceeds, the director may take cues from the sharing after each action structure to develop personal psychodrama sessions that might include the Body Dialogue and other dramas pertinent to individuals within the group.

A good conclusion for the day is having participants share about their dramas and return to the Witness role by standing in front of their Witness card. Each participant in the Witness role speaks to herself in the empty chair, identifying the take-home message of the session.

■ VARIATION

Instead of the Body Dialogue, create a timeline of the body's changes, have each protagonist share what specific changes he or she finds troubling and explore in a psychodrama session.

■ VARIATION

Develop a sociodrama, using roles such as the Critic, the Aging Body, the Aging Face, the Plastic Surgeon, the Fashion Magazine Editor and the Aging Movie Star. Work with the group to identify a specific theme where all of the characters can interact; for instance, selecting a cover photo of the most popular women's fashion or men's body building magazine in the country.

■ VARIATION

Develop a sociodrama, using roles such as the Child self, Teen self, Young Adult self, Middle-Age self and Wise Elder self. Work with the group to identify a specific theme where all can participate.

■ VARIATION

Have the protagonist pick group members to play Child self, Teen self, Young Adult self, Middle-Age self and Wise Elder self and have the auxiliaries stand in line in chronological order right to left and shoulder to shoulder, facing the protagonist. The protagonist is given the opportunity to role reverse with each role, speaking from each role in the present. After reversing back, the protagonist expresses

164

appreciation to each role player for lessons learned that are still carried within the self. The protagonist may be able to step into and claim the Wise Elder; if the protagonist is not yet able to claim the role, she may take the role as a surplus reality scene.

■ VARIATION
Have group members commit to a specific self-care behavior to practice after the workshop. Have them enact behavior in a monodrama in front of the group or create a sculpture with the assistance of others.

Chapter 13

Images of Nourishment

As a body everyone is single, as a soul never.

Hermann Hesse

A picture is worth a thousand words. A picture that can be changed teaches the mind that our lives and behaviors can be transformed from distress and pain to acceptance and peace. We have used art, sculpture, sand tray, photographs, cards and collage as specific stand-alone action activities with individuals and groups in the belief that art helps express and sustain the self in times of turmoil.

Some of these activities may be used as warm-up activities and others as follow-up assignments. As we have noted, the warm-up activities prepare the person and the group for a full-bodied experience of the action; the follow-up activities are designed to deeply integrate the messages and learning within the protagonist.

For instance, Linda assigns a project of integration after each drama that cements the messages learned in the drama that the protagonist wants to keep. She has protagonists identify images and words to connect the right and left hemispheres of the brain to anchor the action insights. Projects may be as simple as a collage with pictures and words illustrating the important insights from the drama, or as complex as a PowerPoint presentation or digital movie with words, images and music.

Karen may assign journaling, picture making or meditation based on useful affirmation or another activity. If a sand tray arrangement was created during the session, she may take a digital photo of the arrangement—or have the protagonist take a photo with his or her phone camera—and advise the client to revisit the image. Some clients decide to make the picture the screen saver on their computer or create a private digital diary online where they post photographs of their work.

Fork in the Road

The Fork in the Road offers the opportunity for a protagonist to visualize and experience the choice-making process and the consequences of specific choices, especially in terms of advancing healthy behavior.

Create a large "Y" on the floor, using scarves, yarn, masking tape or whatever is appropriate. Explain that the "Y" represents the fork in the road of recovery, with the possibility to walk in two directions—one for health and one for sickness.

Have the protagonist stand at the bottom of the stem of the "Y." Ask him or her to identify two possible choices regarding an action with food, personal care, etc.

CASE STUDY: BRIGITTE MAKES A CHOICE ABOUT SODA

Brigitte wanted to abstain from soda, which she identified as her binge beverage. She was not able to stop at one can or glass and, once started, knew that she would continue to crave and drink soda hour after hour. By the end of the day she felt not only bloated and uncomfortable but also guilty about hurting her body and digestive system.

When working with Karen during a session, Brigitte identified one tine of the fork as problematic to health, "a sugary beverage with no nutritional value, one that sets up continued cravings and damages my bones."

The second tine of the fork was health, "feeling good about making healthy choices, stopping sugar cravings and taking care of myself."

Brigitte first role reversed with the problematic choice, speaking as the consequence: "I'm the choice that has no nutritional value, will set you up for cravings all day and make you bloated."

She role reversed with the healthy choice, speaking as the consequence: "I'm the choice that helps you feel good about yourself and protects your digestive system and bones, helping you improve the quality of your life."

Group members were selected to play the roles as Brigitte returned to her original self at the stem of the "Y." The role players improvised with some laughter and some seriousness; Brigitte was given an opportunity to walk toward the healthy choice and feel physically embraced by that choice.

■ **VARIATION**

Use in individual session with stuffed animals or chairs decorated as choices.

■ **VARIATION**

Use in individual session with puppets, with each puppet representing a choice. The protagonist operates one puppet on each hand and speaks through the puppet about the choices and consequences. Use of puppets provides a protective distance from the emotional material, which may be threatening, while bringing in an element of play to the process.

■ **VARIATION**

Use in individual session with sand tray, letting the protagonist pick significant objects for self and choices. Practice with the hand slowly moving the object for self toward each choice, talking about how each choice feels in the body.

■ **VARIATION**

Give the protagonist a support person or other strength (or several strengths) to stand with him or her when listening to consequences. Role reverse the protagonist into the strength and speak to the self, especially if there is wavering or struggling.

■ **VARIATION**

Add music as the vignette concludes. We like Kathy Amdsen's "Road to Recovery" from *Awakening*, but many songs have metaphors of journeys to a new life.

Paper Plate Imagery

Guided imageries help a person's inner images to emerge, revealing surprising and new information that is below consciousness. With Karen's Paper Plate Imagery, we employ both closed-eye imagery and open-eye imagery, in addition to drawing the image on a paper plate. For this activity, you will need plain white paper plates, pastel crayons or colored markers and a music player to provide relaxing music.

If participants are unfamiliar with imagery, you will want to tell the group that the imagery takes us on an inner journey in the mind's eye and that they will hear your voice and the sound of relaxing music.

- Encourage all to become physically comfortable on their chairs or on the floor (providing pillows if necessary).

- Begin with a relaxing introduction, which might involve deep conscious breathing and progressive relaxation.

- Allow images to fully surface and accept whatever images, or thoughts of images, that come.

After the director has begun with the relaxing activity of choice and the participants have relaxed, he or she might say:

You will now find yourself in an open space. It is an open space where you feel completely comfortable, protected and relaxed. Take time to notice how it feels to be in this safe place in every part of your body. Continue to breathe as you experience yourself in this space...

And now, in the space in front of you, become aware of an image of food. Allow yourself to accept whatever image that comes, without judgment or comment....

As the image forms, notice the color or colors of this food, allowing the colors to become vivid and real to you...

Notice the texture of the food, imagining how it might feel to touch, pick up, hold or taste...

Notice the aroma of this food, imagining how it might be to inhale the aroma deeply...

Now take more time with this image, noticing whatever feelings or sensations come forward...

And now, when you feel ready, allow yourself to come back here into this room, feeling your body, being aware of your breathing, and open your eyes.

When group members appear ready for the next step, distribute paper plates, pastel crayons or markers.

- Invite them to draw their images on the paper plates with their crayons or markers.

- Suggest that they draw in silence to focus inward and stay with their process.

- When all have finished their drawings, ask them to put away the art materials, staying in silence.

- Next, have them sit comfortably, hold their plate in their hands and focus on it with soft eyes.

Tell the group that we will be doing a second imagery, this one an open-eye imagery where the answers will come from the image, not from their head. As music plays, ask these questions, leaving a pause after each question:

- "What am I expecting from you?"

- "What do I want you to do?"

- "What do you remind me of?"

- "Do I need you right now?"

- "Are you the food I want right now?"

- "Do you have a message for me?"

Give the group ample time to share the imagery and the messages, feelings, recollections and memories related to each one's particular paper plate image. Refrain from offering interpretations and validate any feelings that may surface.

In itself, this brings the inner drama outward and allows participants to reveal their inner world. The Paper Plate Imagery also serves as a deep warm up, allowing group members or individuals to develop dramas around their relationship with food.

CASE STUDY: LOIS AND HER PAPER PLATE

Lois drew a picture of a wedge of lemon meringue pie, with the fluffy meringue topping taking up most of the picture. In sharing, she voiced confusion about the picture; she didn't binge on pie, including this kind of pie, nor did she think about any kind of pie very much. Her binge foods were likely candy bars and sweets from the vending machine at her work place.

Karen asked Lois to role reverse with the pie. Lois obligingly stood in the center of the circle, her arms raised above her head, both hands touching to demonstrate the "wedge" shape of the pie slice. She started speaking as the pie: "I am thick and creamy and luscious," she said. "My flavor is just the right amount of sweet and sour. And I am homemade..."

She stopped speaking as the pie and exclaimed suddenly, speaking as herself, "My grandmother! My grandmother Anna made this kind of pie! It was her specialty and she always served me a slice of lemon meringue pie with milk!"

Now moving to the second scene, Karen role reversed Lois into her grandmother Anna. As grandmother, Lois proudly talked about her baking skills and how she had won awards for her pies at the community farm fairs where housewives presented their best baked goods. "Lois was my favorite granddaughter," said the protagonist-as-grandmother. "It wouldn't be right to show favoritism, but I could bake this pie for her—that's my way of showing her that she was special."

Karen brought in a double for Lois, and directed that Lois-as-grandmother tell the Lois double how much she loved and cared for her. "You are special to me," said Lois-as-grandmother. "You are the first grandchild and we were so happy when you were born. In my heart, you will always hold a special place."

Lois returned to her own role and listened as another group member, as grandmother, spoke these words to her.

Next, Lois was sent to stand at the side of the group, in the observer role, to watch the scene of grandmother telling her double these words. After saying, listening and watching the scenes, she returned to her role for a final statement and to hear group members tell how they related to her drama.

■ **VARIATION**

A surplus reality scene might be added, having Lois participate, or participate and then watch, in other activities with grandmother that felt special—activities that did not involve food. These activities would be suggested by the protagonist and enacted with the help of the group, so Lois could participate, watch and integrate these new nourishing images.

Magic Shop

Magic Shop is the classic psychodramatic activity developed by J.L. Moreno and expanded and adapted by other psychodramatists through the years. This versatile activity fills the needs of various group members even if their needs are diverse. It also supports each group member taking something of value from the group that he or she may use as a reference in continuing growth or development.

In Magic Shop, there is a shopkeeper—often a wizard-like character—who runs a shop that contains no objects, only intangibles of traits and essences. These personal qualities are bought and sold by the wizard according to what people want to give up or get to improve their lives.

The personal qualities that are wanted may include a range of traits, such as honesty, warmth, ability to take risks, gentleness, self-control, patience or assertiveness. The personal qualities that are to be brought and bartered at the shop may include traits that generally do not serve healthy functioning, such as rigidity, resistance or stubbornness.

Sometimes the shopkeeper's balky personality forces the visitor to bargain or prove that someone else desperately needs the quality that the visitor is trying to sell. Group members may be challenged in using their imagination—and enlisting the imagination of other group members—in negotiation that is sometimes playful. For instance, a group member who wants to give up his rigidity must convince the shopkeeper that someone else may need that rigidity for a more healthy reason; for instance, someone with poor boundaries may need a little rigidity for self-protection.

Basically, the process goes like this:

- The stage or part of the room is designated as the shop, sometimes using props to delineate the space. The shop is stocked with imaginary qualities, essences and other intangibles and the director may take time in warming up the group with the setting of the scene by miming "sweeping" steps or "polishing" the merchandise.

- The director takes the role of shopkeeper by his or her posture, soliloquy or perhaps a special coat, scarf or hat.

- Group members take the roles of customers and are instructed to think of something that "is causing you difficulty" or that "is inhibiting your growth."

- Customers approach the shopkeeper as they are warmed up with a wish for a particular attribute in the shop.

- To barter for the quality that is desired, the customer must trade the intangible: something the customer has in excess, the difficulty or something that another customer values highly.

- The customer receives the new intangible after having made the trade.

A perceptive director may gently challenge group members to promote awareness and insight. For instance, traits like skepticism and stubbornness may serve positive purposes in some circumstances.

A group member may request, " I want to trade in my self-doubt for self-confidence," or, "I want to trade in my isolation for connection."

Making a Mandala

The mandala is a circle shape that was revived by Carl Jung as an expression of the whole self. In this exercise, participants are given a large blank piece of paper and a variety of art materials, such as pastel crayons, colored pencils and tempera paint. Large dinner plates are provided and each participant uses the plate to trace a circle on his or her paper. After the circle is drawn, the plate is put aside and participants are instructed to fill in the circle with their choice of colors and shapes, all representing the strengths that will heal the eating disorder. Sometimes additional items, such as small leaves, magazine pictures or found objects, may be added to the pile of art materials so that the mandala becomes a collage. This activity allows participants to take home a visual reminder of their strengths.

■ VARIATION
Use a real dinner plate, inexpensively obtained from thrift stores or yard sales, and have group members use strong glue or a glue gun to attach their pictures and other objects directly to the plate.

■ VARIATION

Bring the mandala to life by having group members stand in a circle and use scarves and other items to bring color, movement and energy to the image. Have the protagonist observe and walk into the mandala.

Shield of Strengths

A Shield of Strengths may be created for protection from sabotaging self-talk. For instance, a sabotaging self-talk statement such as "You don't deserve to eat" can be identified; then words, pictures and colors can be chosen that fend off this kind of self-defeating thought pattern. The demeaning "saboteur" role is able to meet the "truth teller" role, which says, "Don't listen to lies—everyone deserves to eat."

To make a shield, participants are given a large piece of poster board, which they trim into a shield shape, as well as pastel crayons, colored pencils, tempera paint and a selection of pictures and words from magazines. They may also add personal items, using a paper punch to make holes so strips of yarn, string, leather, ribbon and other objects will hang from parts of the shield. Participants can hold the finished shield in front of the torso and move through the group room in a posture and walk that shows the power of the strengths. This project can be a stand-alone activity or a warm up for a drama; we have found this activity especially meaningful to our male group members.

Chapter 14

Circles of Change
and Transformation

Sticks in a bundle are unbreakable.

Kenyan Proverb

The circle is a powerful symbol of unity and wholeness. We may guess that natural circles, like the sun and the moon, fascinated the ancients, and we know that indigenous people for centuries have gathered in circles for talk, worship and ceremony. J.L. Moreno's original stage in Beacon, New York, was designed as a round stage, with participants sitting in a circle, especially during the sharing part of the process, so that all could see and speak and be seen and heard.

The circle is more than a symbol: it is a living structure that represents connection, protection and communion. Through the years, we have borrowed, adapted and invented many circle structures for our clients to help them build strengths, review behaviors, sort options and grow in awareness. We find these structures to be highly versatile, and the practitioner with training and experience in psychodrama and sociometry should be easily able to develop variations according to group setting and population.

Circle of Strengths

The Circle of Strengths provides a safe container where action takes place. This structure, developed by Kate Hudgins as part of the Therapeutic Spiral Model, is ideal for a group session in itself or as a warm up to deeper healing work. It may be used in group or individual sessions although we find it especially powerful in group, where the whole is greater than the sum of the parts.

The director sets up the room with a pile of scarves and other colorful cloths in the center. We have also used furry auxiliaries, pillows or other props. The director identifies that in times of distress people are sustained by three areas of strength: personal qualities they carry within themselves, past or present relationships that are loving and supportive, and spiritual strengths that are bigger than self or others.

Then we may say:

> Choose a scarf or cloth to represent a strength that you have within yourself—something you can call upon to help your recovery, such as compassion, integrity, courage. Place the scarf on the floor somewhere to concretize that strength. You can stand on that strength and connect to it whenever you need it.

After each person has spoken and presented his or her concretized intrapersonal strength, there is a witnessing breath and the process is repeated with choosing a scarf for an interpersonal strength—strength from a relationship with another being, past or present: grandparent, spouse, friend, aunt or perhaps a pet or group.

Then the transpersonal strengths are concretized—strengths that come from our connection to something larger than ourselves: nature, music, the divine, a 12-step group, God, Jesus, Buddha...

When the circle is complete, the director acknowledges that "We now have a safe container of strengths where we will do the work." The scarves can be visited at any time to reconnect with the strengths they represent.

■ VARIATION

After each person has identified the strength and chosen an object, the director says, "Show us the strength with a movement and sound." The group mirrors back the movement and sound. This enables each person's strength to become embodied not only by the individual but also by all group members.

■ VARIATION

Use small figures, stones, shells and other objects for strengths and arrange in a sand tray or on a large place mat. Include an object to represent the self. Talk about the strengths when the scene is complete. Take a picture so the protagonist can revisit the scene.

■ VARIATION

Provide ribbons, strips of cloth and leather, beads, bells or charms, silk leaves and flowers and other materials. Bring out a large stick (length may vary from six inches to a tall walking stick) and have the participants select items that represent their strengths and tie them around the stick, which will become a talking stick for the group circle. The stick may be used as decorated or infused with Reiki energy (see Chapter 12) to add to the ritual and power of the activity in subsequent use. Participants also may make individual sticks—or wands of power—and share with the group.

■ VARIATION

Use magazine pictures to make a group or individual collage and add words with markers or pastel crayons. Place individual collages on chairs and have participants walk silently around the circle to view the collages.

Walking the Wheel of Change

Because eating disorders hold such powerful defenses, people are often ambivalent about psychotherapy, or perhaps adamantly adverse to change. Sometimes medical consequences have necessitated hospitalization. The person may feel deprived of choice and determined to maintain a sense of control by holding on to the eating disorder. In this vignette, which we call Walking the Wheel of Change, we concretize Prochaska, Norcross and DiClemente's six stages of change from their 1994 book, *Changing For Good: A Revolutionary Six-Stage Program for Overcoming Bad Habits and Moving Your Life Positively Forward*:

- Pre-contemplation, when the person is in denial and not yet able to acknowledge change is necessary.

- Contemplation, when the person is beginning to understand that the behavior is problematic.

- Preparation, when the person starts to identify how to change and may begin to make small changes.

- Action, when the person makes specific behavior changes and acquires new healthy behaviors.

- Maintenance, when a person sustains the new behaviors and is working to prevent relapse.

- Termination, when the person avoids old behaviors. If old behaviors are resumed, the person moves to the alternate "recycling" phase to begin again with new knowledge.

Concretizing these stages, rather than just talking about them, offers a deeper experience and helps people learn that good intentions are not enough: there is a particular process involved with creating and sustaining change, which includes:

- gaining awareness about one's stage in the cycle of change

- identifying blocks in the process of change

- building motivation and strengthening commitment to change

- showing more compassion for self and understanding the contributing factors to relapse.

The Wheel of Change, especially when presented in group, allows participants to explore the consequences of change—and of not changing. When various group members are in various stages of change, this structure enables those in early recovery to learn from those further along. For instance, group members in the contemplation stage can learn from those in the preparation or action stage—or from those who have returned to treatment due to relapse. Those in the action stage or maintenance stage can review and confirm their growth as they witness those in earlier stages.

This structure can be used in inpatient and outpatient settings; in groups and individual therapy, and in educational settings have the director double the protagonist as he or she walks the Wheel.

Using props with the Wheel of Change

Using furry auxiliaries to represent the stages of change not only concretizes each stage but also bypasses the defenses when the protagonist takes the role with the furry auxiliary. For instance, in the contemplation stage, the protagonist may be unable to acknowledge isolation and the negative consequences of the eating disorder, but may be able to take the role of "the contemplative cat" and acknowledge the negative consequences from that role.

In addition, the protagonist is able to try on the various stages of change and experience in action what another stage might feel like. For example, a protagonist in the preparation stage may walk to the action stage and soliloquize from there, then to the maintenance stage and soliloquize from there. This future projection provides the protagonist the experience, hope and wisdom of moving forward in recovery.

Typically, people are not fully in one stage but may experience the pull of two or more stages. "Walking the Wheel" enables a client to show this and to make choices by moving the body, rather than just talking about it: using the body to concretize choice.

■ **VARIATION**
Use a sand tray and small figures to concretize the change stages.

Walk Around the Clock

This action structure is designed to help the eating disorder person and the director explore issues during a 12- or 24-hour period.

It is a simple design based on soliloquy, and the director may serve the double function. It is adapted from eating disorder interventions designed by Monica Callahan (1989) and earlier innovations from Zerka Moreno who developed the clock structure to illustrate time by walking clockwise (into future) and counterclockwise (into past).

Walk Around the Clock may first be used as an assessment tool, providing a sense of the protagonist's behaviors, thoughts and feelings during a full day. For those with eating disorders, this activity will provide a behavioral analysis, revealing triggers for eating disorder behaviors such as restricting, binge eating, purging or compulsively exercising.

This action structure:

- allows the director to learn where the protagonist has been behaviorally, cognitively and emotionally in the previous 12 to 24 hours

- analyzes impulsive behavior so the protagonist goes back in time to identify the trigger, engaging the body

- elicits information that informs the director's follow up

- (with the clock showing different times and representing past, present and future), allows the protagonist to move to where he or she needs to be in order to identify patterns, set goals and the like

- helps the person focus on history as a way to move towards his or her goal

- investigates what the person experienced during the evening and night in a residential setting

- permits identifying when loss—death, trauma, serious medical treatment—occurred so grief work can take place.

The process

Create an imaginary clock face by setting up pillows, chairs or furry auxiliaries to indicate the hours of 12, 3, 6, 9 on a clock; the numbers may also be written on sheets of paper and placed on chairs or the floor. In a group setting, group members can hold roles of the hour by sitting or standing in those positions. Use as much space as the room allows so that when the protagonist "walks the clock" he or she can pause at the hours between the 12, 3, 6, 9. This exercise can be repeated if additional days need assessment.

If the protagonist's appointment is scheduled for 3 p.m., the director can begin the walk at 3 p.m. the day before and have the protagonist walk and talk, beginning from that hour. The protagonist will be directed to soliloquize with the director in the double role.

CASE STUDY: SOLILOQUY WITH DOUBLE: VIGNETTE WITH EILEEN

In this individual session with Eileen, Linda has set up the clock with furry auxiliaries, so the stuffed animals can hold the places of the clock hours. Linda takes the role of the double and expands Eileen's narrative.

Eileen begins: "At 3 o'clock yesterday I was at work and was bored. I went to the vending machine and bought pretzels and a candy bar and a soda."

Linda (as double): "In addition to being bored, I was also..."

Eileen (frowns): "In addition to being bored, I was... I don't know."

Linda (as double): "I was frustrated?"

Eileen: "I *was* sort of frustrated—and tired. Too much dumb, boring work!"

Eileen moves a little past 3 and says, "I just ate everything real fast, drank the soda and..." (hesitates)

Linda (as double): "I felt..."

Eileen: "I felt gross and disgusting and fat!" (walks to 4 on clock) "I went to the bathroom and got rid of it."

Linda (as double): "I purged."

Eileen (sighs): "I purged. Then I washed my hands and face, brushed my teeth, used mouthwash, popped gum in my mouth and went back to my desk."

Linda (as double): "I felt relieved?"

Eileen: "I did feel relieved that I didn't keep all those calories, but I also felt ashamed and guilty." (moves on to 5 on clock) "Thank goodness it's time to leave!" (walks between 5 and 6)

Eileen: "I am so relieved to be off work. I deserve a reward—just a little something for surviving a yucky day, but I don't want to binge again." (walks to 6) "I made it home and I didn't stop for binge food!"

Linda (as double): "I feel proud of myself for not stopping at the store."

Eileen: "Mostly relieved, but I am really hungry." (walks to 6:30) "I look in refrigerator. Nothing appeals. I look through cabinets—I'm starving." (walks to 7) "I open the freezer—ice cream! Just a spoonful till I find something to make. I get a teaspoon and begin eating the ice cream standing there with the freezer door open, right out of the carton—it's like I'm in a trance. I just stand there and eat, teaspoon after teaspoon until I finish the whole half gallon!"

Linda (as double): "I feel better now. Filled up…"

Eileen: "I feel calmer and the phone rings—it's my sister…"

Eileen's soliloquy with the director in the double role continues, revealing the contents of the conversation with her sister, the resulting thoughts, feelings and behaviors; sleep pattern; morning rituals, and events that eventually led up to Eileen's appointment.

Other uses

In addition to the assessment tool, the clock has other uses:

- It can "turn back time" to re-create the previous 24 hours with alternatives to the eating disorder behaviors and to make behavior changes.

- It can enhance future projection and train the protagonist for coping with the challenges of daily life without eating disorder behavior. In doing so, he or she trains for a new role, the role of healthy eater, the good self care-taker, the person who appreciates his or her body.

Adaptations are limited only by the director's imagination.

Medicine Wheel

In indigenous traditions, the Medicine Wheel consists of a cross within a circle, with four equal lines of the cross pointing from the center to the spirits of the North, East, South and West—signifying the elements of earth, air, fire and water—and it plays a vital part in spiritual rituals.

In Karen's Medicine Wheel adaption, we set up the wheel with scarves, pillows, stones or other items. Karen talks about the fact that in the modern Western world medicine is an object, a commodity that one purchases and consumes, but in the indigenous world it has a much wider definition, so that all kinds of activities are "medicine" because they bring us into balance.

The protagonist may set up his or her Medicine Wheel, identifying places of pain and places of growth, as well as "medicine" to take at various times. The medicine may be a prayer, a call to a support group sponsor, a yoga pose, a support group meeting, a cup of herbal tea, lighting a candle, creating a ritual, a talk with a friend—the list is never-ending.

Wheel of Awareness

Dr. Daniel Siegel, psychiatrist and author of *The Mindful Brain* (2007), shows us the power of our innate awareness and how we can return to awareness when distracted. He uses the image of a bicycle wheel, with a center and spokes that connect the center to the rim of the wheel. The center, or hub, is the place of observing and focusing; the rim is sectioned into four areas, with each area representing an experience that we perceive:

- Perceptions of our inner body, including the breath, the muscles and the internal organs.

- Perceptions of the world through the five senses of sight, touch, taste, smell, hearing.

- Perceptions of the activity of the mind, including our thoughts and emotions in the moment, as well as memories.

- Perceptions of social relationships, with experiences of connection and compassion.

This model can be used as a meditation to develop the "mental muscles" of focus and discernment, or we can track our inner life throughout the day, locating ourselves in the wheel.

When starting the meditation, begin with focusing on the breath and centering attention at the hub, also the seat of the Caring Observer. This is the quiet place of focused attention. The rim is the deep, consuming trench of experience. During the meditation you visit the four sectors of the rim, allowing yourself to be fully immersed in sensory information (smell, taste, sound, etc.), bodily sensations (head-to-toe scan), mental activity (thoughts, hopes, feelings), and finally adding social relations (compassion, connection). The four sections develop, differentiate and refine our experience so we become more attuned and present. Developing the hub allows us to become more aware and observing. Developing the rim allows us to be fully present and attuned during experience.

For example, as we meditate, it may be easy to focus on the breath (the hub) and, before we know it, the mind wanders into what is needed at the store, what we'll eat for dinner or the urgency of a forgotten appointment. As we sit in a non-judgmental space, we can observe the comings and goings of the mind, noticing the strength and valor of the rim some days or perhaps a steadier hub on others. This model can be helpful during challenging times, as we learn to bring the caring observer of the hub with us; one who sees with wise eyes how difficult a situation is, compassionately allows us the fullness of the experience, and knows it will pass. The observer understands the power of strong feelings and knows this is not all of who we are; they are just feelings that will pass like the tide.

Connie Lawrence James (2012) has adapted Siegel's Wheel of Awareness and combines it with the Caring Observer that she has designed. She offers these structures in both guided meditation and action, which we find useful when working with eating disorder clients:

Guided meditation

As with other meditations, find a comfortable place and comfortable posture, generally with an upright or elongated spine with feet flat on the floor. The director follows this sequence:

- Begin with awareness of the breath, breathing deeply into the belly, paying attention to the sensations, rise and fall of the belly and chest.

- As you become comfortable with the breath, the rise and fall of the chest, you can imagine making a safe place to rest with the breath. This can be the center of the wheel or the hub.

- Create the rim of the wheel, with the rim an outer circle in the distance. Imagine four spokes.

- In this meditation, we will take a guided tour to each area, each time returning to the hub, slowing down and refocusing on the breath—a resting place. We are going to build four spokes of the wheel.

- The scan of the five senses—sound, sight, touch, taste and smell.

- And now we return to the hub...

- The internal body scan—head-to-toe scan of sensation.

- And we return to the hub again...

- Mental activity—turn on the lamp inside, watching and witnessing thoughts, dreams, hopes and feelings as they arise.

- And we return to the hub again...

- The Relational Self—the web of connections to the people in our circle, expanding to include communities, pets, nations.

- When all is complete, return to the hub and allow the meditation to simply unfold, watching from the place of Caring Observer, without judgment and paying attention to the thoughts (quantity, frequency, valor) and simply returning to the breath.

■ VARIATION WITH ACTION

Concretize the wheel with scarves, pillows or other items to mark the different areas, much like a locogram. Allow participants to walk the Wheel of Awareness, visiting each place on the rim as well as the center hub. Participants can share experiences with a soliloquy, create a group sculpture, or improvise ways to experience the spaces.

Cycles and seasons: Five-Element Flower

The five elements of the Asian philosophy—water, wood, fire, earth, metal—offer a holistic way to view multiple aspects of a person's well-being through emotions, cravings, thoughts, energy and spirituality. Each element is associated with a season, a color that shows up in the hue of one's complexion and tendencies that challenge the person's well-being. In addition, there are nourishing foods connected to each element that promote balance.

Although a full discussion of this complex system is beyond the scope of this book, we have been inspired by key concepts for developing an action structure that helps our clients, who often objectify the body as a "thing" to be managed, controlled or sculpted—in effect creating an energetic disconnection that interrupts, depletes or stagnates the body's life force, the energy which Asians call *chi*.

The five-element approach (Connelly, 1979) is rooted in the philosophy of Taoism and the practice of Traditional Chinese Medicine. We recommend five-element acupuncture as part of the treatment process to lend energetic support for recovery because it focuses on every aspect of the client's well-being rather than on the identification of symptoms that are to be fixed. Educating our clients in this way provides a holistic perspective. This is especially helpful because our clients tend to think in dualistic terms of black and white—and therefore "fat" or "thin," or "beautiful" or "ugly." As they consider this holistic view, they are encouraged to embrace the idea of the body inseparable from mind, heart, spirit and nature—a shift in self-perception.

A good way to visualize the five elements is to imagine a flower with five petals. Each petal is distinct but joined at the center and makes the single flower. When the five elements are functioning in harmony, we feel healthy, nourished and fully alive. When the elements are not in balance, signs will show up in our body, mind, emotions and spirit.

The five elements are:

- Water, associated with winter, the color blue; can be turbulent or serene; exhibits a need to contain and channel energy, and may be prone to fear, anxiety and depression. This person may crave or be repulsed by salty foods.

- Wood, associated with spring, the color green, and anger or lack of expression of anger when that would be appropriate. Splitting of nails, skin cracking in hands and feet and troubles with tendons and ligaments, as well as difficulties with worry and decision making may signal imbalances in the wood element.

- Fire, associated with summer, the color red (although an ashen hue may indicate a lack of fire); may have difficulty with temperature regulation, physically or emotionally, or both. There may be poor circulation, heart ache or sleep problems, as well as feeling "hot and cold" emotionally and difficulty with relationships. The flavor of bitter, as with dark leafy greens or dark chocolate, may be craved or avoided.

- Earth, associated with late summer, the color yellow and the emotion of sympathy—which may appear as deficient or excessive in giving to self, others or both. Earth imbalance may appear in pensiveness, excessive contemplation and overthinking. Vinegary tastes may be craved or avoided; fatty foods may feel soothing. Sweets may be craved or avoided.

- Metal (minerals), associated with autumn, the color white, connected to the lungs (which may evidence trouble through the skin) and large intestine and signal unresolved issues of grief—which may show up through a lack of appropriate weeping or perhaps through somatization, as in "weeping" skin. A drive for perfection is sometimes present. Pungent or spicy foods may be craved or avoided.

Putting the five elements into action

Linda collaborated with colleagues Patti Desert and Nancy Alexander and a team of trained auxiliaries to offer a series of five-element seasonal workshops. When bringing the five elements into action, the director should carefully craft a warm-up process that acquaints the participants not only with the elements but also with the appropriate strengths and sociometric connections.

Prior to the workshop, participants receive an email message describing the five elements. Upon arrival, they are greeted by several wall posters of the seasonal element and given cards made by landscape photographer Alma Nugent that depict scenes of the season.

In one session, all were asked to choose cards to hold the role of the Witness and shared in dyads why they selected that particular card. Then, each participant stepped into the Witness role after choosing another participant or one of the trained auxiliaries to hold the role of their Client self. Each spoke from the Witness role to himself or herself about how a quality of the season would help during the workshop.

For example, "As your Witness, I have the winter's capacity of being serene like still water and am able to notice what is going on both above and below the surface." Or, "As your Witness, I have the wood quality, the Spring quality, of a tall and strong well-rooted tree that sees the big picture."

Next, following introductions, group norms, spectrograms identifying experience with psychodrama and with five-element philosophy, and safe touch preferences, we moved into the Circle of Strengths, which we mentioned earlier in this chapter.

Five locograms in the five colors are placed in a circle on the floor, each identifying an element and its primary characteristics. Participants are invited to:

- stand on the locogram of the element that they most positively identify with and offer a soliloquy

- stand on the locogram that depicts the element that they find most problematic and offer a soliloquy

- state in one sentence the presenting issue that they would address if they were chosen as protagonist.

This warm-up sequence leads to protagonist selection, a drama and sharing. The director and team pay close attention to locogram choices to identify themes that could be woven into action structures during the workshop.

We recommend the creation of a seasonal sculpture with props and art materials for a group project of integration, showing how that season's element and its characteristics have become transformed. Photos of the project may be taken so that each participant has a photo to take home and may elaborate upon with personal words making meaning of the experience.

Circles of support

Studies show that people with social support enjoy a higher level of good health and well-being with lower levels of stress and even physical pain. We are fans of self-help support groups, such as Overeaters Anonymous and Anorexia Nervosa and Related Disorders (ANAD), and we have initiated specialized groups to provide additional support for people with eating disorders. These groups are not considered psychotherapy, but rather informal gatherings where participants may share without judgment what is happening in their daily lives as they recover from eating disorders. The two group rules are confidentiality and avoiding discussion of food, weight and appearance.

The second group norm often surprises first-time attendees who expect to focus on food, weight and appearance; they learn to identify topics that hinder or help their recovery. We have found that 90 minutes is adequate time for this kind of group.

Other group guidelines:

- Do your best to arrive on time.

- If you must leave before the group ends, please tell the group at the start of the meeting.

- We hope to allow time for everyone to speak who wants to speak but sometimes this is not possible due to group the size. If you have something pressing to share, please share early in the meeting.

- Monopolizing time in the group is discouraged.

Chapter 15

Nutrition Nuggets, Mindful Movement, Body Metaphors

To keep the body in good health is a duty...otherwise we
shall not be able to keep our mind strong and clear.

Buddha

Eating disorders and struggles with body acceptance are layered and complex. Action methods, while extremely powerful, are not substitutes for education about nutrition, making changes in eating patterns, identifying food sensitivities that cause cravings and binges, and the necessity of movement for a healthy body.

Our work is typically integrated with other professionals and disciplines, including acupuncture, nutrition evaluation and education, movement, body work and energy work. Asian practices like yoga, tai chi, qigong and other mindful movement quiet the mind so that we are attuned to our internal rhythms. Research has shown that the practice of yoga improves mindfulness of cues about hunger and satiety, and energy work reduces the stress response while balancing the energy meridians and energy centers in the body.

Nutrition education in action:
Grocery Store Tour

Information about nutrition is an important key to recovery. Many people do not know, for instance, that bodies need healthy fat to function, the size of a normal portion or the importance of vegetables.

Linda developed Grocery Store Tour to actively acquaint clients about how the foods they purchase have an impact on the body's functioning. This structure is both lighthearted and serious and may be used with individuals or groups or in educational settings. It goes like this:

Have the protagonist or group write their five most frequently purchased food items on index cards. They may share their selections verbally in dyads or triads before setting the scene of the grocery store with psychodramatic "aisles" of various foods.

Linda asks for a volunteer for "grocery shopping," saying that she will accompany the volunteer on the psychodramatic tour, speaking as the double for the body in response to what is being placed in the cart. For example, the protagonist may stop in the soda aisle and place a six-pack of cola in the imaginary cart. As the body, Linda may say something like, "Oh! The rollercoaster again! Blood sugar up, blood sugar down! Yee-ha!" before falling to the floor with a groan and then a yawn.

This type of humorous drama generally draws laughter, and participants report they have greater awareness of how the body is affected by food choices than by anything they have read.

If a participant chooses a selection of fruits and vegetables, or foods rich in essential fatty acids, Linda as body might improvise into a song that she makes up in the moment, like this one to the tune of "You gotta have heart" from *Damn Yankees*:

> You've gotta have heart
> Miles and miles and miles of heart
> Blood vessels love what's in the cart
> All these colors keeping me pumping along
> So happy and strong—you are so very smart!
> Keeping this healthy heart. I am your grateful heart.

The song might be accompanied by a few steps of "heart happy dancing," and sometimes Linda, as the body, pulls a Valentine heart out of her pocket at these moments and presents the grateful heart to the shopper–protagonist.

■ VARIATION

The grocery tour is also a warm up for vignettes or dramas. At the end of the tour, Linda asks which item on the list wants to talk to the protagonist or group member, and she directs a dialogue to discover what role that food is playing.

■ VARIATION

If you, as director, do not have sufficient knowledge of nutrition, invite a nutritionist to collaborate. The nutritionist will walk with the director, providing the educational information while the director or trained auxiliary acts as the body responding to the food.

Food sensitivities

Although there are many perspectives—and some controversies—about how food and food ingredients affect the body and the brain, we also encourage people to learn if they have food sensitivities that may contribute to cravings.

Many recovering people have identified that certain foods and food ingredients contribute to headaches, cravings and bloating, and find that once they eliminate these foods or food ingredients their cravings greatly diminish and they no longer have the bloated feeling that they interpret as "fat"—a common experience that contributes to restricting food or starting a diet. Some of the common ingredients that have been reported as problematic include sugar, white flour, dairy, wheat and gluten. (Brostoff and Gamlin, 2000; Davis, 2011).

Due to the rising use of antibiotics, there are reports of an increase in digestive problems, resulting from the impact of the antibiotics on the intestinal flora. Antibiotics do not generally discriminate between the "good" bacteria and the infection-causing "bad" bacteria—they simply eliminate most of the bacteria. The "good" bacteria in the intestines not only help produce digestive enzymes, they are also anti-bacterial, anti-viral and anti-fungal. When the "good" bacteria are wiped out, the uncomfortable consequences may include impaired digestion, overgrowth of systemic yeast, food cravings and alternating conditions of constipation and diarrhea.

In the field of nutrition, this condition is sometimes labeled as "leaky gut." Leaky gut affects the intestinal lining so material that should remain in the gut escapes through the gut wall, and material that should be kept out of the gut gets in. Linda has noticed that leaky gut is sometimes a physical metaphor for a person's trouble with boundaries, and she has frequently used physical symptoms as a springboard to explore other kinds of boundary issues being faced.

Naomi, who suffered fibromyalgia, depression and emotional overeating, was referred to Linda by her acupuncturist. Her health history showed a wide range of digestive trouble, symptomatic of leaky gut. After educating Naomi about this condition, Linda asked her if overly permeable boundaries were problematic in her daily life.

The conversation revealed a long history of being in the caretaker role with friends and family and trapped in a cycle of codependent behaviors. When relationships were difficult or unsatisfying, Naomi would eat to comfort herself, particularly choosing foods that did not agree with her body. With Naomi's permission, her acupuncturist and Linda shared health information and worked to repair Naomi's gut wall lining and build skills in setting and keeping appropriate boundaries. Linda used role training, helping Naomi to set boundaries with family and friends.

Naomi practiced real-life scenarios in 1-1 consultation room work using empty chair, role reversal and Linda's doubling from the director's role. She gradually was able to set boundaries with others and herself, developing a closer relationship with her body's needs and her emotional needs. Her acupuncture appointments were often scheduled immediately before or after appointments with Linda; the acupuncturist and Linda communicated at day's end and kept in regular contact to maintain a net of support so there were no leaks, emotional or physical, for Naomi.

Meals

Group sessions and workshops that take place before meals—for instance, before lunch or dinner or during an extended period of time such as all-day, weekend or week workshops—provide excellent opportunities to prepare people to approach eating in a safe way. It is helpful when the final vignette or closing activity includes strengthening the group or a specific group member for the meal experience. Participants can then eat without gulping, worrying or dissociating. With planning, directors can also introduce new foods, identify opportunities for socialization and explore novel ways of making meal time less threatening and more joyous.

Water is always available during sessions, which may be consumed hot, warm or room temperature. We do not serve ice with water, as the Asian traditions of medicine consider icy beverages and foods to inhibit digestion. Beverages that might be available during longer sessions include herbal teas, juice without sugar and mineral water. Snacks are always healthy, such as nuts (raw or roasted without additives), fresh fruit, fruits dried without sugar and fresh vegetables. We check with clients prior to intensives to learn if they have sensitivities or allergies to nuts, other foods or food ingredients, and, if so, we include alternative foods or eliminate a certain item completely. If whole-grain breads are served, there are alternatives such as corn chips, corn tortillas or whole-grain rice cakes or breads to accommodate those with wheat allergy or gluten intolerance.

In addition, we often provide information about why we are serving a particular food item in a handout, as part of an educational discussion or with a small sign on the table. We might acknowledge that the presence of certain foods may serve as an informal warm up to someone's work, particularly if a food was force fed or denied in childhood. Such experiences are used to open an exploration of participants' responses to the meal offerings.

Participants may be requested to bring a healthy main dish to share during a day-long workshop. Part of the meal might include saying grace as a group or individually, lighting candles, singing or some other ritual (Scott and Crowther 1994) that supports people being emotionally present and connected.

Listening to body cues

In workshops, we sometimes designate at least one meal or snack break as a time to eat in silence, allowing participants to focus on the experience of preparing for and eating the meal, with the option to journal their experience before sharing verbally when the group resumes.

At other times, we have used meals as a time to listen closely to the body and its cues.

At a meal break during an intensive program, for example, Linda might pause the meal three to four times to ask participants to attune to inner cues for hunger and fullness, asking them to rate their experience from one to ten. One is defined as feeling "empty," with ten defined as feeling "fully stuffed." She also suggests attention to tastes and sensations of foods—smooth, chewy, creamy, crunchy, salty, sweet and sour.

In one workshop—focusing on self-care and eating issues—the group visited a restaurant for a shared lunch. On request, the restaurant provided a large table, separated from the main dining room by a folding screen. After all the participants had taken their seats, they were asked to:

- look at the menu and, before ordering, take a few slow deep breaths

- notice on a scale of zero to ten their levels of hunger, with zero meaning, "I feel absolutely empty, I am famished," and ten meaning, "I am already full, I really am not hungry at all, I am completely filled up"

- notice what kinds of foods they felt drawn to

- notice if they were craving anything in particular

- notice if they wanted anything special.

After ordering, the group was guided to express gratitude for the meal and the opportunity to come together to do the work. When the food arrived, participants were asked to monitor every few minutes if their level of hunger changed.

Linda directed all to notice the following:

- The taste of the food: Is it sweet? Is it sour? Is it bitter? Is it salty?

- The various characteristics of the food: Is the texture creamy? Is it crunchy? Is it smooth? Is it warm, icy or room temperature? Is the arrangement of the food on the plate pleasing to the eye?

From time to time, group members were directed to place their forks on the table, take a sip of water, take a few deep breaths and again check their level of hunger and fullness. At the end of the meal, Linda asked the group to check:

- hunger and fullness cues

- how satisfied they were, not by the hunger and fullness, but whether their taste buds were "happy."

Linda often teaches about the difference between the body being satisfied with hunger and fullness, but the taste buds wanting something else—and being able to discern the difference.

After a meal, group members are invited to share their discoveries. It is not uncommon for participants to be shocked that they don't know what exactly they tasted. Many are surprised that they noticed that they were full earlier in the meal. There are often pleasant surprises—taste bud delights that diners enjoyed when they took time to notice. Others learned that they took more time to eat because they were actually experiencing the tastes and textures of the food and had a more satisfying experience. Sometimes diners risked ordering an item they wouldn't normally have, which opened more conversation:

- "Are there other areas of life where you make the same choices?"

- "How might taking a bit of a risk lead to some growth?"

Other areas of conversation might be as follows:

- "Is there anything you wanted to have but didn't?"

- "Was that food available?"

- "Why did you not choose it if you wanted it?"

- "Was there something you chose that you were sorry you chose?"

- "Did talking distract you from conflicted feelings about food?"

Mind to the Muscle

Although many people with eating disorders exercise excessively as a way to purge, others report problematic or even traumatic experiences with exercise and physical activity, resulting in avoidance of exercise.

- In high school, Ramona tried for a girls' softball league one year and the lacrosse team the next year, but was never picked for the teams. She had a difficult time throwing and catching and could not seem to handle the lacrosse stick properly, constantly bumping into others' knees. Embarrassed about being clumsy, she refrained from most physical activity as an adult. In talking with Karen, she was surprised when Karen asked if she had been born prematurely. She discovered new information about the fact that premature births frequently contribute to problems with reflexes and for the first time began to forgive herself for feeling awkward.

- Timothy, at the age of 60, was encouraged by his physician to begin a regular exercise program to address risk factors for heart disease. While telling himself that he "should" follow his doctor's advice, go to the gym or at least begin a regular walking program, he noticed reluctance to engage in any type of physical activity. He mentioned childhood experiences where his rope-climbing skills never met the expectations of the physical education teacher. His repeated failure to meet designated fitness challenges made him the object of teasing by his peers and evoked statements of disappointment from his parents, leaving him feeling inadequate and embarrassed and lacking trust in his body.

- Carmen had enjoyed lively participation in an African drumming class and was excited about taking an African dance class at a retreat center in anther state. She went to great lengths to travel to the program; however, minutes after the class started, she found herself breaking into tears because the dance instructor yelled at the students like a drill sergeant, criticizing every move as not performance worthy. She stopped dancing and sat out most of the program with the drumming group.

Before a person is able to participate in physical activity, it is best to design experiences of repair to move past old beliefs about the body and transform criticism into encouragement and failures into successes.

For instance, Ramona felt relief when she learned about the connection between her awkwardness and her reflexes and premature birth; Karen referred her to a specialist in the Masgutova Method of Neuro-Sensory-Motor and Reflex Integration (Rentschler, 2008) who could assign simple exercises to improve her delayed developmental reflexes. She also had the option to forgive herself in role play for her self-judgment.

Timothy can speak to the physical education teacher and to his younger self in a dramatic vignette. From his compassionate adult self, he can tell his child self that he understands the child's struggles, and he can express to the coach his truth about the negative impact of the coach's teaching style.

Carmen had the opportunity to have her psychodrama group become a reparative African dance class as some members drummed and some members danced. Through role reversal, she modeled being the kind of teacher who treated students with gentle encouragement and respect, and everyone enjoyed dancing together in the concluding scene.

Movement Metaphors

The focus on appearance often obscures the understanding and appreciation of the body's functions. Linda combines her fitness trainer skills with mindfulness to address a greater appreciation of the body. After assessing a person's health and fitness profile and receiving medical consent for exercise, she brings in simple gym equipment—such as free weights, a ball and bands—and takes the client through exercises that focus on major muscle groups and their functions as they relate to activities in daily life.

Metaphors can be used in all forms of physical activity by applying exercise principles and elements to recovery. Linda employs mindfulness during her strength-training sessions with clients, guiding them to move slowly to feel the subtle movements of the muscles and develop appreciation of their functions. She may call attention to how the pectoral muscles help us push away what we want to distance from and the latissimus dorsi help us pull toward us what we want closer. On the psychodrama stage, the creative director can use these metaphors in sculptures, vignettes and dramas, enlivening these concepts so that physical activity is no longer compulsive or avoided but a route to personal growth:

- Endurance is the ability to go the distance, the ability to persist, to stay with treatment as long as it takes.

- Strength assists in overcoming obstacles in recovery; for example, the ability to overcome denial and the ability to set limits to the amount of weight lifted, the number of repetitions and self-sabotaging behaviors.

- Flexibility not only relates to muscles and connective tissues but the ability to move through patterns of rigid behavior and thoughts.

- Balance, either static or in motion, is the ability to stay centered and grounded, avoiding excesses of too much or too little.

- Coordination is the ability to integrate movements with one another in time and space, making mind–body integration not just a phrase but a reality within the human being.

- Breathing refers to the ability to take in what is needed and release what is not needed. For those neglecting exercise, remember you cannot continuously exhale; you need to inhale to nurture yourself. If you are overexercising, remember just as it is necessary to inhale it is also necessary to let go.

- Rest is essential for muscle recovery and in the recovery process.

CASE STUDY: STEP BY STEP, ANNABEL BUILDS HER STRENGTH

Annabel came to Linda after giving birth to her first child at the age of 30. Her main concern was her appearance; she had gained 90 pounds during the complicated pregnancy and wanted a quick fix for weight loss.

After educating Annabel about the dangers and inevitable backfiring of crash dieting, Linda began a social history, learning that Annabel had lost her parents at the age of five and had grown up with a rage-filled alcoholic uncle. When talking about her body, Annabel admitted that she was often short of breath, having great difficulty getting up and down stairs to care for her baby. She agreed to a reasonable food plan and to begin a mindful movement program, provided she could bring the baby because of a lack of child care. Linda agreed that the baby sit in a stroller and that they would meet in a nearby park on good weather days and at the local mall otherwise.

The program began with slow walking while Annabel pushed the stroller; Linda encouraged her to tune in to the muscles that were working during various parts of the walking motion. For example:

> Notice how the ball of the foot and the contracting calf of the back leg push away from the pavement while the hamstrings—the muscles in the back of the thigh—stretch to pull the front leg ahead, moving the body forward, and all muscles work as a team. Notice how the muscles of the arms and chest push the stroller [and so on].

As Annabel progressed, Linda guided her through a series of movements at the park pavilion—first using Annabel's own body weight and later adding bands to the routine—accompanied by rhythmic breathing and labeling each working muscle group. Linda prompted Annabel to speak about the working body part for which she was grateful, such as: "I am so grateful my arms can hold the baby," or "I am glad my legs are strong enough that I can get out of the rocking chair while holding the baby."

In addition, Linda used the Triple Double during psychodrama sessions to help Annabel identify and express feelings while practicing how to soothe and contain. Using metaphors of fitness, they discussed how each showed up in Annabel's daily life, identifying her strengths and what needed more attention. Endurance, for example, was linked to Annabel's physical, mental and emotional fatigue and her ability to build her physical capacities. When the walk around the lake was easily accomplished, hills were added as a metaphor for climbing the challenges of life. As the baby grew heavier, the work of pushing the stroller became the concretization of steadily pushing through life's "heavy loads" using personal strengths to move forward without straining.

Linda directed Annabel to soliloquize about her food-feelings connections while Linda took the double role—revealing that her emotional eating was partly driven by the attempt to "stuff" unprocessed childhood anger about the loss of her parents and her uncle's abuse. She associated her anger with the consumption of crunchy foods like potato chips and pretzels. As Annabel's fitness level improved, Linda recommended cardio kick-boxing classes to use the breath and movement to release old anger trapped in the body. The Witness role was enlisted to observe the process, with follow-up journaling. Psychodrama and Reiki followed if additional clearing was necessary.

Because stress played a role in Annabel's overeating, breath work was included in the recovery plan. She learned to calm her nervous system by inhaling deeply through the nose, followed by very slow exhalations, working up to extending the exhalations twice the length of the inhalations. Breath awareness helped Annabel tune in to her body so she could recognize hunger and fullness cues, manage the stress response and mindfully attend to her body's rhythms. Linda introduced the principle of entrainment in which the use of music, synchronized with movement and breath, restores the body systems to rhythmic patterns which have been disrupted by trauma or disordered eating. When Annabel walked without Linda, she used music designed for walking at a specific pace (3 mph and later 4 mph) and paced herself accordingly, always using breath awareness to adjust her walking pace.

This multi-modal approach helped Annabel reach a new state of well-being and fortified her self-care role, which supported her functioning in her mother role. Today, Annabel recalls with delight the joy she felt during a ski trip she took after six months of her work with Linda—she skied all day and loved being in touch with the strength of her legs and lungs, and the exhilaration of gliding through the mountains.

Yoga and body work

Yoga is a valuable practice that enhances psychodramatic enactments at every stage of the action. Yoga is a centuries-old Eastern discipline that means "union," referring to integration of mind, body and spirit; the combination of breathing and movement assists the growth of strength, flexibility, balance and relaxation, eventually enabling the mind to quiet.

Yoga philosophy offers a framework of support for those with eating and body image problems: non-violence, which includes being respectful of one's own body; avoiding self-harm; respecting personal limits and letting go of attachments to pre-conceived notions about what the body should be or not be. In practice, its Witness role is helpful in supporting people to observe themselves in a neutral, or at least non-critical, perspective and is compatible with psychodrama's Observing Ego role.

A good yoga teacher will emphasize a non-judgmental approach and the importance of listening to the body, attuning to subtle cues so the practitioner can continue at his or her own pace. Linda, who is a certified yoga instructor, regularly encourages her class members to rest as needed, refrain from staying in postures that are painful and take sips of water from time to time. She tells class members to listen to their bodies and truly care for themselves rather than performing or competing with each other.

She employs yoga before or during group psychodrama sessions as well as with individual clients to embody the lessons of recovery. For example, Linda encouraged Dora, a woman approaching 30 who was struggling with bulimia and injuries from excessive exercise, to begin a yoga practice. Yoga gradually transformed Dora's experience of exercise from self-punishing to self-caring and became a source of personal growth. Linda asked Dora to use her Witness role during her yoga practice to notice how the practice of yoga provided wisdom and transformed her life perspective.

In her journal, Dora wrote about: "Life lessons from my body—wisdom learned through yoga." She listed how rigidity became stability, vulnerability became flexibility, scattered became focused and anxious became energized. Her patterns of dissociation were replaced with grounded awareness, and she realized her responsibility to take ownership of her life in the present moment.

"I used to try to outsmart the system, moving forward too quickly without having a firm foundation in place to support growth or a higher level of functioning," she wrote. "Now I am systematically moving forward and have replaced compulsive exercise with mindful activity."

From a psychodramatic perspective, Dora actually was discovering new roles to play within her world. She also learned to listen to the "voices" of her body: "My back has shown me how distanced I've been from my body. Healing occurred when I brought my full attention to my back, accepted my limits, honored my strengths and let the Holy Spirit do its work."

Energy work

Reiki is one of several modalities of natural healing that uses universal life energy channeled through a practitioner's hands to restore a sense of well-being. As Amy Z. Rowland points out in her (1998) book *Traditional Reiki for Our Times*, a Reiki treatment is similar to massage, with two important differences: the client lies on the treatment table while fully clothed and the practitioner's hands on the client are usually still, moving only when the practitioner notices shifts in the flow of energy. This modality often feels more comfortable to people who have experienced abuse, assault, rape or other body violations. In addition, faith in the effectiveness of Reiki treatment is not required by the client or the Reiki practitioner.

Reiki energy may be channeled into places and objects, and clients can learn a basic form of Reiki, known as a Level 1 attunement, to treat and calm themselves. Both Karen and Linda have been trained in Reiki, and Linda is a certified master Reiki practitioner who periodically gives Reiki treatments before or after a psychodrama session. We speculate that psychodrama combines well with Reiki because, in the view of licensed Reiki teacher Colleen Benelli (2012), the energy modality activates the right brain, which is the location of our imagination, guidance and spiritual connection. Linda has used Reiki to bless the group space and to energize symbolic and archetypal objects for ritual use. More information on using Reiki to infuse objects is discussed in Chapter 12.

CASE STUDY: REIKI AND PSYCHODRAMA WITH RHODA

During a psychodrama weekend workshop, Rhoda requested a Reiki treatment, stating that she always felt better after such sessions.

At 45, Rhoda had a history of childhood sexual abuse and a long history of self-harm through chronic dieting, overexercise, nicotine and alcohol abuse, and trichotillomania. In recent years, she had been diagnosed with an autoimmune disorder that caused severe joint and muscle pain, which she was suffering that weekend.

During the Reiki session, Linda assessed Rhoda's body with an energetic scan and focused on parts that drew the most energy. These were parts where Rhoda reported the most pain at the beginning of the Reiki session and, later, relief. Linda began a methodical treatment of the entire body; when her hands came to the large muscles of the left thigh, she felt a strong current of energy moving like a large ocean wave. This current remained after several minutes of Reiki focused in that area, and Linda continued directing the Reiki there until the energy settled.

After the Reiki session, Rhoda talked about body parts that had been in pain and were helped by the session. Linda asked permission to ask a question about her thigh, and Rhoda agreed.

> Has there ever been an occasion when you wanted to use this leg to kick, perhaps to kick someone away, and you were unable to do so?

Surprised, Rhoda said such a scene came to mind that might be the theme of her drama that day. In fact, the scene focused on her early abuse in which she wanted to kick the perpetrator but was too small to have the strength. During her psychodrama session, she was able to safely replay the scene and re-write the ending, using her leg to push the perpetrator away. In the concluding scene, Linda gave additional Reiki to energetically wash away the perpetrator energy and infuse positive light into Rhoda's body.

Following this combination of Reiki and psychodrama, Rhoda reported significant reduction in self-harming behaviors.

Body-friendly placement

Karen has collected an assortment of simple hand placements that she teaches to clients to use at home and at work and before, during and after psychodrama enactments. These hand placements are physically comforting while also reconfiguring the body's energy, offering multiple layers of healing.

Triangle Fingers

One placement, which she calls Triangle Fingers, involves sitting and placing the hands gently on the lap, with the tips of the fingers and thumbs lightly touching. The person places the feet flat on the ground and practices conscious breathing; most people report feeling calmed in as little as 30 to 90 seconds. The eyes may be open, partly closed or closed.

Heart and Hand

Another placement, Heart and Hand, involves having the client place one hand on the heart and the other hand on the abdomen and practice conscious breathing. Again, the client is likely to feel calmed.

Karen may sit in front of the client—staying in her psychotherapist role—and instruct the process, or alternatively she may sit next to the client and guide him or her from the Double, Body Double or Containing Double role. The client may also be asked to say aloud: "Dear Body, we are safe."

With these simple practices, clients learn they have options in working with their energy systems rather than to binge or impulsively reach out to unhealthy coping mechanisms. Karen also encourages clients to pursue training in Reiki and other energy modalities so they can use these practices for themselves.

Chapter 16

The Ancestor Connection

In Iroquois society, leaders are encouraged to remember seven generations in the past and consider seven generations in the future when making decisions that affect the people.

Wilma Mankiller

Psychotherapy traditionally looks at the condition of eating disorders related to mother, father or immediate family—or specific traumatic incidents in the life of the person seeking help. However, the healing process of systemic constellation work also known as family constellation work, offers the new perspective that many of our problems may have roots in intergenerational family trauma.

Family constellation work

When we suspect that the ancestral family system is the root of the problem, we have found that the integration of psychodrama and constellation work is especially valuable in the treatment process. (Carnabucci and Anderson, 2012). Anne Ancelin Schützenberger was the first psychodramatist to document findings about hidden ancestral connections in her 1998 book, *The Ancestor Syndrome: Transgenerational Psychotherapy and the Hidden Links in the Family Tree*. Since then, a new approach known as systemic constellation work, has become invaluable to make the historic trauma visible so we can see the underlying energetic patterns and acknowledge them and heal them (Hellinger and ten Hövel, 1999; Hellinger, Weber and Beaumont, 1998).

Although the practice of constellation work, which employs a complex combination of fact-finding, phenomenology and sensing of body energy, is not within the scope of this book, we have developed, modified and adapted certain activities, sculptures and action structures to show the family connection. Karen, who is also a certified constellation facilitator, is likely to select from options of these methods, singularly and in combination, according to the needs and inclination of the people she is working with.

Historic trauma with food and deprivation

However, whatever the method, when we look at families in the context of historical events, we will discover that many suffered due to poverty, famine, war, slavery, immigration and other trauma where food or lack of food was a significant experience of pain and deprivation. The facilitator of systemic constellation work must be extremely careful, though, not to make assumptions about one trauma or another but faithfully follow the process as the energy of the family system unfolds. In the end, it may be revealed that a craving for sweets is related to a forgotten child who died two generations ago, or that anorexia is related to an unknown great-grandfather who was a prisoner of war.

Certainly, as we look across the cultures and across the centuries, we will find many stories of deprivation: the great famines in Europe, especially Ireland and Italy; the Native American children who were sent to boarding schools and separated from their traditional foods; the struggles for sustenance during the Great Depression in the United States; the starvation in Nazi Germany's concentration camps and the scarcity of food in Germany, the Netherlands, Russia and Japan after World War II.

New evidence is suggesting that such deprivation is not simply a historical and intellectual memory but a deep experience that alters our genetic structure; after all, we get our bodies from our ancestors. A 2008 video by NOVA, *Ghost In Your Genes*, suggests that what we eat, drink, breathe or experience leaves an enduring imprint, not just in our bodies but in future generations. For instance, researchers studied harvest records and births and deaths from Överkalix, a remote town in northern Sweden, and discovered that famines affected the life expectancies of the grandchildren of those who had suffered in the famine.

Two methods, similar and different

Psychodrama typically explores our conscious knowledge about a situation, and we use role reversal and other techniques to explore the situation from multiple perspectives. In contrast, constellation work eliminates role playing, and asks people to "represent" the important figures related to the problem, note sensations within their bodies and report on their moment-to-moment physical experiences.

The first set of structures in this chapter focus on psychodramatic vignettes that employ intergenerational themes with eating disorders and body distress, and later vignettes in the chapter focus on the use of constellation work. As we have said earlier, we continue to advise training in these methods for best practices, the effectiveness of the intervention and the safety of the clients.

Showing family connections

After a warm up of talking about, diagramming the family social atom or journaling about family relationships with food, eating behaviors and body dissatisfaction, you may instruct group members to do the following:

- Create a sculpture of their present-day family. Identify the distorted relationships with food, eating behaviors, body problems or compulsive behaviors.

- Create a sculpture of their family of origin. Identify the distorted relationships with food, eating behaviors, body problems or compulsive behaviors.

- Create a sculpture of their family of origin and their parents and others in the family, even if the group members did not know them or they died before he or she was born. Identify the distorted relationships with food, eating behaviors, body problems or compulsive behaviors.

Family Table

The family dinner table is the stage where the drama with food is enacted in real life. We bring the idea of the dinner table into the psychodrama room to support our clients in exploring the feelings, attitudes and traditions at the family dining table, both past and present.

Karen employs a guided imagery in which she takes an adult through a deep relaxation session that leads the person to the current-day kitchen and dining table. The imagery might go like this:

When you are in the kitchen, take time to look around. Notice how it feels to be here in this moment.

Notice if there are any smells or aromas in this room...

Take time to open the cupboards, the refrigerator and other places where food is stored or prepared...

What do you see there? Are these foods that you like or enjoy? Are there any foods traditional to your culture, your ethnic background or your ancestry?

Is there anyone preparing a meal here today? Who is responsible for the meals and what conversation is taking place as they are prepared? Is there anything else taking place at this time...

When meal time comes, how is the food served?

And now, as you sit at the table, notice who is sitting next to you...

Notice who is sitting across from you...

What is the conversation at the table? Are there rules about food, about meals, about manners?

What might happen if you asked for something at the table? And what might happen if you broke the rules?

What are the punishments? And what are the rewards in this household at meal time? You may wish to place your hand on your stomach right now, just to notice how it feels to be here...

Stay with the feelings, honoring your experience, and then allow yourself to come back into the room here...

When you feel ready, open your eyes…

And when you feel ready, allow yourself to sit up if necessary, or stretch, being gentle with yourself…

Participants may share in dyads and then in the larger group about their imagery experience. Ask who wishes to sculpt the dinner table scene with members of their group taking roles of self and others.

■ VARIATION

Take the adult to meet the inner child and together go to the childhood home and childhood dining table. If there is significant trauma in the family of origin, it is advised to be extremely cautious to make sure the adult person is well resourced with personal, relational and spiritual strengths on the journey. If there is concern that the imaginary visit may stir dissociative episodes or other trauma material, you may have the client or group journal about the dinner table in the family of origin instead.

■ VARIATION

Have the protagonist choose an object in the room to hold the Witness role—something that can metaphorically "know" what has taken place at the family table for generations, such as a clock, an old painting, a mirror. The director tells the protagonist that the "witnessing object" sees, hears and knows whatever there is to know about this family. The protagonist assigns group members to roles of current family members at their places at the table.

Next, the protagonist role reverses with each family member auxiliary and is given a three-part statement to complete:

- "How I feel about food is…"

- "How I feel about my body is…"

- "How I feel about myself is…"

To deepen the process, group members may be enlisted to double or the director may double. After each family member has spoken, the director role reverses the protagonist into the "witnessing object" role with a reminder that it watches accurately and without judgment. The director asks the protagonist in role of "witnessing object" to look at the protagonist's chair at the table and report what was seen, heard and felt; the director or group members may double as necessary.

The director asks the protagonist (in Witness role) who from past generations is standing behind the chairs of each family member. If enough group members are available, ancestors may be portrayed by participants; if the group is small, the ancestors may be represented by empty chairs or place mats.

The protagonist, still in the Witness role, makes a statement to the ancestors, then to the current family members and finally to self. If there is anger, it is recommended that the anger is expressed respectfully and directly. The protagonist returns to his or her role at the table to make a final statement.

Family Photo

Many of us have photographs of ourselves at the dining table for holidays, birthdays, family reunions and other special events. Sculpting the photo allows us to learn more about ourselves and our relationship to food and family—a pictorial variation on a social atom.

The warm up begins when participants are invited to find photos relating to food and eating to bring to a session.

The warm up begins prior to the session when participants are invited to find photos relating to food and eating to bring to a session. At the start of the session, the photographs may be placed on a table, wall, bulletin board or other central location to be viewed. Next, participants pick up their photos and are instructed to select a partner and share each other's photograph. Sharing begins with common questions—Who is in the photograph? What is the occasion? Why is this photograph important to you?—and progresses to informal sharing as everyone feels comfortable.

Participants are invited to sculpt their photos, asking group members to take the roles of those in the photographs. The auxiliaries pay special attention to the posture of each person shown in the photo — hands, arms, heads, eyes—and a person who is only partially shown in the photo may be added. During the set up, we notice who is turned toward or away from whom, who is looking at whom, and so forth. Invite the protagonist to soliloquize about looking at this "live" photograph. The protagonist may role reverse with each person in the scene, including himself or herself.

The director may ask: "Is there any way you would like to change this scene?" and give the protagonist the option of rearranging the auxiliaries, adding a missing person or making another kind of change.

Messages from generations

In conversations with our clients, we invariably talk about the messages in their heads that feed the eating disorder. "Whose voice is that?" we are likely to ask when a protagonist brings up a well-embedded statement.

Clients are encouraged to breathe and calm themselves to determine if the voice and its message is their own or if it is rooted in another person, especially from a family member, such as a parent, sibling or previous generation.

CASE STUDY: ALICE DISCOVERS GENERATIONAL DIRECTIVES

Alice, for instance, became aware that the statement "Appearance is what matters—no one will love you if you're fat," had been with her as long as she could remember.

Linda asked, "Who taught that eating disorder voice?"

"My mother," Alice quickly answered. She knew that her mother had gotten similar messages from her own mother.

Linda pulled in four chairs, putting Alice's chair in the front, and then a row of chairs behind her.

When all the chairs were placed, there were three generations behind Alice's chair; Alice identified which family member "sat" in each chair. Linda directed Alice to place hats and scarves to concretize each person, and identify who had given which message that contributed to Alice's eating disorder.

Linda asked Alice to take each role: her role, her mother's role, her grandmother's role and her great-grandmother's role.

A separate chair was placed to the side and designated as the Witness. Alice was directed to reverse with each role, one at a time, to learn the perspective of the mother, the grandmother and the great-grandmother about food, dieting and body appearance.

Linda then directed Alice to speak to each family member about the impact of each message; in the next scene, Alice was asked to state from her "truth teller" role what messages she wished had been passed on instead:

> Mom, you said no one would love me because I was fat. I need you to say that I am always loveable no matter what my body size.

> Grandmother Ruthie, you told mom that she had to lose weight to get a man, and mom passed that message to me. I wish you had said that other qualities of a woman matter so much more.

> Great-grandmother Irma, I never knew you, but you told Grandmother Ruthie that she would never survive in the world without getting married and she would never get married without the "right figure." I wish you had said that women are strong and resourceful regardless of size.

Alice also sat in the chair of the Witness role, so the Witness could make a final statement about multigenerational impact of messages to herself. "All these messages told you that your survival and acceptance depended on your weight and appearance. However, I see how strong and resilient you are—and these have nothing to do with your size or appearance."

This session could easily be adapted for a group setting, with group members selected to play the roles.

Acknowledging ancestral patterns

At other times, a person may have little or no knowledge of specific family messages about food or knowledge about any kind of personal trauma. Here, the ancestral message or pattern is not conscious but the behavior is very much present as the person continues to respond to the ancestral legacy.

CASE STUDY: SHEILA AND CONSTELLATION WORK

Sheila, a well-educated attorney, struggled during most of her life with compulsive overeating. With psychotherapy, including action therapy, and the help of the support group of Overeaters Anonymous, she had been able to greatly diminish her episodes of binge eating and had lost a significant amount of weight through the years. However, when she was served food in a restaurant, the panicky thought of "It's not enough!" automatically sprang to Sheila's mind even though her meals were well spaced throughout the day and the actual servings were abundant.

When she learned about constellation work, she remembered that an elderly aunt from Ireland had told a story about an earlier family member becoming ill after eating spoiled food. Sheila realized that she may have been carrying the experiences of these food-deprived villagers even though they had immigrated to the United States at the turn of the twentieth century and their children and grandchildren, including Sheila, were financially successful and well-provided for.

Karen directs all group members to stand at one side of the room, taking the "places" of anonymous poverty-stricken ancestors who never had enough to eat—those people who were likely to have spoken or thought those very words of "It's not enough." Sheila stood at the other end of the room, looking at the ancestors. There is no role playing; the direction is to stay silent and mindful of any and every physical feeling that emerges in the bodies of those standing.

Slowly the participants representing the ancestors identify an assortment of sensations and feelings: a hurting abdomen, a small ache on the left side of the head, a tingling in the hands, tightness in the neck and locking of the throat. Sheila, looking at the group, notices that she begins to feel very sad, and tears fill her eyes.

Karen, as director, gives specific healing sentences that acknowledge the suffering of the ancestors while confirming Sheila's survival.

Karen directs: "Please say, 'I see your suffering and deprivation.'"

Sheila repeats: "I see your suffering and deprivation."

Karen says: "I honor those who died and those who lived and prevailed to pass on life."

Sheila repeats: "I honor those who died and those who lived and prevailed to pass on life."

Karen says: "I have made it. I have enough now."

Sheila repeats: "I have made it. I have enough now."

Karen says: "When I sit with my meal, I will remember you and it will be enough."

Sheila repeats: "When I sit with my meal, I will remember you and it will be enough."

The standing "ancestors" report feeling lighter and calmer, their feelings of tightness and achiness fading. Sheila, now silent, breathes more easily. She also reports feeling calmer and more present.

Objects as representatives

Objects may serve as "representatives" in individual sessions; Karen has used sand tray objects as well as plastic place mats and plastic or paper cups. When using place mats, she makes an arrow with masking tape on the mat to show what "direction" the object is looking; with paper cups, she draws one arrow on the underside of the cup with a marker.

CASE STUDY: ANGELA AND THE HUNGER CUP

In an individual session, Angela, an elementary school teacher, discussed a feeling of strong hunger that had been with her as long as she could remember. She learned about portion size and low-fat choices with the help of a commercial weight loss group and benefited from its social support. When she learned that sugar appeared to accelerate food cravings, she stopped its use. However, even though she had lost weight and abstained from sugar, white flour and most processed foods, she continued to feel this strong hunger at the age of 60. She periodically suffered insomnia, which was only soothed by visiting the pantry for a late-night snack. She sometimes sat impatiently when waiting for the next meal, which she demonstrated by tapping on the chair arm of the sofa where she was sitting. She wanted to feel pleasantly full after a meal and practice consistent self-care. She reported that her ancestors came from a poor village in southern Italy and that her grandparents immigrated to the United States in the early 1900s to find work as coal miners.

Karen gave Angela two cups, one to represent herself, the other to represent Hunger, and asked her to place them upside down on the carpeted floor with little thinking about their arrangement or meaning.

Karen placed the cup labeled Hunger some distance away from Angela, almost on the other side of the room. She placed the cup labeled with her name closer to her but in the same line as Hunger and looking away. Karen asked that Angela sit meditatively with the arrangement and report her feelings, sensations and any other spontaneous reactions as they emerged.

Angela turned her cup to "look" toward Hunger. Karen asked her if she might move her cup closer to Hunger. After some time, Angela moved her cup slightly closer to Hunger. She looked silently at the floor for a while.

"I just imagined myself lying on the carpet near my cup," she said.

"That's fine," Karen answered. "Feel free to do that if you wish."

Angela dropped to the floor on the right of the cup, laying on her right side as she curled her body slightly around the cup. She felt her body stiffening and her eyes open wide, as if she was awake in the middle of a long sleepless night. From her vantage point, Angela noticed a Catholic religious symbol on the wall of the retreat center.

"What do you want to say to the crucifix?" asked Karen.

"You never helped," said Angela somewhat forcefully and bitterly. "You had all the money, but you didn't help us— we were starving!" She paused, seemingly surprised by her outburst, then sat up. "I grew up Catholic," she announced, "but I left the church when I was 12."

After a pause, she said, "I can move closer to Hunger." The cups were now standing together near the other side of the room, rim to rim. More time passed, as Angela sat quietly.

"What's happening now?" asked Karen.

"I'd like the two cups to kiss!" Angela reported, seemingly surprising herself again.

She leaned and picked up the cups, touching them together lightly, almost in a toasting fashion. "It's an affectionate kiss," she added, explaining this spontaneous reaction. There was more meditative silence. Angela returned to her original side of the room with her cup.

At Karen's request, she agreed the Hunger cup could move closer; as Karen moved the cup, Angela swallowed with nervousness; Karen responded to these body signals by slowing the movement of the approaching cup and speaking softly. Finally, the two cups were together again, close to Angela. Angela began tapping the bottoms of her cups with fingernails, just like she had been tapping before—but this time the tapping was playful rather than impatient.

"Like the tarantella?" Karen asked with a smile, referring to the popular Italian folk dance, as Angela smiled in return.

Karen asked Angela to place the Hunger cup back in the past, its original location, and tell Hunger, "You are in the past. I leave you in the past." Then Karen placed a third cup on the sofa cushion where Angela had been sitting. This cup, she announced, represented the long-ago ancestors who had plenty—at a time where there was no hunger, only celebration, feasting, abundance, love and laughter. Angela was invited to sit on the floor, leaning back against the sofa seat and feeling its support while she closed her eyes.

As Angela listened, Karen described the scene around the dining' table of Angela's ancestors, describing the pungent smell of tomato sauce and basil, the smiling and happy faces of the family and camaraderie among all. Angela was invited to embellish the image in her mind and "take in" the experience of the scene. After the session, she was given the labeled cups to take home and to revisit the final scene in her mind's eye so it would be fully experienced and integrated.

CASE STUDY: LUCILLE UNCOVERS A SECRET

Lucille, a 36-year-old professional woman, sought psycho-therapy to address anxiety that she described as relentless. In individual sessions, she acknowledged that she had developed patterns of "Look how good I am," "Look how cute I am," "Look how smart I am" in her family of origin to attract their approval, and had continued those behaviors in her marriage. As an adult, Lucille was struggling with a number of life choices, both in her marriage and in her career. She often felt herself wavering, deciding to please her husband rather than attending to her own wishes and needs.

She participated in Karen's ongoing constellation groups, which were open to any topic brought by group members. During a group session, Lucille identified a desire to know her "truth."

Two representatives were chosen: one for Lucille, another for her Truth. After placement of each representative, the Lucille representative's eyes grew big, and she described herself as feeling curious. The Truth representative, however, lowered her head and pulled inward with her body, saying she felt repressed and condensed, bending closer to the floor, saying she felt as if she could not get small enough.

The Lucille representative became increasingly curious, starting to touch Truth, but then pulled back, feeling cautious and fearful. Truth did not respond but announced more agitation and became smaller, curling herself on the floor on top of a pillow. She pulled a nearby blanket over her head, saying she wanted to hide.

At one point Truth doubled over and reported "something" coming up inside of her, much like stomach reflux. The representative stopped and, speaking as herself, said she felt like she was going to vomit; she sat up quickly. She was not sure that she could continue in the session because she was feeling so sick.

However, Lucille, watching from the mirror position, as is customary with constellation group sessions, confirmed the representative's feeling of illness as not belonging to the representative but to herself. Lucille admitted that she vomited periodically, especially when she felt agitated and full of pressure—the throwing up seemed to release the agitation, she said.

After this information was revealed, Truth felt calmer, noting that her stomach now was settled.

Lucille recalled a family secret that she had discussed during the genogram-making intake session several months prior. Her paternal great-grandfather left his wife and family in Portugal to travel to the New World—where he married another woman and started a new family, with the "new" children given the same names of the children he had abandoned. The secret family was discovered only after this death.

Karen brought in one chair for the great-grandfather, who had abandoned his first family in Europe, as well as a second chair for the first family and a third chair representing the second family.

As the three chairs were set up, Truth reported feeling more agitated. The Lucille representative cautiously moved closer.

Lucille, watching from the side, said she did not know why the great-grandfather left his family and home town in Portugal.

Karen asked the Lucille representative to say this healing sentence to the great-grandfather chair: "Whatever happened in this family and whatever was done, you are still my great-grandfather and I will always honor you as my great-grandfather."

With this statement, Truth reported the agitation lessening.

Lucille's representative was asked to say to the chair representing the first wife and family, "You are also my family. I accept you as part of my family. Whatever happened in this family and whatever was done, you are still my great-grandfather's family and I will always honor you as part of my family."

With this healing sentence, Truth reported increasing calmness. She settled under the blanket, nestling on pillows, reporting feeling calm and content.

The Lucille representative wanted to pull out the blanket and pillow that was covering Truth and tugged at it, but Truth held on to the blanket.

Lucille was asked to come into the scene and stand with the Lucille representative and say, "I thought you were my truth, but now I know that you are the truth of the family and you belong to the ancestors. I now look for my own truth—the truth that belongs to me."

After she spoke these words, Lucille noticed she felt a sigh of relief. Truth, underneath the blanket, continued to feel content and calm.

Lucille was asked to anchor the statement again, this time holding her abdomen, breathing and saying to herself, "Dear Body, we are safe."

Follow up with Lucille

Nearly six months later, Lucille, still in psychotherapy that employs psychodrama, imagery, meditation, sand tray and constellation work, reported that she no longer felt an urge to vomit when anxious.

"I had never felt the urge to throw up again when dealing with a situation I could not digest or support," she reflected.

"The best thing about this session and the other sessions is that step by step they put me nearer to my own truth—they give me light and happiness."

She is now able to meditate, which she described as impossible in the past. "I can stand still long enough to be in contact with myself. I think more and more I am learning to separate what is mine and what is from others. Maybe I am learning to digest. This session was an important step that led to this evolution."

Chapter 17

Spirituality and Eating Disorders

Health is a state of complete harmony of the body, mind, and
spirit. When one is free...the gates of the soul open.

B.K.S. Iyengar

When we work with people with eating disorders, we must help people learn to nourish the body and nurture the spirit.

Disconnection from the spirit leads to hopelessness and despair, which leads to depression, as Carolyn Coker Ross notes in her 2009 book *The Binge Eating and Compulsive Overeating Workbook: An Integrated Approach to Overcoming Disordered Eating*, citing a variety of studies relating to physical and emotional illnesses. Yet tending to our spiritual needs appears to provide important healing for people with eating disorders, and there is growing empirical evidence that spiritual approaches to treating clients with eating disorders are as effective, and sometimes more effective, than secular ones, particularly with religiously devout clients. The book *Spiritual Approaches in the Treatment of Women with Eating Disorders* by P. Scott Richards, Randy K. Hardman and Michael E. Berrett in 2007 cites a study showing that individuals with eating disorders who participated in a spirituality support group during the first month of inpatient treatment improved more quickly than those in an emotional support group or cognitive behavioral therapy group.

Nancy Bailey, writing in her 2012 doctoral dissertation, *The Healing Experiences of Women: Psychodrama and Eating Disorders*, notes that the process of allowing psychodrama group members to become vulnerable without shame in the presence of others also encouraged inner growth and the ability to engage in a greater spiritual connection.

We have psychodramatic, action and arts-based routes to explore spiritual themes with individuals and groups. Role reversal and other psychodramatic techniques give us multiple opportunities to travel to the realm of surplus reality and explore our relationship with whatever is greater than ourselves. Dr. J.L. Moreno, the developer of psychodrama and sociometry, wrote regularly about our connection to the divine, which he termed the Cosmos, and developed a specific kind of drama, known as axiodrama, to explore issues of ethics, cosmic relationships and values. More recently, psychodramatist Connie Miller (2010) has created a process called Souldrama to provide a specific path for spiritual development.

Introducing spirituality

When we introduce the theme of spirituality, we are careful to remember that our clients may come from diverse religious backgrounds, perspectives, experiences and beliefs. Some may feel alienated from their religion for a variety of reasons, including the fact that religion has sometimes been associated with abuse, high levels of judgment or messages that the body is "bad" or "sinful."

We make an effort to welcome all points of view about religion and spirituality, and we believe it is important to distinguish religion, the practice of a set of beliefs, from spirituality, which we consider a more personal connection to the divine not associated with an institution or dogma.

To start the exploration of spirituality, we use the locogram developed by colleague Cathy Nugent with five categories for the individual or group to choose:

- Religious and spiritual.

- Neither religious nor spiritual.

- Religious, not spiritual.

- Spiritual, not religious.

- Other.

These categories support clients to consider their experience and definition of spirituality. The "other" choice allows clients to disclose their spiritual orientation when it does not neatly fit into the first four categories or if the answer is "don't know" or "not sure." This sociometric exploration also gives us information about our clients' spiritual practices so we can craft suitable warm ups and action structures that most suit a group.

For instance, if the group is primarily Christian, we may invite them to encounter God or Jesus to engage in dialogue, asking questions and participating in role reversal so that a greater experience of these relationships is possible. Our Jewish clients may relate to the story of Moses in the desert and the provision of manna from heaven—which might serve as a warm up to explore the many food and fasting rituals in the Jewish tradition. If there are orientations that are more alternative, the encounter may focus on a wise entity or spiritual force of some kind. We always aim to respond spontaneously to the variations within the group and with individuals so that we are not responding to stereotypes, neither making assumptions about others' beliefs nor excluding any beliefs.

Circle sociometry

We strive for respect for all spiritual beliefs and practices and make a container that is open to everyone. For example, step-in sociometry allows people to claim specific religious or spiritual criteria. With these action disclosures, they are able to find commonalities with other group members and we, as directors, learn information that allows us to respond sensitively to the variations of the group, just as we would be culturally sensitive to a variety of ethnic groups and cultures.

Some step-in criteria might include:

- I have a specific connection to a religious congregation.

- I am Christian.

- I am Jewish.

- I am Hindu.

- I am Buddhist.

- I am Muslim.

- I am Native American.

- I have a spiritual community or religious study group.

- I was raised in a religious home but no longer practice the religion of my family.

- I was not raised in a religious home and am just beginning my spiritual journey.

- I have been following a guru as part of my spiritual journey.

- I have felt betrayed by a spiritual or pastoral leader.

- I have involvement in a 12-step group that supports the concept of a higher power.

Warm ups

Cards, such as Angel Cards, SoulCards, Gaian cards and others, serve as an evocative doorway to exploring spiritual themes. Nature walks, photographs, music, poems and holy readings generate warm ups to connect with awe, sacredness and sources of inspiration.

We each keep a library of music that we find suitable for inspiration for a variety of themes and a variety of clients. Offering songs written and sung by women and men give directors a variety of voices to present to our clients. We include music with many styles and from many cultures, so our libraries include Native American flute songs, African drumming and Asian chanting.

We make sure to have music that is soothing; Rebecca Ridge (2012) points out that sound is a potent trigger of neuroception—the perception of the brain's neural system—according to Stephen Porges's (2011a) Polyvagal Theory. Lullabies, love songs and the songs from folk musicians share a similarity to a mother's voice, a modulation of high frequencies. For instance, Prokofiev's *Peter and the Wolf* is an excellent example of acoustic stimulations; the friendly characters are the violin, the clarinet, flute and oboe while the predator wolf is signaled by low-frequency sounds.

Blessings

We have borrowed blessing traditions from a variety of cultures for our group and for ourselves. Before the group begins, we may variously "bless" the group space with a prayer, with smudging with sage or with Tibetan singing bowls or chimes to clear lower vibrations and invite higher vibrations into the space. We bless the room with Reiki energy and improvised prayer before a session begins. Instead of smudging, we might use a bowl of water with a few drops of sage oil that is passed around the circle for people to dip their fingers in and bless themselves. The use of the bowl bypasses concerns about people with respiratory problems but still offers the clearing and the ritual.

Variously, we may include the group in a blessing ritual as part of the warm up. For instance, we may ask group members to bless the space according to their traditions, whether Christian, Native American, Jewish or others. We also have simple musical instruments, such as small drums and rain sticks, to use during warm ups and dramas.

Transpersonal strength

To move to a higher level of warm up, we ask group members to identify a transpersonal strength, whatever they perceive as greater than themselves "which could help you recover from your eating disorder." This might be God, or Jesus or Buddha—or it may be the life force, nature, music, art, the group or a vaguely named Higher Power. They can take that role and speak to the present self about how they can work together towards recovery.

■ VARIATION

Concretize the spiritual strength with a scarf or cloth, small figure, empty chair, pillow or other object that seems suitable.

Prayers

Prayers may be used as warm ups and as grace for meals during all-day or all-weekend workshops. One favorite prayer that Karen has used through the years involves a kind of call-and-response practice that includes everyone and builds community:

We give thanks…
(We give thanks…)

We give thanks for being…
(We give thanks for being…)

We give thanks for being here together.
(We give thanks for being here together.)

Other meditations

The short "Verses for Eating Mindfully" from *Present Moment, Wonderful Moment* by Thich Nhat Hanh (1990) are also easy to use as meditations before a meal or interspersed before, during and after a meal.

The spirituality of food and eating

In the past two decades, a number of spiritually oriented writers are redefining the way that cookbooks are presented. Moving from the functional perspective of traditional cookbooks to an approach that honors the origins, traditions and rituals of food and eating, we have *Cooking for the Love of the World: Awakening Our Spirituality through Cooking* by Anne-Marie Fryer Wibolt and *Chakra Foods for Optimum Health* by Deanna Minich as examples. There also is *Serving Fire: Food for Thought, Body, and Soul* by Anne Scott and Catherine Rose Crowther, which encourages kitchen and serving rituals.

With knowledge of action methods, it is easy to take information presented in the book and bring it to action. For example, in *Cooking for the Love of the World: Awakening Our Spirituality through Cooking*, the author invites us to observe the creative life force in a carrot, with gravity pulling down the thick dense root and the sun drawing up the delicate green leaves. This scene could easily be enacted in a group setting, stimulating participants to consider their connection with nature and cosmic forces.

Meditation and mindfulness

Meditation offers multiple health benefits. We have noted earlier the Harvard Medical School study (Hözel *et al.*, 2011) which showed that just eight weeks of meditation for 30 minutes daily increased the size of the brain's hippocampus—excellent news for trauma survivors whose hippocampus has been damaged by trauma. We suggest clients consider meditation as part of their personal growth process and we introduce them to simple meditation skills during individual and group sessions. Because most students who are new to meditation have difficulty sitting still for more than five minutes, Linda often starts with a physical activity such as yoga or tai chi.

Participants may be sitting or standing as the meditation begins. Here is a typical meditation that Linda often uses:

> Feel all four corners of each foot firmly grounded on the floor. Feel under the ball of the big toe and little toe, both sides of the heel, under the ball of the foot. Now, just begin to breathe naturally—in through the nose, out of the nose, softening the face and the gaze, allowing the shoulders to drop down away from the ears...

> Now, breathe in the energy of the earth, breathing in through the soles of the feet, all the way up the torso to the heart and into the heart and out of the heart...

> Now breathe in the energy of the universe through the crown of the head, down through the face and neck to the heart...

> Allow any tension that you have to drop off the ends of the fingers like raindrops and be in the heart space with the breath...

After the meditation, Linda moves into yoga practice, typically starting with the posture of the Sun Salutation.

Spirituality Timeline

The timeline, mentioned in Chapter 7, is adaptable to explore clients' spiritual evolution. Here, we ask our clients to identify the various points within their lives when they felt a spiritual connection or spiritual disconnection, and how these events and experiences influenced their relationship with food, love of self, body and self-care. In this timeline we may explore:

- childhood teachings and perceptions of a higher power

- rules about food and eating according to religious dogma and tradition

- times of spiritual loss or change

- abuse or trauma associated with religion

- interactions with cults, gurus or other charismatic leaders

- new spiritual discoveries and connections.

This timeline is rich for creating dramas for deeper investigation and resolution, whether they are role reversals with God—"What does God want me to eat?"—or the child self who may have held images of wonderment, curiosity or confusion that must be revisited. At all times, we as directors strive to remain open to what is revealed by our clients and the truth of the protagonist. Being open to their truth, no matter how strange or unexpected, is the essence of discovering and directing a meaningful drama.

CASE STUDY: JOSEPH EXAMINES HIS SPIRITUAL JOURNEY

Joseph had been attending a psychodrama group for several months, making significant strides in his ability to accurately label feelings, to distinguish feelings from thoughts, and to double and to role reverse with others. A divorced father in mid-life, he reached a stage in his recovery when he was warmed up to look at his spiritual journey. He realized that he must sort through the messages about spirituality and religion that he had received through the years, with willingness to let go of the messages that no longer served him and to honor the spiritual strengths and lessons that supported him.

Following the warm-up segment of the drama, Joseph agreed to revisit scenes of his early church experiences, to identify the messages that were no longer serving him and to re-enforce the ones he wished to carry with him into the future. In the opening scene, he identified strengths and picked group members to portray them. The second scene revisited his childhood church, where the pastor had vigorously preached lessons about a God of harsh criticism and judgment of self and others.

This scene contrasted with the next scene, which recreated the church that he joined as a young adult. Here, the minister taught lessons of compassion for self and others and encouraged the congregation to become involved in community service to make the world a better place. In the drama, Joseph expressed gratitude for these lessons in compassion and service to the minister (played by an auxiliary) and then role reversed into the role of the minister, telling himself that he was proud of the man that he had become. Role reversing back into himself, he heard the praise of the minister.

Taking the strengths of this scene with him, he went back to the earlier scene and spoke his truth to the early church pastor (another auxiliary in role) and accurately labeled which of those messages he now chose to leave behind while recognizing love and compassion for those early messages because they had served a purpose in his life at that time.

He ended the drama by setting his intention to fully embrace his "divine feminine" side. As his closing statement, he asserted, "Love and hate cannot occupy the same heart-space at the same time." The drama led to deep and heartfelt sharing from group members, especially the other men in the group who expressed resonance with the need to own the feminine energy within themselves.

One-Minute Gratitude

As we have seen, one of the aspects of an eating disorder is strong self-criticism; eating disorder people tend to bring this criticism and anger to the body and body parts. Because gratitude is a practice that shows up in most spiritual traditions, Karen has created an action structure, One-Minute Gratitude, which has a multitude of uses.

In this structure, people are invited to identify specific parts of the body that they are able to appreciate for just one minute. The short time is often a relief for people who initially see the activity as difficult because they are critical of their bodies.

The director or another group member may take the role of timekeeper. One person agrees to take the role of protagonist, willing to identify the parts of the body that he or she feels gratitude about.

The other members of the group take the role of the "chorus," standing in a cluster and saying, singing or shouting multiple lines of "thank you."

For instance, the protagonist may say, "One thing I'm grateful for is that my eyes can see sunrises and sunsets."

The chorus, standing nearby, may respond, "Thank you, thank you, thank you!"

The protagonist adds, "My ears can hear music."

The chorus adds, "Thank you, thank you, thank you!"

"My hands that drive me to work."

The chorus adds, "Thank you, thank you, thank you!"

"My brain that helps me make good decisions."

The chorus adds, "Thank you, thank you, thank you!"

This activity may be solemn and reverent or playful and joyful. We are mindful to let the group character emerge rather than teaching that spirituality must show up in a particular way.

Wonders of the Body

Here is a variation that combines gratitude with education about the wonders of the body. In this action structure, we first ask group members to think and talk about functions of the body parts, such as kidneys, liver and spleen.

Linda shares pre-written index cards about a body part's functioning such as the following:

- The human heart beats 103,689 times in 24 hours.

- We breathe 23,040 times in one day.

- We exercise seven million brain cells.

- My body needs nutrients to function.

Group members pick a card and are asked to create a moving sculpture showing the function of each part—brain, heart, liver and so forth—moving together. Each part speaks its function aloud in role, with every group member having a turn to step out into the mirror position and observe the moving sculpture. The protagonist in the mirror position may then make a statement like, "What I am most grateful for is…"

Chakra warm up and chakra-grams

When we speak of the body, we consider not only the physical aspects of the body but also its energetic components.

In the yoga tradition, great attention is directed to the body's chakra system. The word "chakra" comes from the Sanskrit word "wheel" and refers to energy centers that yoke mind–body and heart–spirit centers with the divine. These seven energy wheels are stacked one atop the other from the base of the spine to the crown of the head. Each is associated with a color and sound as well as issues of self-development and balance.

Linda and colleague Kathy Amsden developed chakra locograms—calling them chakra-grams—to use as warm ups for a psychodrama workshop.

For this structure, you will want to have ready:

- colored thick paper or card in the chakra colors of red, orange, yellow, green, blue, purple and white

- scarves or lengths of cloth in the chakra colors of red, orange, yellow, green, blue, purple and white

- sound, provided by a musician or pitch pipe.

Write each chakra name on the corresponding color of thick paper or card along with the related element, sound, challenges and personal or emotional issues.

For example, the first chakra is root chakra, color red; associated with earth; sound "oo" pitch C; located at the perineum, and relates to issues of survival. The balance challenge is stability and groundedness. Unresolved issues in this energy center are likely to show up emotionally as fear or anger. In eating disorders, these may be expressed either in starvation or overeating.

The second chakra, the sacral chakra, is orange; element water; located at pelvis below the naval; sound is "oh" pitch D; related to issues of giving and receiving nurturance. The balance challenge is healthy sexuality and self-love. Unresolved issues here may show up as shame. We often see trouble here in clients with bulimia.

Third chakra, the solar plexus chakra, is yellow; element fire; sound "awh" pitch E; located at arch of ribs; issues here are self-definition, independence, will. Balance challenge here is strength of will and purpose and spontaneity. Unresolved issues here may show up in a pattern of "shoulds"—what we should or should not eat; what one's body should or should not weigh, etc.

Fourth chakra, the heart chakra, is green; center of chest; element air; sound "ay" pitch F; related to issues of loving and being loved. Balance challenge is self-acceptance and compassion for others. Unresolved issues here may show up as lack of joy; difficulty forgiving self and/or others. Sometimes we see the eating disorder show up here in the self-punisher role; or as a way of enacting relationship troubles.

Fifth chakra, at the throat, is blue; located at base of neck; element is sound; "ih" pitch G; issues here are truth telling, responsibility for self; expression. Balance challenge is to communicate clearly and be heard. Unresolved issues may present as sadness, blame, developing a false self. We have found that music, sound and psychodrama are especially helpful here in giving the client a way to communicate in lieu of the eating disorder—hence, clearing this chakra.

Sixth chakra, at the "third eye" in the center of the brow, is purple/ violet; element is light; sound "om" pitch A. Issues involve seeing clearly, understanding. Balance challenge is imagination and accurate intuition. Unresolved issues show up as confusion and may result in anxiety. We have found the practices of yoga and meditation, along with axiodrama, especially helpful in clearing this chakra.

Seventh chakra at the crown (top of head) is white; sound is silence; element is universe, or the divine. Issues are disconnection of self with spirit. Challenge is to live in consciousness and wisdom and maintain spiritual connection while living in the world. Unresolved issues result in apathy and depression. We have found meditation and sacred dance and movement helpful in coming to the peace of what poet T.S. Eliot described as "At the still point, there the dance is" (p.119).

Having placed the locograms on the floor, we give a brief teaching about the chakra and invite participants to take time to visit each chakra-gram and to stand on the one they feel most closely reflects their energy in the moment. Then, each participant shares why he or she chose this place. Next, we invite participants to revisit the chakra-grams and find one that reflects strength that they have that would help them clear unresolved issues from the first-named chakra. One at a time, each member says the chakra, the strength, makes that chakra's sound, and takes a posture or yoga pose to embody the strength. Then, the group mirrors that posture or pose. This process continues until everyone has identified a chakra strength and been mirrored by the group.

Each member picks a scarf the color of the "strength chakra" and walks to the originally chosen chakra-gram and states his or her goal of psychodramatic work if chosen as the protagonist. A protagonist is selected and each group member places his or her chakra scarf on the floor, creating a "sacred chakra circle of strengths" similar to the one used in the Therapeutic Spiral Model. Within this circle is where the psychodramatic action takes place. As appropriate, the sound, color, yoga pose of the chakra strength becomes a role taken by an auxiliary chosen by the protagonist and the director calls role reversals as needed. The drama progresses until the contract is met and the protagonist reports a shift in his or her internal energy; for instance, heaviness in the heart now feels light. A "chakra celebration" with scarves, sound and movement concludes the session.

After traditional psychodrama sharing, group members vocalize each chakra sound in order, from root to crown, ending in silence. We conclude with the Namaste gesture, with the palms pressed together in front of the heart. The person making the gesture also makes a slight bow to the other person. The meaning of the gesture is, "The light in me honors the light in you."

Role training in finding meaning and purpose

People finding meaning and purpose in their lives becomes an important part of the spiritual journey. Role training and future projection provide a way to rehearse or experience how we can contribute to others.

CASE STUDY: IRIS DEVELOPS MULTIPLE ROLES IN RECOVERY

Iris has integrated a number of activities in her life that allow her to maintain her recovery and give her life meaning. At the age of 50, she has a history of severe childhood trauma and abuse and a long struggle with food and weight issues. Through the years, she worked diligently to recover first from anorexia and then from a binge eating disorder, and to develop regular self-care practices that included working with a personal exercise trainer and a daily practice of meditation. She also developed her talents as a landscape photographer and poet as well as a dedicated gardener. In addition, she has rescued and trained dogs to become certified therapy dogs, and volunteers at nursing homes and day care centers, knowing that she is bringing joy to the very young and the elders. She has taken training in Reiki and offers sessions at no charge to people who want them. She considers these activities as parts of her spiritual practice that allow her to maintain her recovery and give her life meaning and purpose.

Blessing Table

Karen initiated a "blessing table" for concluding an intensive group or for saying goodbye to group members when they are leaving treatment. For this activity, Karen places a table in the center of the group, decorated with a special cloth and perhaps a candle or even a sprinkling of glitter, and gives group members the opportunity to place a personal item—such as glasses, ring, bracelet, scarf, keys or gloves—on the table. She explains that in the group interaction and dramas we are healers of each other, as a basic tenet in psychodrama, and that our experiences will continue to heal us and that we can carry the connections within us.

The group is invited to place the palms of their hands near or above the objects, sending whatever healing and loving energy they wish to send to these belongings. They may recite a favorite prayer or spontaneously create a wish or blessing for each other. At the conclusion of the ritual, each retrieves his or her personal item.

Finally...

When the body is the battleground, there is anger, distress and pain that have a great impact on the human spirit. With attention to an individual's spiritual exploration and growth, the person begins to feel more connected to a greater purpose and meaning in life and generates hope for the future. Most of all, there is peace within the body, mind, heart and spirit.

We close now with this intention for our readers and for all whose lives have been touched by eating disorders, with the words from Plato's *Phaedrus*:

> Once you have set foot upon the upward pilgrimage, do not go down again into darkness and to journey beneath the earth, but live in light—always.

Expected Changes in
the Fifth Edition of the
Diagnostic and Statistical Manual
of Mental Disorders (DSM-5)

- Binge eating disorder, likely the most common eating disorder, is now a separate diagnosis. This disorder has significant health complications and the designation as a separate diagnosis represents the importance of treatment.

- The requirements for the diagnosis of anorexia nervosa no longer involve the criteria of amenorrhea, the loss of a woman's monthly period. This recognizes that many women with low weight still menstruate and also permits the possibility of men to be recognized as anorexic.

- The diagnosis for bulimia nervosa has been changed, reducing the purging episodes per week from three or four to one. This change will result in more people with bulimia being able to access health care.

- Eating Disorder Not Otherwise Specified (EDNOS) signals variations of disordered eating that do not meet the diagnostic criteria for other eating disorders but that require treatment and are just as serious as other disorders. This diagnosis is expected to be modified as Feeding or Eating Disorder Not Elsewhere Classified.

Signs, Symptoms and Consequences of Eating Disorders

A distorted relationship with food and eating

- Constant dieting, restricting of food and fasting.

- Binge eating—a typical binge consists of large amounts of foods being gobbled in a short amount of time with little chewing and often secretly.

- Purging—by self-induced vomiting, laxative abuse, use of ipecac, diet pills, diuretics or compulsive exercise.

- Food rituals such as cutting and dicing food into small pieces, arranging food in a particular way on the plate, chewing a certain number of times before swallowing or spitting.

- Obsessively collecting recipes, cook books, cooking utensils and the like.

- Obsessing about food, counting calories and carbohydrate and fat grams.

- Cooking and baking for others, but not eating the food themselves.

- Discomfort when eating with others.

- Hoarding or secretive eating of food.

- Intense preoccupation with food, weight, appearance, body image, shape and size.

- Intense fear of becoming "fat."

Relationships with people

- Isolation and withdrawal.

- People-pleasing behavior, seeking external validation.

- Lack of intimacy: issues of trust, honesty and control.

- Difficulty asking for help.

Thinking

- Dichotomous ("all or nothing") thinking.

- Obsessive thoughts.

- Distorted body image, such as feeling fat when thin; or sometimes, with severely obese persons, feeling thin or average weight with little understanding of their actual body weight.

- Limited or distorted perception of actual body weight and size.

- Difficulty concentrating.

Behaviors

- Suicide attempts.

- Compulsive behaviors.

- Perfectionism.

- Poor impulse control.

- Excessive activity, restlessness, insomnia, early morning awakening.

Emotions

- Difficulty identifying and expressing feelings.

- Irritability and low tolerance of frustration.

- Fear of inability to stop eating.

- Anxiety, especially difficulty handling stress.

- Low self-esteem.

Adjunctive behaviors

- Shoplifting and petty thievery, often to get food.

- Chemical dependency, including nicotine dependency.

- Promiscuity, especially when there is a history of sexual abuse.

What's in the Psychodrama Room?

Basic props and supplies

- Extra chairs, camp stools or other furniture for sitting.

- Scarves or lengths of cloth.

- Pillows.

- Stuffed animals, puppets and dolls.

- Sand tray and small figures.

- Music player.

- Plastic, paper mache or cloth objects of food, especially for children, that might include fruits, vegetables, eggs and fast food items like cheeseburgers and French fries.

Other props, particularly those that allow a variety of projections, may include the following:

- Plastic spoons.

- White paper plates.

- Paper or plastic cups.

- Stones and geodes.

- Baskets and other containers.

- Blankets, towels or sheets.

- Yarn, ribbon or rope.

- Masking tape in various colors.

- Sponge balls and sponge blocks of various sizes.

- Large inflatable balls used for yoga or exercise.

- Wide elastic bands used for stretching, exercise and group activities.

- Hats.

- Masks.

- Commercial card decks, such as Tarot cards, Deborah Koff-Chapin's *SoulCards* and other interesting picture cards such as *Medicine Cards*, the Louise Hay *Healthy Body Cards* and the Cheryl Richardson's *Self-Care Cards*. We have found card decks that especially focus on health and affirmations and have used photographs and made our own cards with pictures clipped from magazines.

- Pictures or posters on the wall.

Art materials may be available as follows:

- Paper of various sizes and weights, including large rolls of newsprint.

- Markers, pastel crayons, paint such as tempera paint and fabric paint.

- Glue.

- Scissors.

- Magazines or magazine pictures, appropriate to the task.

- Push pins or tape to display the art on the wall.

Paper, pens, pencils and markers are helpful for making social atoms and other diagrams and journaling. A music player and musical instruments, even simple ones like rattles and drums, are not only visual props but provide sound during a warm up or drama.

Some directors like to have smaller props, such as small figures and toys that can be arranged in a sand tray or on a carpet square or table mat for display. Others create a clothes tree, closet or box of dress-up clothes that can be used to show shadow sides and playful sides.

Candles and other burning objects should be handled carefully if they are used at all. The best props are non-breakable and would not hurt people or property if they were thrown, dropped or mishandled in impulsive or accidental situations.

Music

For fun explorations of themes about food and movement with children, Linda uses many songs—several about food, movement, and having fun in the body—from the music series *Music Together*, developed by the Center for Music and Young Children in Princeton, New Jersey.

Songs that celebrate the fun of movement include The Wiggles' "Walk," and "Shake Your Sillies Out," "The Monkey Dance," "Ponies" and "Dancing with Wags the Dog" although professionals are encouraged to seek out the many excellent children's songs that are available from a variety of artists.

We have found music from singer–songwriter Karen Drucker extremely suitable, especially her *Sounds Of The Spirit* series. Favorites include: "Oh Mother God"; "Are You Ready to Receive"; "God is my Source"; "I Am the One Within You"; "The Healing Song"; "The Praising Prayer"; "How Could Anyone Ever Tell You"; "I Send My Love"; "I Give Myself Permission"; "Woman's Spirit"; and "Loving Kindness." There are many others.

There is John Lennon's classic "Beautiful Boy" from the album *Double Fantasy* and "Imagine" from the album of the same name and George Harrison's "Here Comes the Sun," "The Inner Light" and "My Sweet Lord." The Beatles' "In My Life" and "Let It Be" and Simon and Garfunkel's "The Sound of Silence" are evocative on many levels. Cat Stevens's (later Yusuf Islam) albums offer "The Hurt," "Morning has Broken," and "Peace Train." For integration, there is Jackson Browne's "It is One."

We also like the instrumental music of Steven Halpern, George Winston and Yo-Yo Ma. Specific favorites with lyrics are "Meaning in Life" in Kathy Amsden's CD *Awakening*. Martina McBride's "Any Way" in the album *Wake Up Laughing* helps with accessing spiritual strengths, and Josh Groban's "You Raise Me Up" from his album *Josh Groban* speaks to the importance of strengths as well.

Traditional gospel songs such as "Oh Happy Day" and "Pass Me Not, Oh Gentle Savior," which are respectively upbeat and plaintive offer a spiritual perspective. Many also enjoy the chanting of Snatam Kaur and others.

Songs

"I've Found My Voice Again"

Ahhhh...

I have a voice.
I have a choice.

OOOOooooo
Loud and clear.
Without fear.

Ahhhh—come on, join me this time

I have a voice.
I have a choice.

OOOOooooo
Loud and clear.
Without fear.
Ahhhh...
Breathing...the music signals the ending is near.
Ahhhh...
Ahhhh...
Ahhhh...

VERSE 1

Running to and fro.
Don't know where to go.
Try to let it go,
Right here and now.
From this moment on,
I will carry on.
Must transform this song,
Into my life.

REFRAIN

I found my voice again.
Lost way back when.
Silenced by years of pain.
Waiting to be born again.
And I have a voice,
And I have a choice.

VERSE 2

Harboring this pain.
Silencing my name.
Cannot stake my claim,
Unless I'm heard.
No more silent nights.
I'll put up a fight.
Search for inner peace,
Before I die.

REFRAIN

Can you hear me loud and clear?
I speak my truth without fear.
Yearning to be whole once more.
Must reclaim my soul for ever more.
And I have a voice.
And I have a choice.

Can you hear me loud and clear?
I speak my truth without fear.
Yearning to be whole once more.
Must reclaim my soul for ever more.
I have a voice.
I have a choice.
This is my voice.

© Katherine M. Amsden (2003)

"Road to Recovery"

Walking down the road of no return
What's a guy gonna do?
Umm?
Walking down the road of no return
What's a guy gonna do? Yeh
What's a guy gonna do?

REFRAIN

There's a road to recovery
And it's a road in the right direction
There's a road to recovery
And it's a pathway to joy.

STANZA

I look around, I can't believe
What I'm seeing
How to hell did I get myself here? Umm
I wonder how I'm ever gonna
Get out of this one
Where did it all go wrong?
Yeh, where did it all go wrong?

STANZA

I don't see a pathway out of this one
Yet I gently hear her call
She says, there is a road to recovery
Yet, I don't know which way to go
No, don't know which way to go.

(Spoken, not sung)

REFRAIN

You know in that movie
Where Indiana Jones
Is in search of the Holy Grail
And he comes to that part where
He's right at the edge of the cliff.

Well, it's like that!
You just gotta take that leap of faith.

REFRAIN

Years have gone by. I look back in awe
God, how things have changed
How I've grown. It's amazing how
It all fits together
There is a road to recovery
Yes there is a road to recovery.

FINAL STANZA

Just take it…"one step at a time"
"Easy does it"…"one step at a time"
"Take it slowly"…"one step at a time"
"Keep it simple"…"one step at a time"
One step at a time… (repeated and fade)

©Katherine M. Amsden (2003)

"Getting to Know You"

Getting to know you
Getting to know all about you
Getting to like you,
Getting to hope you like me.

You are my body
Where would I be without you?
I'd be a no-body
Then where would I be?!

Here is my good brain
Inside my head so nicely
Very precisely
Where—it ought to be!

Here are my biceps
You help me to lift and carry
You never tarry
When work is to be done.

Here is my dear chest
You are protecting my heart
You are just so smart
You help me push right on through.

Moving back around
Here are the lats that pull down;
Glutes to sit down
And get up again.

Here are my shoulders
You do so much to help me
Raise up and lower
Circling all around.

Quads, you help me move fast or slowly
Hamstrings, you and quads are a team
Calves, although you are lean
You are the strong-est in my body!

Here are my abdominals
You really are phenomenal
You keep my insides
Inside of me!

Here is my low back
What a lot of work I give you
Bending and twisting, amazingly.

Dearest body, you truly are amazing
All you do for me astonishes me
I know more how you are really meant to move, so
I promise to improve—in caring for you…

Getting to love you
Learning to take good care of you
I am so thankful for all you've given me
You are my body
Where would I be without you?
I'd be a no-body
Then where would I be?

I could go on singing your praise forever
But it's time to go now, so I'll say so long—
And I'm sorry for all the times I ever
Took you for granted.

Getting to love you
Learning to take good care of you
I am so very thankful for all that you've given,
And without you—what would I live in!

Instead there's all the
Beautiful and new things
I'm learning about you
Day by day!

Linda Ciotola, inspired by
"Getting to Know You" from *The King and I*

Resources

There are many resources to learn about the chakra system; we have used *Intuitive Living: A Sacred Path* (2001) by Alan Seale, *The Inward Arc* (2000) by Frances Vaughan and *Chakra Foods for Optimum Health* (2009) by Deanna Minich.

When considering books for parents, a current favorite author is Ellyn Satter, a registered dietician and clinical social worker who has written books for parents to prevent power struggles about food, attending to children's nutritional requirements and encouraging them to try a variety of foods. Her 2000 book, *Child of Mine: Feeding with Love and Good Sense* is widely considered the leading book about nutrition and feeding infants and children.

Another excellent resource is *What Chefs Feed Their Kids: Recipes and Techniques for Cultivating a Love of Good Food* by Fanae Aaron, published in 2012. The chefs talk enthusiastically about introducing children to the wonders of whole foods as an evolving adventure for parent and child. Rather than assuming that toddlers prefer bland foods, children are encouraged to experiment according to their natural curiosity and explore textures, flavors and unique qualities—richness, sour, sweet, salty.

Movement and play for children

We also recommend ideas for parents about the importance of free play—as an alternative or addition to structured sports—for children who may need encouragement to get moving. *Last Child in the Woods: Saving Our Children from Nature-Deficit Disorder* by Richard Louv in 2008 points out the value of exposure to nature for physical and emotional health. Even children who do not have easy access to nature should be encouraged to spend time outdoors; involvement in a community garden can serve multiple aspects of contact with nature, observations of seasonal cycles, learning about fresh locally grown food and improving nutrition. More suggestions from the *IDEA Fitness Journal* (2012), which we brainstorm, include:

- letting children get dirty while playing outdoors

- playing with your children and showing them the kinds of activities you did outdoors when younger, such as jumping rope, riding your bike, roller skating on the sidewalk

- having rules about electronic devices, such as restricting the amount of time spent on them and keeping them out of kids' rooms

- fostering an active culture at home—as we would say, "Be a role model."

Index of Action Structures and Experiential Activities

Glossary

Abandoning Authority role: According to the Therapeutic Spiral Model, the trauma-based role that represents the part of self that abandons the person during a traumatic incident. This introjected role creates a challenge with self-care.

Action methods: A form of personal and professional growth work derived from psychodrama that facilitates the person's shift from narration (verbally telling the story) to motor representation (showing through use of the body as well as the voice).

Appropriate Authority role: According to the Therapeutic Spiral Model, the role that is created when the Abandoning Authority role is transformed, enabling the protagonist to internalize the ability of taking appropriate action on his or her own behalf. In other words, this is a self-care taker role.

Anorexia nervosa: An eating disorder of self-starvation, often life-endangering, characterized by a distorted body image, excessively low weight and the relentless pursuit of thinness.

Auxiliary or auxiliary ego: The person playing a role in a psychodrama for the protagonist.

Binge eating: Recurrent episodes of quickly eating a large amount of food in a short amount of time while feeling out of control.

Body Dialogue: Action structure with specific steps in which the client role reverses with the body to develop an empathic relationship with the body, developed by Linda Ciotola.

Body Double: A prescriptive role first used in the Therapeutic Spiral Model that decreases dissociation and helps people experience their bodies in a healthy state.

Bulimia nervosa: Binge eating followed by purging behaviors such as self-induced vomiting, laxative abuse or excessive exercise in an attempt to avoid weight gain.

Circle sociometry: An action structure in which a group member stands in a circle, names a criterion that is true for himself or herself and asks that others who meet the criteria step into the circle. For example, "I am an only child—anyone else who is an only child, please step into the circle." This sociometric test builds safety and group cohesion.

Client role: A prescribed role in the Therapeutic Spiral Model assigned when there is a need to increase observation beyond that of the Observing Ego. It holds the executive ego.

Containing Double: A prescribed role in the Therapeutic Spiral Model used to increase cognitive processing and narrative labeling to contain the trauma response when trauma material emerges.

De-roled or de-roling: When auxiliaries who play roles in the protagonist's drama release identification with their roles at the conclusion of the drama; for instance, "I am Sondra. I am no longer your mother."

Director: The person who facilitates a psychodrama session. The director typically is the group leader or the client's psychotherapist, but sometimes a visiting consultant directs the session while the psychotherapist watches. There may be a co-director or an assistant director to help with various roles.

Dissociation: A psycho-physiological defense developed during a traumatic experience to defend against pain, which is re-activated when traumatic memories and flashbacks occur. This disturbance in functions of identity, memory or consciousness may result in the person feeling "out of body" or in losing time.

Double: In classical psychodrama, the protagonist is joined by an auxiliary, either a co-therapist or group member, who speaks as the protagonist's inner voice. The double is a basic technique in psychodrama.

Eating Disorder Not Otherwise Specified (EDNOS): Variations of disordered eating that do not meet the diagnostic criteria for other eating disorders but that require treatment and are just as serious as other disorders. This diagnosis is expected to be modified in the *DSM-5* as Feeding or Eating Disorder Not Elsewhere Classified.

Experiential psychotherapy: Experiential therapies define the facilitation of experiencing as the key therapeutic task, and the therapeutic relationship as potentially creative. Experiential approaches emphasize the importance of process-directive intervention procedures oriented toward deepening experience within the context of a person-centered relationship.

Food atom: An action structure adapted from the social atom. The food atom connects food, feelings and relationships.

Future projection: The enactment of a specific scene in the future; it may include sub-scenes such as the hoped-for outcome, the most-feared event, an exaggerated reaction, a realistic expectation, or simply an exploration of an upcoming situation. In role training, the technique becomes an opportunity for rehearsal of new behaviors.

Locogram: A sociometric activity that designates locations on the floor that represent certain roles or preferences about specific questions in a given moment.

Mirror(ing): The protagonist stands out of the scene and watches while his or her role is played or replayed by an auxiliary.

Observing Ego: A long-standing role in psychodrama that observes the self; in the Therapeutic Spiral Model, it has been established as the role in the Trauma Survivor's Internal Role Atom (TSIRA) where the protagonist or others can neutrally observe and label his or her behaviors.

Prescriptive roles: In the Therapeutic Spiral Model, the roles are "prescribed" to the survivor for containment, observation and restoration before engaging with traumatic material. They include the strength-based roles (interpsychic, interpersonal and transpersonal) and the Observing Ego, the Containing Double and the Body Double.

Protagonist: The person who presents an issue to be explored in dramatic action and plays the main role in the enactment.

Protagonist-centered drama: A classical psychodrama in which the story of the main actor, called the protagonist, is enacted. This differs from the Central Concern Model (Buchanan, 1980) in which a group theme is enacted.

Psychodrama: The action method developed by Dr. J.L. and Zerka Moreno that uses improvisation to facilitate problem solving. It is mostly known as an experiential and expressive arts therapy—as are drama therapy, music therapy, art therapy, dance/movement therapy, poetry therapy. This powerful modality has applications in psychotherapy, education, business, law, theological exploration and more.

Reiki: Method of natural healing, in which the practitioner channels universal life-force energy through his or her hands to create a state of relaxation and well being in the client.

Role diagram: A pencil and paper drawing of roles that comprise an individual's personality at any given time. After diagramming on paper, it may be put into action.

Role play: Role playing seeks the best approach to solve a problem and generally is not aimed at discovering the deeper feelings within a person's behavior. It is often used in business, industry and education.

Role repertoire: The roles available to an individual. J.L. Moreno believed that a well-rounded role repertoire signified good mental health, spontaneity and creativity, enhancing an individual's ability to respond appropriately to any given situation.

Role reversal: The major participants in the drama change roles as part of the enactment. When a protagonist role reverses, he or she not only demonstrates how the "other" behaves in the scene—warming up the auxiliary and giving non-verbal cues to the auxiliary so that the scene is played close to the protagonist's experience—but also transcends habitual limitations of egocentricity. Role reversal is indicated when it is appropriate for the protagonist to empathize with the other's viewpoint. Role reversals may also be used intra-psychically, when the client role reverses with another part of self.

Self-soothing voice: Based upon neurobiology and object relations theory, this musical prescriptive role developed by Kathy Amsden (2004) uses the elements of sound, rhythm, tone, melody and lyrics to calm the limbic system, facilitate developmental repair and lay the groundwork for meaning making.

Sharing: The final phase of a psychodrama, when the auxiliaries share their experiences from the roles they played and everyone tells how a role they played is relevant to their lives. The protagonist has a chance to listen and feel connected to the group. In the Therapeutic Spiral Model, shared experience becomes shared meaning to carry into the future.

Social atom: A sociometric exercise showing an individual's significant social connections, drawn as a diagram on paper. After diagramming on paper, it may be put into action.

Sociodrama: A social issue, rather than a personal issue, explored through enactment.

Sociometry: The science and art of evaluating roles as they are played out in social relationships. Sociometric tests for this evaluation include the spectrogram, the locogram and step-in (or circle) sociometry, among others.

Soliloquy: The protagonist shares aloud feelings and thoughts normally kept hidden. The protagonist may be engaged in a solitary activity, such as walking home, winding down after an eventful day, or preparing for an event in the near future.

Systemic (or family) constellation work: An experiential healing process developed in Germany by Bert Hellinger that explores and heals intergenerational or systemic trauma by discovering energetic blockages in the family system.

Three Faces of Eating Disorders: An action structure developed by Kathy Metcalf and Linda Ciotola to "connect the dots" between food, feelings and relationships.

Timeline: A linear representation of a series of important events that are concretized in some way. We have used role players, small figures, stuffed animals, magazine pictures and other items to concretize timelines.

Trauma Survivor's Intrapsychic Role Atom (TSIRA): The clinical map of the essential internal roles in the self-organization and personality structure of a trauma survivor according to the Therapeutic Spiral Model. It shows the impact of trauma on self-organization as defined by role theory.

Trauma Triangle: An action structure from the Therapeutic Spiral Model, adapted from the Karpman Triangle. It illustrates how roles learned through trauma are re-enacted by the trauma survivor.

Triple Double: A term coined by Linda Ciotola when the classic Double, the Containing Double and the Body Double are used with the same protagonist in the same session, with moment-to-moment application according to the client's needs.

Vignette: Short scene enacted with one or two auxiliaries chosen by the protagonist; if auxiliaries are not available, props may be used.

Warm up: The pre-drama activity that develops group cohesion and focus and readiness to work. A warm up may be designed to create a special atmosphere, orientation or theme in a group.

Witness: A role adapted from yoga philosophy, sometimes called "the see-er within the see-er." Often used interchangeably with the term Observing Ego and able to observe one's thoughts, feelings, impulses, behaviors, etc. without judgment and without becoming engaged in feelings, behaviors or thoughts. The term Witness also incorporates a transpersonal perspective.

Bibliography

Aaron, F. (2012) *What Chefs Feed Their Kids: Recipes and Techniques for Cultivating a Love of Good Food.* Guilford, CT: Lyons Press.

Allen, J.G. (2001) *Traumatic Relationships and Serious Mental Disorders.* Chichester: John Wiley and Sons.

Amen, D.G. (2011) *The Amen Solution: The Brain Healthy Way to Lose Weight and Keep It Off.* New York: Three Rivers Press.

Amsden, K. (2003) *Awakening: Original Music for Inspiration and Healing.* CD. Windham, ME: Pine Point Productions. For musical clips and ordering see http://cdbaby.com/cd/kathyamsden, accessed on 15 September 2012.

Amsden, K. (2004) "A Musical Road to Recovery: Healing the Effects of Trauma with Music and Experiential Methods of Practice." Unpublished manuscript.

Anderson, A., Cohn, L. and Holbrook, T. (2000) *Making Weight: Men's Conflicts with Food, Weight, Shape and Appearance.* Carlsbad, CA: Gurze Books.

Andersen, A.E. (1992) "Eating Disorders in Males." In R. Lemberg (ed.) *Controlling Eating Disorders with Facts, Advice, and Resources.* Phoenix, AZ: Oryx Press.

Anderson, N. (2006) *Women and Weight Loss.* IDEA Personal Trainer Conference.

Archer, S. (2012) "Is Yoga Safe?" *IDEA Fitness Journal,* July–August, 116–125.

Badenoch, B. (2008) *Being a Brain-Wise Therapist: A Practical Guide to Interpersonal Neurobiology.* New York: W.W. Norton and Company.

Badenoch, B. (2011) *The Brain-Savvy Therapist's Workbook: A Companion to Being A Brain-Wise Therapist.* New York: W.W. Norton and Company.

Bailey, N. (2012) "The healing experiences of women: Psychodrama and eating disorders." Ph.D. thesis, Capella University.

Banks, A. (2011) *The Smart Vagus: Exploring The Social Wisdom of Our 10th Cranial Nerve.* DVD. Wellesley, MA: The Wellesley Centers for Women.

Bannister, A. (1997) *The Healing Drama: Psychodrama and Dramatherapy with Abused Children.* London: Free Association Books.

Banting, W. (1869) *Letter on Corpulence, Addressed to the Public.* London: Harrison. Available at www.subdude-site.com/WebPages_Local/Blog/topics/health/WilliamBanting_LetterOnCorpulence1864.pdf.

Baratka, C. (2012) Personal communication, 12 February.

Baratka, C. (2013) "Healing Your Body: The Therapeutic Spiral Model With Eating Disorders." In K. Hudgins and F. Toscani (eds) *Healing World Trauma with the Therapeutic Spiral Model: Psychodramatic Stories from the Frontlines.* London: Jessica Kingsley Publishers.

Barbour, A. (1992) "Purpose and strategy behind the magic shop." *Journal of Group Psychotherapy, Psychodrama and Sociometry 45,* 91–101.

Bellofatto, M. (2012) Personal communication, 20 January.

Benelli, C. (2012) "Reiki talking stick." *Reiki News Magazine,* Spring, 13–17.

Berne, E. (1978) *Games People Play*. New York: Ballantine.

Blatner, A. (2000) *Foundations of Psychodrama: History, Theory and Practice*, 4th edition. New York: Springer Publishing Company.

Brewerton, T.D. (2005) "Psychological trauma and eating disorders." In S. Wonderlich, J. Mitchell, M. De Zwann and H. Steiger (eds) *Eating Disorders Review, Part 1*. Academy for Eating Disorders, Milton Keynes: Radcliffe Publishing, pp.137–154.

Brooke, S.L. (2007) *The Creative Therapies and Eating Disorders*. Springfield, IL: Charles C. Thomas Publishers.

Brostoff, J. and Gamlin, L. (2000) *Food Allergies and Food Intolerance*. Rochester, VT: Healing Arts Press.

Buchanan, D.R. (1980) "The Central Concern Model: A framework for structuring psychodramatic production." *Group Psychotherapy 33*, 47–62.

Bulik, C.M. (2012) *The Woman in the Mirror: How to Stop Confusing What You Look Like With Who You Are*. New York: Walker and Company.

Burden, K.B. and Ciotola, L. (2002) *The Body Double: An Advanced Clinical Action Intervention Module in the Therapeutic Spiral Model to Treat Trauma*. Available at www.vsjournals.de/pdf/body_offener_beitrag_032007.pdf, accessed on 15 September 2012.

Callahan, M. (1989) "Psychodrama and the Treatment of Bulimia, in Experiential Therapies for Eating Disorders." In L.M. Hornyak and E.K. Baker (eds) *Experiential Therapies for Eating Disorders*. New York: The Guilford Press, pp.101–120.

Campbell, D.G. (1992) *Introduction to the Musical Brain*, 2nd edition. St. Louis, MO: MMB Music.

Carnabucci, K. (in press) *The Psychodrama Notebook: Little Articles for the Curious Professional, the Psychodrama Student and the Exam Candidate*. Self published.

Carnabucci, K. and Anderson, R. (2012) *Integrating Psychodrama and Systemic Constellation Work: New Directions for Action Methods, Mind-body Therapies and Energy Healing*. London: Jessica Kingsley Publishers.

Carnabucci, K. and Fullin, K. (2013) "Two Programs: The Therapeutic Spiral Model in Domestic Violence Work with Perpetrators and Survivors." (In K. Hudgins and F. Toscani, (eds) *Healing World Trauma with the Therapeutic Spiral Model: Psychodramatic Stories from the Frontlines*. London: Jessica Kingsley Publishers, pp.333–350.

Carrington, H. (1997) *The Natural Food of Man*. Whitefish, MT: Kessinger Publishing (scanned from the original book from 1912).

Carson, D. (1988–2012) *Medicine Cards: The Discovery of Power through the Ways of Animals*. New York: St. Martins Press.

Ciotola, L. (1998) *Eating Disorders*. San Diego, CA: Greenhaven Press.

Ciotola L. (2006) "The Body Dialogue." *Journal of Group Psychotherapy, Psychodrama and Sociometry 59*, 1, 35–38. Washington, DC: Heldref Publications.

Ciotola, L. (2009) "Giving voice to the unspoken: Triple Double." Maryland National Association of Social Workers Conference handout for co-presentation with Nancy Alexander, Baltimore, MD.

Ciotola, L. and Kenna, J. (2004) "Using Furry Auxiliaries in Individual Therapy." Handout for workshop for Mid-Atlantic Chapter of the American Society of Group Psychotherapy and Psychodrama, Silver Spring, MD.

Connelly, D. (1979) *Traditional Acupuncture: The Law of the Five Elements*. Laurel, MD: Tia Sophia Institute (formerly Traditional Acupuncture Institute).

Davis, W. (2011) *Wheat Belly: Lose the Wheat, Lose the Weight, and Find Your Path Back to Health*. Emmaus, PA: Rodale Books.

Dayton, T. (n.d.) "An interview on psychodrama with Zerka Moreno." Available at www.tiandayton.com/wp-content/news/news3.html, accessed on 15 September 2012.

Dayton, T. (1994) *The Drama Within: Psychodrama and Experiential Therapy*. Deerfield Beach, FL: Health Communications.

Dayton, T. (1997) *Heartwounds*. Deerfield Beach, FL: Health Communications.

Dayton, T. (2000) *Trauma and Addiction: Ending the Cycle of Pain through Emotional Literacy*. Deerfield Beach, FL: Health Communications.

Dayton, T. (2005) *The Living Stage: A Step-by-Step Guide to Psychodrama, Sociometry and Experiential Group Psychotherapy*. Deerfield Beach, FL: Health Communications.

Doktor, D. (ed.) (1994) *Arts Therapies and Clients with Eating Disorders*. London: Jessica Kingsley Publishers.

Dykema, R. (2006) 'How your nervous system sabotages your ability to relate: An interview with Stephen Porges about His Polyvagal Theory. *Nexus*, March–April. Available at www.nexuspub.com/articles_2006/interview_porges_06_ma.php, accessed on 15 September 2012.

Elliot, T. S. (1952) *Burnt Norton, In the Four Quartets in the Complete Poems and Plays 1909–1950*. New York: Harcourt Brace and World Inc.

Erikson, Erik H. (1959) *Identity and the Life Cycle*. New York: International Universities Press.

Farhi, D. (1996) *The Breathing Book: Good Health and Vitality through Essential Breath Work*. New York: Henry Holt and Company.

Garcia, A. and Sternberg, P. (2000) *Sociodrama: Who's in Your Shoes?* 2nd edition. Westport, CT: Praeger.

Goode, E. (2000) "Thinner: The male battle with anorexia." *The New York Times*, 25 June. Available at www.nytimes.com/2000/06/25/health/thinner-the-male-battle-with-anorexia.html?pagewanted=all&src=pm, accessed 30 October 2012.

Hanh, T.N. (1990) *Present Moment, Wonderful Moment: Mindfulness Verses for Daily Living*. Berkeley, CA: Parallax Press.

Hansen, R. with Mendius, R. (2009) *Buddha's Brain: The Practical Neuroscience of Happiness, Love and Wisdom*. Oakland, CA: New Harbinger Publications.

Hay, L. (2002) *Healthy Body Cards*. Carlsbad, CA: Hay House.

Hellinger, B. and ten Hövel, G. (1999) *Acknowledging What Is: Conversations with Bert Hellinger*. Phoenix, AZ: Zeig, Tucker and Theisen.

Hellinger, B., Weber, G. and Beaumont, H. (1998) *Love's Hidden Symmetry*. Phoenix, AZ: Zeig, Tucker and Theisen.

Hinz, L.D. (2006) *Drawing from Within: Using Art to Treat Eating Disorders*. London: Jessica Kingsley Publishers.

Hoey, B. (1997) *Who Calls the Tune? A Psychodramatic Approach to Child Therapy.* New York: Routledge/Taylor and Francis.

Hözel, B., Carmody, J., Vangel, M., Congleton, C., Yerramsetti, S.M, Gard, T. and Lazar, S.W. (2011) "Mindfulness practice leads to increases in regional brain gray matter density." *Psychiatry Research: Neuroimaging 191*, 1, 36–43.

Hudgins, M.K. (1989) "Experiencing the Self through Psychodrama and Gestalt Therapy, in Anorexia Nervosa." In L.M. Hornyak and E.K. Baker (eds) *Experiential Therapies for Eating Disorders.* New York: The Guilford Press.

Hudgins, M.K. (2002) *Experiential Treatment for PTSD: The Therapeutic Spiral Model.* New York: Springer Publishing Company.

Hudgins, K. (2008) "Nourishing the Young Therapist: Action Supervision with Eating Disordered Clients Using the Therapeutic Spiral Model." In S.L. Brooke *The Creative Therapies and Eating Disorders.* Springfield, IL: Charles C. Thomas Publisher.

Hudgins, K. and Toscani, F. (eds) (2013) *Healing World Trauma with the Therapeutic Spiral Model: Psychodramatic Stories from the Frontlines.* London: Jessica Kingsley Publishers.

Hudgins, M.K. and Ciotola, L. (2003) "The Body Double: An experiential intervention for eating disorders." *IADEP Connections Newsletter,* August.

Hudgins, M.K. and Kiesler, D.J. (1987) "Individual experiential psychotherapy: An initial validation study of psychodramatic doubling." *Psychotherapy 24,* 245–255.

IDEA Fitness Journal, "Exercise for young athletes." July–August, 144.

Isaacson, W. (2011) *Steve Jobs.* New York: Simon and Schuster.

James, C.L. (2012) "Sowing the seeds of the caring observer." *Global Association for Interpersonal Neurobiology Studies Newsletter.* Summer (unpublished).

Joynt, C.R. (2012) "Former White House Pastry Chef Recalls Bill Clinton's 'Scary' Appetite," *The Washingtonian,* 6 January. Available at www.washingtonian.com/blogarticles/22186.html, accessed on 15 September 2012.

Karpman, S. (1968) "Fairy tales and script drama analysis." *Transactional Analysis Bulletin 7,* 26, 39–43.

Kellermann, P.F. and Hudgins, M.K. (2000) *Acting Out Your Pain: Psychodrama with Trauma Survivors.* London: Jessica Kingsley Publishers.

Kessler, D.A. (2004) *The End of Overeating: Taking Control of the Insatiable American Appetite.* New York: Rodale (distributed by Macmillan).

Keys, A. (1950) *The Biology of Human Starvation.* Minneapolis, MN: University of Minnesota Press.

Koff-Chapin, D. (1996) *SoulCards.* Langley, WA: The Center for Touch Drawing.

Kolata, G. (2007a) "Chubby gets a second look." *The New York Times,* 11 November. Available at www.nytimes.com/2007/11/11/weekinreview/11kolata.html, accessed on 15 September 2012.

Kolata, G. (2007b) *Rethinking Thin: The New Science of Weight Loss—and the Myths and Realities of Dieting.* New York: Farrar, Straus and Giroux.

Landy, R. (2008) *The Couch and the Stage.* Lanham, MD: Jason Aronson.

Lemberg, R. and Stanford, S. (2012) "Men with Eating Disorders: Under-diagnosed, Undertreated and Misunderstood." Handout for Eating Disorders Assessment for Men: Exploring Gender Differences and Introducing the First Male Specific

Diagnostic Instrument, presented at the conference of the International Association of Eating Disorders Professionals. Available from http://library.constantcontact.com/download/get/file/1101827005091-540/Handout+for+Eating+Disorders+in+Males.pdf.

Louv, R. (2008) *Last Child in the Woods: Saving Our Children from Nature-Deficit Disorder.* Chapel Hill, NC: Algonquin Book of Chapel Hill.

Marineau, R. (1989) *Jacob Levy Moreno 1889-1974.* London and New York: Tavistock/Routledge (English version 1992).

Maté, G. (2010) *In the Realm of the Hungry Ghosts.* Berkeley, CA: North Atlantic Books.

McVea, C. (2009) "Resolving painful emotional experience during psychodrama." PhD thesis, Queensland University of Technology.

McVea, C. (2013) "The Therapeutic Alliance between the Protagonist and Auxiliaries." In K. Hudgins and F. Toscani (eds) *Healing World Trauma with the Therapeutic Spiral Model: Psychodramatic Stories from the Frontlines.* London: Jessica Kingsley Publishers.

Miller, C. (2010) *Starve the Ego: Feed the Soul!* Spring Lake Heights, NJ: International Institute of Souldrama.

Minich, D.M. (2009) *Chakra Foods for Optimum Health: A Guide to the Foods that Can Improve Your Energy, Inspire Creative Changes, Open Your Heart, and Heal Body, Mind, and Spirit.* San Francisco, CA: Conari Press.

Monroe, M. (2011) "It's all in the brain: Unlocking the secrets of overeating with neuroscience." *IDEA Fitness Journal,* November–December, 38–46.

Moore, R. and Gillette, D (1991) *King, Warrior, Magician, Lover: Rediscovering the Archetypes of the Mature Masculine.* New York: HarperCollins.

Moreno, Z.T. (2012) Personal communication, 3 August.

Morgan, J.F. (2008) *The Invisible Man: A Self-help Guide for Men with Eating Disorders, Compulsive Exercise and Bigorexia.* Abingdon: Routledge.

Music Together. (2003, 2004) Center for Music and Young Children. Princeton, NJ. Available at www.musictogether.com, accessed 3 December 2012.

NOVA (2008) *Ghost in Your Genes.* DVD. Boston, MA: WGBH; originally broadcast by the BBC © 2006.

Ortiz, J.M. (1997) *The Tao of Music: Sound Psychology.* York Beach, ME: Samuel Weiser.

Paulson, T. and McShane, J.M. (2008) *Why She Feels Fat: Understanding Your Loved One's Eating Disorder and How You Can Help.* Carlsbad, CA: Gurze.

Perry, B.D. (2006) "Applying Principles of Neurodevelopment to Clinical Work with Maltreated and Traumatized Children in Working with Traumatized Youth." In N.B. Webb (ed.) *Child Welfare.* New York: Guilford Press pp.27–52.

Peterson, T. (2006) "Dennis Quaid: I battled anorexia." *People Magazine,* 10 March. Available at www.people.com/people/article/0,,1172023,00.html, accessed on 16 September 2012.

Porges, S.W. (2011a) *The Polyvagal Theory: Neurophysiological Foundations of Emotions, Attachment, Communication, and Self-Regulation.* New York: W.W. Norton and Company.

Porges, S.W. (2011a) *Somatic Perspectives on Psychotherapy.* Available at www.stephenporges.com/images/somatic%20perspectives%20porges.pdf, accessed on 16 September 2012.

Prochaska, J.O., Norcross, J.C. and DiClemente, C.C. (1994) *Changing for Good: A Revolutionary Six-Stage Program for Overcoming Bad Habits and Moving your Life Positively Forward.* New York: Avon Books.

Rentschler, M. (2008) *The Masgutova Method of Neuro-Sensory-Motor and Reflex Integration: Key to Health, Development and Learning.* Available at www.masgutovainstitute.com/badania/6-Masgutova.pdf, accessed on 16 September 2012.

Richards, P.S, Hardman, R.K. and Berrett, M.E. (2007) *Spiritual Approaches in the Treatment of Women with Eating Disorders.* Washington, DC: American Psychological Association.

Richardson, C. (2001) *Self-Care Cards.* Carlsbad, CA: Hay House.

Ridge, R.M. (2012) "Embracing the future: Putting social engagement systems theories into action." Handout for the conference of United States Association for Body Psychotherapy, 9–12 August, Boulder, CO.

Ross, C.C. (2009) *The Binge Eating and Compulsive Overeating Workbook: An Integrated Approach to Overcoming Disordered Eating.* Oakland, CA: New Harbinger Publications.

Rowland, A.Z. (1998) *Traditional Reiki for Our Times: Practical Methods for Personal and Planetary Healing.* Rochester, VT: Healing Arts Press.

Salas, J. (1996) *Improvising Real Life: Personal Story and Playback Theatre.* Dubuque, IA: Kendall/Hunt Publishing Co.

Satter, E. (2000) *Child of Mine: Feeding with Love and Good Sense.* Boulder, CO: Bull Publishing Company.

Scalzo, K. (2001) *Polycystic Ovary Syndrome. After the Diet, Volume I, Issue IV,* Winter. Glendale, AZ: Better Way Consulting.

Schützenberger, A.A. (1998) *The Ancestor Syndrome: Transgenerational Psychotherapy and the Hidden Links in the Family Tree.* London: Routledge.

Schwartz, M., Galperin, L. and Gleiser, K.A. (2009) *Attachment as a Mediator of Eating Disorder: Implications for Treatment.* Available at www.castlewoodtc.com/wp-content/uploads/2011/07/attachment_as_a_mediator.pdf, accessed on 16 September 2012.

Scott, A. and Crowther, C.R. (1994) *Serving Fire: Food for Thought, Body and Soul.* Berkley, CA: Celestial Arts.

Seale, A. (2001) *Intuitive Living: A Sacred Path.* San Francisco, CA: Red Wheel/Weiser.

Shannahoff-Khalsa, D.S. (2006) *Kundalini Yoga Meditation: Techniques Specific for Psychiatric Disorders, Couples Therapy, and Personal Growth.* New York: W.W. Norton and Company.

Sharot, T. (2011a) *The Optimism Bias: A Tour of the Irrationally Positive Brain.* New York: Pantheon Books.

Sharot, T. (2011b) "The optimism bias." *Time Magazine,* May 28. Available at www.time.com/time/health/article/0,8599,2074067-3,00.html, accessed on 16 September 2012.

Shiltz, T. (2005) *Males and Eating Disorders: Research.* National Eating Disorders Association. Available at www.nationaleatingdisorders.org/nedaDir/files/documents/handouts/MalesRes.pdf, accessed on 16 September 2012.

Siegel, D. (2007) *The Mindful Brain: Reflection and Attunement in the Cultivation of Well-being.* New York: W.W. Norton and Company.

Siegel D. (2010a) *Mindsight: The New Science of Personal Transformation*. New York: Bantam.

Siegel, D. (2010b) *Wheel of Awareness I, Wheel of Awareness II*. Podcast, 27 July. Available at http://drdansiegel.com/resources/wheel_of_awareness, accessed on 17 September 2012.

Siegel, D. (2012) *The Developing Mind: How Relationship and the Brain Interact to Shape Who We Are*, 2nd edition. New York: Guilford Press.

Sinclair, U. (1906) *The Jungle*. New York: Doubleday.

Thompson, R.A. and Sherman, R.T. (1993) *Helping Athletes with Eating Disorders*. Champaign, IL: Human Kinetics Publishers.

Thompson, R.A. and Sherman, R.T. (2010) *Eating Disorders in Sport*. New York: Taylor and Francis Group.

van der Kolk, B. (2002) "In terror's grip: Healing the ravages of trauma." *Cerebrum* 4, 1, 34–50.

van der Kolk, B.A. (2003) "The neurobiology of childhood trauma and abuse." *Child and Adolescent Psychiatric Clinics 12*, 293–317.

Vaughan, F. (2000) *The Inward Arc*. Available at www.iUniverse.com, accessed on 17 September 2012.

Warren, M. (2000) *The DSM V and Eating Disorders*. Available at www.eatingdisorderscleveland.org/blog/bid/31155/The-DSM-V-and-Eating-Disorders, accessed on 16 September 2012.

Wiggles, The (1999, 2003, 2007) *Yummy Yummy*. Audio CD. Ply Ltd., Koch Entertainment.

Wiboltt, A.F. (2008) *Cooking for the Love of the World: Awakening Our Spirituality through Cooking*. Benson, NC: Goldenstone Press and East Monpelier, VT: Heaven and Earth Publishing.

Winton-Henry, C. (2009) *Dance—the sacred art: The joy of movement as a spiritual practice*. Woodstock, VT: Skylight Paths Publishing.

Wylie, M.S. (2004) "The limits of talk: Bessel van der Kolk wants to transform the treatment of trauma." *Psychotherapy Networker 6*, 1, 30–41, 67.

Zerbe, K.J. (2008) *Integrated Treatment of Eating Disorders: Beyond the Body Betrayed*. New York: W.W. Norton and Company.

Index

Author Index

23253258R00151

Printed in Great Britain
by Amazon